Rational
Expectations and
Economic Policy

A Conference Report
National Bureau of
Economic Research

Rational Expectations and Economic Policy

Edited by   Stanley Fischer

The University of Chicago Press

Chicago and London

The University of Chicago Press, Chicago 60637
The University of Chicago Press, Ltd., London

Library of Congress Cataloging in Publication Data
Main entry under title:

Rational expectations and economic policy.

(A Conference report–National Bureau of Economic Research)
Proceedings of a conference sponsored by the National Bureau of Economic Research, held at Bald Peak Colony Club, N.H., in Oct. 1978.
Bibliography: p.
Includes index.
1. United States—Economic policy—1971– Congresses. 2. Monetary policy—United States— Congresses. I. Fischer, Stanley. II. National Bureau of Economic Research. III. Series: National Bureau of Economic Research. Conference report–National Bureau of Economic Research.
HC106.7.R3   338.973   79-22661
ISBN 0-226-25134-9 (paper)
      0-226-25136-5 (cloth)

Since this volume is a record of conference proceedings, it has been exempted from the rules governing critical review of manuscripts by the Board of Directors of the National Bureau (resolution adopted 6 July 1948, as revised 21 November 1949 and 20 April 1968).

Contents

Acknowledgments

The conference at which the papers in this book were presented was funded by a grant from the National Science Foundation to the National Bureau of Economic Research. Maureen Kay, Martin Feldstein, and Charles McLure of the Bureau did much of the hard work for the conference. I am indebted to David Modest, John Huizinga, and Matthew Butlin for substantial assistance at different stages in the editing of the book.

S.F.

Introduction

Stanley Fischer

The papers and discussions contained in this volume were presented
at a conference on rational expectations and economic policy sponsored
by the National Bureau of Economic Research and held at Bald Peak
Colony Club, New Hampshire, in October 1978. Developments in the
theory of economic policy associated with rational expectations have
aroused considerable professional and public interest in the last few
years, and it seemed desirable to bring together a group of economists
and policymakers to summarize and discuss these developments and,
if possible, to focus on outstanding unresolved issues.

Herschel Grossman's introductory chapter surveys and explains developments in economic theory that underlie most of the remaining
papers in the volume and briefly outlines the contents of those papers.
There would be no point in providing a second introduction, but it
should be useful to explain the rationale for the choice of papers for
the conference and then to summarize the issues that surfaced in the
discussion.

The paper by Robert Barro and Mark Rush summarizes and extends
Barro's earlier work on the effects of unanticipated changes in money
on output and prices. Barro had moved empirical work on rational
expectations to a point where it was clearly understood by many
economists and provided apparently strong support for the view that
anticipated monetary policy has no real effects. Since the earlier work
used annual data, the results needed to be checked against quarterly
data: that is what the present paper does.

The Barro and Rush paper presents reduced form evidence that unanticipated money has real effects. The precise mechanism through
which changes in unanticipated money affect the real economy deserves
careful study: this is the topic generally known as the "monetary

1

mechanism." The paper by Olivier Blanchard explores the monetary mechanism, paying particular attention to the differences in impact of anticipated and unanticipated money on the economy. In order to do this, Blanchard had to face the challenge of building an econometric model whose structure would remain approximately invariant to changes in economic policies.

The paper by Robert Shiller is designed to focus on a key point in most theories of the effects of monetary policy on the economy, namely, its impact on real interest rates. In some theories, anticipated changes in the money stock affect real output. According to these theories, anticipated changes in money typically affect the expected rate of inflation and thus the expected real interest rate, which in turn affects inventory or fixed capital accumulation and/or labor supply. Other theories predict that unanticipated changes in the money stock will affect real interest rates and thus the intertemporal allocation of leisure—individuals work more when real interest rates are high and save to have more leisure later. In either case, the impact of money on the real interest rate is crucial. Since the real interest rate that is relevant to economic decisions is the *expected* real rate, which is not observable, it is no simple matter to examine the effects of monetary changes on real rates.

Most of the discussion of economic policy associated with the rational expectations literature has centered on monetary policy. The strong position that anticipated monetary policy could have no real effects has occasionally been transferred to fiscal policy. However, it is clear that changes in tax rates are likely to have real effects and that anticipated fiscal policy stands on a footing very different from that of anticipated monetary policy. For instance, no one would doubt that a preannounced temporary change in the investment tax credit could affect the rate of investment, though many would doubt that a preannounced temporary change in the growth rate of money would have real effects. The proposition that fiscal policy has real effects does not, however, mean that it should be used to mitigate the trade cycle. The Kydland and Prescott paper was invited to discuss optimal fiscal policies in the light of the nonneutralities associated with tax and expenditure changes.

My paper was in part supposed to serve a similar purpose with regard to nonneutralities of anticipated changes in money. A variety of mechanisms through which anticipated changes in money might have both long- and short-term effects on the economy have been studied, and the paper is intended to summarize and evalute these nonneutralities as the possible basis for activist monetary policy.

The papers by Robert Lucas, Robert Solow, and William Poole were originally to be presented in a discussion of what policy should have been in 1973–75. The purpose of this session was to concentrate attention on the different policy prescriptions that might be made depending on acceptance or rejection of the rational expectations approach to policy. Robert Lucas argued that the question was not meaningful and wrote a paper on the proposal that monetary growth be kept constant. The three papers taken together do point very clearly to differences of opinion on the role of monetary and fiscal policy that reasonable economists still have.

The major unresolved issue that emerged in the discussion of the papers was that of the clearing or nonclearing of markets. Several participants observed that differences between the authors were a result of their views on whether markets are continuously in equilibrium rather than their views on rational expectations. The only paper that developed a non-market-clearing analysis formally is that by Solow; the question of how one would distinguish empirically between the clearing and nonclearing of markets could usefully have been discussed (Robert Gordon's comment on the Barro and Rush paper addresses that important question), especially given a tendency by proponents of the market-clearing approach to develop analyses of apparent nonclearing phenomena in terms of unobserved market-clearing prices. The associated issue of the rationale for the stickiness of prices received some attention and will continue to receive further attention.

A second unresolved issue concerned the mechanism underlying the Lucas supply function, which suggests that the intertemporal substitution of leisure plays a major role in the propagation of the trade cycle. It would have been useful to have had a paper examining the evidence for the view that there is a substantial short-run elasticity of labor supply in response to transitory changes in real wages or interest rates.

A third unresolved issue, which did not receive much attention, concerns the evaluation of past policy. It is frequently asserted that recent monetary policy has been very poor, but there has been little documentation of this—and the view that econometric policy evaluation is difficult presents some obstacles to making such an appraisal. Nonetheless, the argument that some particular policy rule would be better than current types of policy requires serious appraisal of alternative policies that might have been followed in the past.

The papers themselves leave many other important issues unresolved. But it would not be fair to rob the reader of the opportunity for discovering those issues for her or himself.

1 Rational Expectations, Business Cycles, and Government Behavior

Herschel I. Grossman

Government and Business Cycles

Irregular fluctuations in economic activity, as measured by aggregate production and employment, are a persistent characteristic of market economies. What is the relation between these business cycles and the government's monetary and fiscal policies, by which we mean its regulation of the quantity of money and its total spending and taxation? From an historical perspective, have governmental monetary and fiscal actions exacerbated or mitigated business cycles? With regard to prospects for the future, what are the possibilities for prescribing monetary and fiscal policies that can improve the cyclical performance of the economy?

A decade or so ago, the belief was widespread that economists knew the answers to questions such as these, or at least knew how to find the answers. This belief is now severely shaken. The previous optimism derived mainly from the reasonably satisfactory completion of the research program associated with the Keynesian revolution. This program involved the resolution of long-standing theoretical and empirical

This paper provides an introduction to the subject of the conference on rational expectations and economic policy and a selective summary. In preparing this paper, my intent has been to identify critical theoretical and empirical questions, to review the state of knowledge about these questions, and to give a balanced view of the main issues of contention. I have not attempted to survey the literature. The selected references are not exhaustive and are intended only to supplement my summary of difficult points.

Stanley Fischer, the organizer of the conference, gave me considerable advice on the preparation of this paper. Robert King and many other people gave me helpful comments on preliminary drafts. The National Science Foundation provided support for the conference as well as for my research relating to the subject of the conference.

issues concerned with the role of various factors, including monetary and fiscal actions, in the determination of aggregate demand for output and labor services. It seems clear, however, that this work has not resulted in mastery of the business cycle.

Two sets of events have contributed to the loss of confidence in the power and beneficence of economic knowledge and expertise. First, the actual ability of models of the economy to predict business cycle developments has failed to meet the expectations of the builders and users of these models. Second, the government has failed grossly to deliver on official assurances regarding its ability to mitigate the business cycle. The optimism prevalent in the mid-sixties, associated most vividly with the idea of fine tuning the macroeconomy, has soured in the face of recession and inflation in the seventies.

These disappointing developments, in conjunction with basic innovations in economic analysis, have prompted a fundamental reconsideration of accepted ideas about the economic behavior that is responsible for business cycles and have cast doubts on previously established ways of viewing the effects of government behavior on the economy. Specifically, we can identify three distinct but complementary changes in thinking about the relation between government and business cycles. These changes are (1) the development and general acceptance of "the natural rate hypothesis," which relates cyclical fluctuations in aggregate employment to inaccuracy in inflationary expectations, (2) the widespread questioning of the ability of the political process to produce good economic policies, and (3) the fundamentally innovative idea of "rational expectations." Before discussing at some length the meaning and significance of rational expectations, it will be useful to consider briefly the other two developments.

The Natural Rate Hypothesis

Prior to the formulation of the natural rate hypothesis, conventional wisdom about the relation between inflation and economic aggregates, such as output, employment, and unemployment accepted the hypothesis of a stable Phillips curve. This hypothesis associated lower levels of unemployment with higher rates of inflation and implicitly assumed the terms of this supposed trade-off to be independent of both past and current monetary and fiscal actions. Accordingly, government could use monetary and fiscal policies to keep output and employment as high as it desired if it were willing to accept the given rate of inflation associated with these chosen levels of output and employment.

The natural rate hypothesis contradicted this conventional wisdom by asserting that a fixed relation exists, not between economic aggregates and the rate of inflation, but between these aggregates and the difference between the actual rate of inflation and expectations about the rate of inflation. More specifically, the natural rate hypothesis asserts that, given the microeconomic structure of the economy, the behavior of private economic agents—businessmen, workers, and consumers—that is based on correct expectations about the rate of inflation generates unique levels of aggregate output, employment, and unemployment, denoted for obscure historical reasons as "natural" levels. Levels of aggregate output and employment above, equal to, or below their natural levels are associated with rates of inflation higher than, equal to, or less than inflation rates that have already come to be generally expected.

The natural rate hypothesis does not imply that monetary and fiscal actions do not affect the level of aggregate demand for output and labor service, nor does it deny that aggregate demand affects the actual levels of output and employment. It does, however, imply limitations on what government policy can accomplish. Many factors, including fiscal policy actions such as changes in income tax rates and unemployment benefits, can cause the natural levels to change over time. But the natural rate hypothesis implies that monetary and fiscal policies have to affect the difference between actual and expected inflation rates to make actual levels of output and employment change relative to their natural levels. Moreover, if, as seems reasonable, the experience of actual rates of inflation higher or lower than expected tends to increase or decrease inflationary expectations, the natural levels of output and employment are the only levels consistent with a constant rate of inflation. Levels of output and employment above the natural level involve steady increases in both the expected and actual inflation rates, and, as the converse proposition, reductions in the expected and actual inflation rates require a period of recession, with levels of output and employment below their natural levels. Thus, the natural rate hypothesis implies that no tenable monetary or fiscal policy can permanently keep output above and unemployment below their natural levels.

The natural rate hypothesis and its implications are robust propositions, for they can be derived under a variety of assumptions about the determination of economic aggregates. Specifically, some models that imply the natural rate hypothesis assume that market-clearing conditions are satisfied—that is, actual quantities realize all perceived or predicted gains from trade. These models relate differences between the actual and natural levels of the aggregates to differences between actual inflation and expectations of actual inflation (Phelps 1967, Friedman 1968). An alternative model of output and employment that also implies the natural rate hypothesis allows that wage or price stickiness or both can cause markets to fail to clear. This model relates differences between the actual and natural levels of the aggregates to differences between actual inflation and expectations of what the rate of inflation would be if markets were to clear (Barro and Grossman 1976, chap. 5). These examples indicate that the natural rate hypothesis and its implications do not depend on particular assumptions about market clearing. These assumptions become critical when we consider the idea of rational expectations.

The Limited Capability of the Political Process

Prior to the current decade, discussions of the government's role in the economy typically accepted, at least implicitly, the notion of achieving "the public interest." To make this notion operational, economists commonly portrayed the political process as operating as would a rational being facing a maximization problem that is well defined and has a consistent solution. But both recent and distant history suggest that this view does not provide a good basis for understanding the government's monetary and fiscal policies.

This observation does not imply that government behavior is unpredictable. In principle, appropriate positive models of the political process could account for actual monetary and fiscal actions, including both stochastic and nonstochastic components. Yet these models presumably would not be based on the idea of the government's maximizing an unambiguous objective function subject to realistic constraints.

One consideration that would be important in a realistic model of government behavior is the failure of economists, despite their devoting considerable resources to the task, to produce firm enough knowledge about the structure of the economy to support confident adoption of any specific "stabilization policy." Other relevant considerations concern the responsiveness of representative democracy to the electorate and the specific possibility of duplicity on the part of politicians and bureaucrats.

The most basic problem, however, seems to be the inherent weakness of politics as a process for making economic decisions. Experience suggests that the political process has limited ability to specify consistent goals, establish priorities, and choose between competing objectives about economic matters, especially when these decisions require comprehension of complex technical issues and constant processing of complex information. The difficulty of reaching a political consensus about complicated economic issues would seem to be sufficient, even if we had reliable models of the economy and all officials were public spirited, to preclude the adoption of consistent objectives and the explicit acknowledgment of relevant constraints, both of which are prerequisite to using a maximization calculus to prescribe actual policies.

For example, while economists investigate the dynamic relation between unemployment and inflation and argue specifically about whether a tradeoff between unemployment and inflation is possible, the political process has had difficulty accepting even that such a trade-off might be necessary. ?

Actual government behavior seems to alternate, almost mindlessly, *is this mindless?* between giving priority to reducing unemployment and giving priority to reducing inflation. It is noteworthy that the alleged independence of the Federal Reserve system has not avoided this situation. In the present context, the main implication of a realistic view of government behavior and the political process would seem to be that, even assuming that the derivation of optimal feedback control rules for monetary and fiscal *but see Kydland + Prescott.* policies, using economic models and mathematical optimization techniques, were technically feasible, the practical applicability of such an approach is questionable.

Rational Expectations, Neutrality, and Nonneutrality

The idea of rational expectations is distinct from, but complementary to, these other changes in thinking about the relation between government behavior and business cycles. The natural rate hypothesis associates variations in economic aggregates relative to their natural levels with expectational errors involving differences between actual and expected rates of inflation. The idea of rational expectations takes this line of thought one fundamental step further by proposing a general theoretical approach to the study of expectations. The resulting analysis suggests that monetary and fiscal policies may not be able to produce systematic expectational errors, and this implies that the ability of the government to improve the aggregate performance of the economy is even more limited than we inferred either from the natural rate hypothesis or from a realistic view of the political process. Specifically, the idea of rational expectations suggests that it may not be feasible to design monetary and fiscal policies that can actively stabilize aggregate output and employment relative to their natural levels. More generally, the idea of rational expectations suggests a new set of questions about the causes of business cycles and their relation to government behavior.

Models that incorporate rational expectations have three main components. One component, which provides a framework for working out the implications of rational expectations, involves assumptions about the structure of the economy. These assumptions specify the relevance of expectations and perceptions for the market activities of private agents, the relation between the perceptions of government officials and their monetary and fiscal actions, and the interaction of the behavior of the private agents and government to determine the aggregate variables—output, employment, and unemployment—and the rate of inflation.

Full development of these structural assumptions is a large undertaking and would be necessary for a complete understanding of business cycles, but only a couple of assumptions are critical for deriving the implications of the idea of rational expectations. One of these assumptions is that the information that is potentially relevant for private agents includes both knowledge of the specification of the structure of the economy itself and knowledge of the past and current data that this structure identifies as consequential. A second critical assumption is applicability of the natural rate hypothesis.

The second important component, which is also the primary distinguishing feature of rational expectations models, is the general principle (we can call it "the rational expectations postulate") that private economic agents gather and use information efficiently. This postulate treats informational activities the same as any other activity that economic man undertakes. In this context, efficiency means that the amount of resources private agents devote to gathering and using information is such that the marginal alternative cost of these resources equals the marginal benefit from the information.

Acceptance of both the natural rate hypothesis and the rational expectations postulate leads directly to the idea that problems of obtaining and utilizing information are critical factors in the generation of business cycles. Thus, the third component of these models, the relevance of which follows directly from the other components, involves specification of the availability and usability of information. The development of this component has led to a research program that focuses on the relations between various information problems, monetary and fiscal policies, and the nature of business cycles. The carrying out of this program in the last few years has involved considerable ingenuity.

A central theoretical result of this effort has been the formulation of a set of assumptions about information sufficient for the apparently paradoxical juxtaposition of the two propositions about government behavior and business cycles that have become associated with the idea of rational expectations. One proposition, which we can denote the neutrality hypothesis, is that the time pattern of differences between actual and natural levels of aggregate output and employment, which forms the main component of business cycles, is independent of monetary and fiscal actions that involve systematic responses to business cycle developments (Sargent and Wallace 1975, 1976). According to this proposition, systematic monetary actions affect only nominal variables, such as the level of prices and the rate of inflation. The other proposition, which we can denote the nonneutrality hypothesis, is that the pattern of business cycles nevertheless depends in a significant way on an important subset of monetary and fiscal actions (Lucas 1972, 1975*b*, 1977; Barro 1976).

The precise nature of these propositions should be clarified. First, the neutrality hypothesis does not say that systematic government behavior in general cannot affect aggregate output and employment. Rather, the hypothesis is that systematic government behavior affects economic aggregates only to the extent that it alters the microeconomic structure of the economy and changes the natural levels of these aggregates. For example, according to the neutrality hypothesis, if, as economic theory suggests, these natural levels are largely independent of monetary phenomena, systematic monetary actions can have little effect on the actual levels of these aggregates. A corollary of this proposition is that the analytical exercise of calculating optimal feedback control rules for monetary policy is not efficacious (Sargent and Wallace 1975, 1976; Lucas 1976).

Second, the neutrality and nonneutrality hypotheses are not contradictory. Specifically, the neutrality hypothesis does not say that historically monetary and fiscal policies have not been important, perhaps the most important, factors in generating real macroeconomic fluctuations. Rather, the neutrality hypothesis implies only that the systematic part of monetary actions has not been consequential in this respect. A separate question is whether the neutrality and nonneutrality hypotheses are consistent in the sense of being joint implications of a plausible model.

Third, neither the neutrality hypothesis nor the nonneutrality hypothesis follows directly from the natural rate hypothesis and the rational expectations postulate alone. The set of additional assumptions about information is crucial. The most important assumptions in this set seem to be the following:

First, private agents know enough about the structure of the economy to foresee correctly on average the effects of monetary and fiscal actions, if they either perceive or predict these policies accurately. This assumption means that the subjective probabilities that private agents attach to the possible effects of perceived or predicted monetary and fiscal actions are equal to the true probabilities associated with these effects.

Second, private agents readily adjust their behavior in accord with these perceptions or expectations. This assumption means that actual quantities realize all perceived or predicted gains from trade. In other words, aggregate output and employment satisfy market-clearing conditions, a situation that, as mentioned above, some derivations of the natural rate hypothesis already subsume.

These first two assumptions imply that private behavior involving incorrect expectations about the rate of inflation cannot result from correctly perceivable or predictable monetary and fiscal actions. Given the natural rate hypothesis, this implication means that perceivable or predictable monetary and fiscal actions on average do not affect the time pattern of differences between actual and natural levels of output and employment.

Third, if monetary and fiscal policies involve systematic responses to business cycle developments, which would include the case of a feedback control rule, even if the government does not announce its behavioral pattern, private agents will figure it out. This assumption means that systematic monetary and fiscal actions are accurately predictable, and this, together with the prior two assumptions and the natural rate hypothesis, implies the neutrality hypothesis.

Fourth, many monetary and fiscal actions are neither readily predictable, that is, systematic, nor readily perceivable. These actions generate private behavior that is based on incomplete information and possibly incorrect expectations about the rate of inflation. For example, an unperceived monetary contraction can cause private agents to reduce employment and output because they perceive decreased demand for productive services that they supply to be at least in part symptomatic of a worsening of the real terms at which they can indirectly exchange their services for goods that they consume, rather than to be merely symptomatic of a general deflation in the nominal values of the goods they buy as well as the services they sell. This assumption about incomplete information generates the nonneutrality hypothesis and permits the model that implies the neutrality hypothesis to allow as well for the apparent empirical relation between monetary and fiscal actions and business cycles.

A fifth assumption, which extends the theory beyond the neutrality and nonneutrality hypotheses, is that the degree of inaccuracy in beliefs about the state of the economy that results from a given unpredictable and unperceivable monetary or fiscal action depends inversely on the magnitude and frequency of such actions, that is, on the variance of monetary or fiscal policies. This assumption, like the first and third assumptions, is essentially a reflection of a more general and basic assumption that private agents who behave according to the rational expectations postulate do not make systematic mistakes.

This fifth assumption implies the proposition, which we can denote as the variance hypothesis, that the larger the variance of monetary and fiscal behavior, the smaller the effects of given unpredictable and unperceivable monetary and fiscal actions on aggregate output and employment (Lucas 1973, Barro 1976). The variance hypothesis represents an elaboration of the nonneutrality hypothesis. A corollary of the variance hypothesis is the proposition, which we can denote as the misallocation hypothesis, that the larger the variance of monetary and fiscal behavior, the more likely are private agents to misinterpret other economic disturbances and to fail to make the adjustments in resource allocation that these other disturbances would otherwise call for (Barro 1976).

Are the Neutrality and Nonneutrality Hypotheses Consistent?

Critical evaluation of this model that combines rational expectations and incomplete information has involved both considerable discussion of the a priori plausibility of the assumptions of the model and tentative attempts at direct econometric testing of its implications. On a priori grounds, the assumption about incomplete information, which says specifically that a significant part of monetary and fiscal actions are neither systematic nor perceivable, seems to me to be the most troublesome. The problem is that, although it seems reasonable to suppose that much government action is not systematic, the identification of specific and significant monetary and fiscal actions that are not perceivable is not immediately obvious. After all, both published data that measure values of monetary and fiscal variables and price indexes, which indicate the aggregate state of the economy, are readily available. Consequently, this assumption about incomplete information seems to require that either the noise or the reporting lag involved in these measurements is operationally significant. The one empirical study that directly addresses this issue suggests, however, that imperfections in the published data do not play a significant role in determining the behavior of economic aggregates (Barro and Hercowitz 1978).

Such results, if supported by further empirical research, would make it hard to accept the juxtaposition of the neutrality and nonneutrality hypotheses. Specifically, without this assumption about incomplete information, the other assumptions listed above would imply the neutrality hypothesis but would not imply the nonneutrality hypothesis. In this case, acceptance of the proposition that systematic monetary and fiscal policies cannot affect the course of business cycles would seem to imply that no monetary and fiscal actions affect business cycles. This implication is not only implausible but would leave us without a convincing theory of why economic aggregates fluctuate at all. Alternatively, preservation of the nonneutrality hypothesis would require rejection of other assumptions, which seem to be necessary for the neutrality hypothesis.

Pursuing this line of thought, what can we say about the plausibility and significance of the other assumptions? As suggested above, the assumptions that concern knowledge about the structure of the economy and the systematic behavior of government seem in spirit to be simple extensions of the rational expectations postulate, which in turn is an application of the concept of economic man. Thus, it would seem hard to reject these assumptions without rejecting the presuppositions of neoclassical economic theory (Lucas 1975a, McCallum 1979).

A more contentious aspect of the derivation of the neutrality hypothesis is the assumption, which concerns the utilization of information, that aggregate output and employment satisfy market-clearing conditions. Of particular interest in this context are recent variations on the so-called non-market-clearing approach, which is both the primary paradigmatic rationalization for Keynesian models of business cycles and the principal alternative to the incomplete information approach to explaining the causal relation between monetary and fiscal actions and economic aggregates. The traditional attraction of the non-market-clearing approach has been that it explicitly takes into account alleged evidence of the chronic failure of markets to clear, such as layoffs and other apparent symptoms of nonwage rationing of employment.

Recent non-market-clearing models incorporate the natural rate hypothesis, the rational expectations postulate, and the assumptions that private agents understand the structure of the economy and the systematic behavior of government; however, these models also assume that long-term contracts fix wages or prices and prevent the realization of advantageous transactions that were unpredictable when these contracts were being made but are perceived or become predictable during the term of the contracts (Fischer 1977, Phelps and Taylor 1977, Taylor 1979). This non-market-clearing assumption implies that monetary and fiscal actions that are perceivable, though not predictable sufficiently in advance, can affect the course of business cycles. In these models assumptions about incomplete information are redundant. Moreover, an additional assumption that the government can react to business cycle developments faster than private agents revise their contractually fixed wages and prices implies that the neutrality hypothesis does not hold and that systematic monetary and fiscal policies are efficacious.

Although these non-market-clearing models are superficially appealing, they are also problematic. For one thing, the argument that contractual rigidity is real is not conclusive. Recent theoretical work based on the idea that labor market transactions involve arrangements for shifting risk from workers to employers suggests that the allegation that actual markets chronically fail to clear may reflect an incorrect interpretation of the facts. These risk-shifting models provide a rationale for observed stickiness of wage rates and explain alleged symptoms of employment rationing, such as layoffs, while allowing markets to clear and private agents to realize all perceived gains from trade (Grossman 1979).

Non-market-clearing models are also subject to the basic a priori objection that contractual arrangements restricting perceived and mutually advantageous transactions would not be viable in competitive markets unless there were costs involved in taking advantage of information about potential gains from trade (Barro 1977b). But the existing literature has not identified any convincing costs of this type. Thus, these models of contractual rigidity do not explain the failure of markets to clear.

Another problem with the incomplete-information model that implies both the neutrality and nonneutrality hypotheses is sometimes alleged: even if some monetary and fiscal actions are not currently perceivable, it is not plausible that such misperceptions would persist over time. This argument leads to the claim that this model is not consistent with observed persistence in the effects of monetary and fiscal actions on aggregate output and employment. Various extensions of the model show, however, that an absence of serial correlation in misperceptions does not preclude serial correlation in the effects of these misperceptions resulting from gradual adjustment in, for example, demands for labor services, inventories, or physical capital (Blinder and Fischer 1978, Lucas and Sargent 1978, McCallum 1979). In addition, careful empirical analysis suggests that the amount of persistence in employment and unemployment is much less than one might infer from casual inspection of the data (King 1978).

Formal econometric analysis of models incorporating rational expectations has involved experimentation with a variety of approaches. One interesting example is the development of operational statistical distinctions between predictable and unpredictable changes in the stock of money (Barro 1977a, 1978), and another is the testing of the variance hypotheses as applied to monetary disturbances (Lucas 1973, Hanson 1978), but none of the econometric studies have yielded a clear-cut test of the key neutrality hypothesis (Lucas 1977b, Barro and Hercowitz 1978, McCallum 1979). Moreover, some of the results of such studies seem to be weak in the face of small changes of specification (Small 1979).

In sum, the present state of the theory of the business cycle and the role of monetary and fiscal policy is unsatisfactory. The research program associated with the natural rate hypothesis and the rational expectations postulate has raised basic questions but so far has provided fewer answers. The ingenious incomplete information model that implies both the neutrality and nonneutrality hypotheses is not wholly convincing, but a sound basis for preferring any other existing model of the business cycle is still wanting.

Significance of Rational Expectations

The neutrality hypothesis implies that attempts to design optimal systematic monetary and fiscal policies are pointless except to the extent that such policies affect the natural level of output. Whether or not we accept this hypothesis and its radical implication, however, the rational expectations postulate has had profound effects on our way of thinking about government behavior. For example, within the recent vintage of non-market-clearing models, analysis of the determination of the degree of contractual rigidity as a balancing of adjustment costs and benefits would seem to imply a version of the variance hypothesis. Specifically, the larger the effort government makes to use systematic monetary and fiscal policies to manage economic aggregates, the larger the incentive private agents have to modify the form of their contracts to mitigate these effects (Gray 1978). Thus, even in a model in which the neutrality hypothesis does not hold, acceptance of the rational expectations postulate implies limitations on the potential effects of systematic monetary and fiscal policies on aggregate output, employment, and unemployment.

The importance of the positive analysis associated with rational expectations, moreover, does not depend on whether or not actual monetary behavior results as if from the solution of a postulated social optimization problem. The discussion of the limited capability of the political process suggests that the conventional conception of basing monetary and fiscal policy on a maximization calculus is largely irrelevant and that adoption of a consistent stabilization policy is not a practical possibility. Thus, the implications of rational expectations regarding the potential effects of stabilization policy and the feasibility of the optimal control approach may have little practical relevance. Nonetheless, the hypotheses associated with rational expectations have essential implications for understanding the effects of government behavior, however it is generated.

These hypotheses, in addition, do not imply that government behavior—or, more basically, the institutional framework within which government behavior is determined—is without normative significance, although discussion of the normative implications of these hypotheses requires the additional specification of a relevant normative standard. For example, acceptance of the neutrality hypothesis and the misallocation hypothesis suggests as a standard of optimality the hypothetical outcome that the behavior of economic agents would generate in a world of complete information. This standard implies that the best policy the government can pursue is dissemination of any information it has and minimization of the nonsystematic aspects of its own behavior (Barro 1976). In this context, particular instances of nonsystematic government behavior on average do not improve the performance of the economy, but the possibility of such disturbances tends to mislead private agents about the nature of other economic disturbances, thereby worsening the average performance of the economy.

The idea of rational expectations also has profound implications for research strategy, which reflects our way of looking at the behavior of private economic agents and its relation to government behavior. Most basically, it no longer seems reasonable to analyze the effects of government behavior without taking into account the reactions of private agents behaving in accord with the rational expectations postulate. Acceptance of this view implies, among other things, rejection of the methodology underlying conventional economic forecasting models (Lucas 1976). One might speculate that the fact that the idea of rational expectations threatens to make obsolete a substantial amount of professional capital, which is associated with forecasting models as well as with the methodology of optimal control, helps to explain the amount of heated professional controversy it has provoked.

A final question is whether the implications of rational expectations are good news or bad news for the man in the street. The neutrality hypothesis is surely disturbing to those who view government as an economic doctor attempting to use stabilization policy to treat a periodically ailing private economy. In this view, past failure to mitigate the business cycle has resulted from bad luck or potentially avoidable mistakes.

An alternative view, however, is that monetary and fiscal policy has a sorry historical record that is the inevitable consequence of the political process by which policy is formulated. For those who hold this pathogenic view, the implications of rational expectations are both good and bad. On the one hand, the variance hypothesis implies basic limitations on the potential for systematically misguided government behavior to do harm to the economy. On the other hand, the misallocation hypothesis implies that chronic unpredictability of government behavior worsens the average performance of the economy. From this point of view, the basic structural reform suggested by the idea of rational expectations is the adoption of stable and readily predictable monetary and fiscal behavior.

Summary of Conference

The papers and discussions of the NBER conference touch on most of the issues raised in the preceding sections. The paper by Robert J. Barro and Mark Rush, "Unanticipated Money and Economic Activity," reports extensions of Barro's earlier econometric analysis that focuses on the distinction between predictable and unpredictable growth in the stock of money. The main innovations in the conference paper involve refining the calculations of predictable and unpredictable money growth to take account of the relations between money growth and economic aggregates and testing of these cross-equation restrictions. Barro and Rush conclude that the new evidence, both annual and quarterly, provides further support for the finding that aggregate output and unemployment respond to unpredictable money growth, but not to predictable money growth. They are less successful, however, in explaining changes in the price level. For example, the pattern of response of the price level to unpredictable money growth does not seem consistent with the pattern of response of aggregate output. Barro and Rush stress that this inconsistency is discomforting for non-market-clearing models as well as for incomplete information models. Another problem is the lack of close correspondence between the pattern of price response for annual data and that for quarterly data. These difficulties reaffirm the need for further development of the theoretical framework underlying the empirical analysis.

In his discussion of the paper by Barro and Rush, Robert Weintraub questions whether the assumption that monetary policy reacts to unemployment implicit in Barro and Rush's calculations of predictable money growth is consistent with the neutrality hypothesis. Weintraub also expresses doubt that the data would contradict other assumptions about monetary policy.

Robert J. Gordon's discussion of the paper by Barro and Rush stresses the difficulty of reconciling the estimated response pattern for prices with the incomplete information model. Moreover, Gordon emphasizes the apparent reality of the non-market-clearing assumption and the apparent falsity of the incomplete information assumption.

The paper by Robert J. Shiller, "Can the Fed Control Real Interest Rates?" sets up a model embodying assumptions that imply both the neutrality and nonneutrality hypotheses and shows that these hypotheses also extend to the rationally expected real interest rate, defined as the difference between the nominal interest rate and the rationally expected rate of inflation. Although prima facie evidence suggests that monetary actions can affect the rationally expected real interest rate, Shiller's analysis implies that such evidence does not contradict the neutrality hypothesis and does not mean that systematic monetary policy can control the time pattern of this interest rate. Shiller discusses various observations that bear on the plausibility of the neutrality hypothesis and stresses doubt about the crucial market-clearing assumption. Shiller's main point, however, is that existing data on seasonal or cyclical time patterns of realized real interest rates do not provide a logical basis for an empirical test of the neutrality hypothesis.

The paper by Olivier Jean Blanchard, "The Monetary Mechanism in the Light of Rational Expectations," presents a non-market-clearing model of the recent vintage that incorporates the idea of rational expectations. Specifically, Blanchard assumes that aggregate demand determines aggregate output, with output prices either rigid or adjusting gradually in response to non-market-clearing situations, but that expectations of future wage income, which affect consumption demand, and expectations of eventual market-clearing prices, which serve as a target for actual price adjustment, are accurate. Blanchard simulates the effects of monetary disturbances on aggregate output, asset prices, and output prices, using some parameter estimates reported in another paper and some made-up parameters. The simulations draw the important distinction between anticipated and unanticipated disturbances, and they suggest in general that assumptions about expectations are quantitatively important for dynamic adjustments in this type of model.

Bennett McCallum's discussion of Blanchard's paper presents a critique of the econometric procedure that produces parameter estimates used in the simulations. This critique brings out the inherent difficulty of drawing confident quantitative conclusions about the structural relations of the macroeconomy, especially when the model of the economy takes expectations and their formation carefully into account. Michael Parkin's discussion stresses the basic objection that the non-market-clearing assumption, which, in Blanchard's model, allows monetary disturbances to affect aggregate output, lacks a firm basis.

Stanley Fischer, in his paper "On Activist Monetary Policy with Rational Expectations," argues that the type of model specified by Blanchard is realistic. Specifically, Fischer asserts that various costs of utilizing information provide a plausible a priori basis for the non-market-clearing assumption. Fischer also explains that Barro's econometric analysis, which suggests that predictable monetary actions do not affect aggregate output, is consistent with the idea of rational expectations but does not provide a test of the neutrality hypothesis. In particular, Barro's evidence does not imply that systematic monetary policy cannot affect the course of business cycles by reacting to new information faster than private agents. Fischer stresses that, if we accept the non-market-clearing assumption and the implied potential for effective systematic monetary policy, the key issue becomes whether the policy-making process is capable of taking good advantage of this potential. Fischer discusses various economic and political considerations that seem relevant to this issue and reaches cautiously optimistic conclusions. Mark Willes's discussion of this paper stresses the point that the idea of rational expectations at the least has shaken confidence in the ability of economists to design effective stabilization policy and has shifted the burden of proof to those who advocate activist policy.

Finn Kydland and Edward C. Prescott investigate the implications of rational expectations for choosing among alternative fiscal policy rules in their paper "A Competitive Theory of Fluctuations and the Feasibility and Desirability of Stabilization Policy." Kydland and Prescott consider a model in which the neutrality and nonneutrality hypotheses both obtain, and their analysis focuses on the effects of changes in technology and shifts in fiscal policies on aggregate employment. In their model, these effects are persistent, but not permanent. Kydland and Prescott conclude that tax rates should not respond either to fluctuations in economic aggregates or to temporary changes in public expenditures. Robert Hall's discussions of this paper and of Fischer's paper stress both the crucial role that the assumptions about market-clearing and non-market-clearing play in the analysis and the lack of a convincing case either for accepting or for rejecting these assumptions.

In the paper "Rules, Discretion, and the Role of the Economic Advisor," Robert E. Lucas argues that the idea of rational expectations provides a powerful tool for analyzing the consequences of various fixed policy rules but also implies that economic analysis cannot hope to predict the consequences of discretionary policies. Lucas acknowledges that the rational expectations postulate by itself does not imply the neutrality hypothesis and, hence, does not preclude consideration of systematic monetary and fiscal policies.

The paper by Robert M. Solow, "What to Do (Macroeconomically) When OPEC Comes," discusses what monetary and fiscal policies should have been during 1974–75 on the basis of a non-market-clearing model that is not restricted to conformity either to the natural rate hypothesis or to the rational expectations postulate. Solow characterizes actual policy during this period as "mindless."

The paper by William Poole, "Macroeconomic Policy, 1971–75: An Appraisal," reviews the record of monetary and fiscal actions and price controls during that period and concludes that these discretionary policies were a cause of substantial fluctuations in economic aggregates. Poole attributes much of the bad record of macroeconomic policy to political considerations that impinge on all policy makers. He suggests that legislated policy rules would improve the performance of policy.

A summary of the conference also provides a summary of the current state of thinking about the issues relating to rational expectations. Four main observations seem warranted. First, nearly all of the participants accepted the rational expectations postulate, at least as a working assumption. Second, most of the participants expressed a priori reservations about both the incomplete information approach and the non-market-clearing approach to understanding business cycles. They agreed that there do not seem to be firm a priori grounds for either accepting or rejecting the neutrality hypothesis. Third, the participants agreed that at present no solid empirical evidence exists relating to the neutrality hypothesis, and they were not sure about how to produce such evidence. Fourth, the participants expressed the prevailing skepticism about activist stabilization policy. This attitude seemed to result in part from acceptance of the idea of rational expectations and in part from the disappointing record of actual monetary and fiscal policies.

References

Barro, R. J. 1976. "Rational Expectations and the Role of Monetary Policy." *Journal of Monetary Economics* 2:1–32.

———. 1977a. "Unanticipated Money Growth and Unemployment in the United States." *American Economic Review* 67:101–15.

———. 1977b. "Long-Term Contracting, Sticky Prices, and Monetary Policy." *Journal of Monetary Economics* 3:305–16.

———. 1978. "Unanticipated Money, Output, and the Price Level in the United States." *Journal of Political Economy* 86:549–80.

Barro, R. J., and Grossman, H. I. 1976. *Money, Employment, and Inflation.* New York: Cambridge University Press.

Barro, R. J., and Hercowitz, Z. 1978. "Money Stock Revisions and Unanticipated Money Growth." Unpublished.

Blinder, A. A., and Fischer, S. 1978. "Inventories, Rational Expectations, and the Business Cycle." Unpublished.

Fischer, S. 1977. "Long-Term Contracts, Rational Expectations, and the Optimal Money Supply Rule." *Journal of Political Economy* 85:191–205.

Friedman, M. 1968. "The Role of Monetary Policy." *American Economic Review* 58:1–17.

Gray, J. A. 1978. "On Indexation and Contract Length." *Journal of Political Economy* 86:1–18.

Grossman, H. I. 1979. "Why Does Aggregate Employment Fluctuate?" *American Economic Review* 69:64–69.

Hanson, J. 1978. "The Short-Run Relation between Growth and Inflation in Latin America: A Quasi-Rational or Consistent Expectations Approach." Unpublished.

King, R. 1978. "Dynamics of Unemployment and Employment: A Reevaluation of the U.S. Time Series, 1950–1976." Unpublished.

Lucas, R. E., Jr. 1972. "Expectations and the Neutrality of Money." *Journal of Economic Theory* 4:103–24.

———. 1973. "Some International Evidence on Output-Inflation Tradeoffs." *American Economic Review* 63:326–34.

———. 1975a. "Review of 'A Model of Macroeconomic Activity' by R. C. Fair." *Journal of Economic Literature* 8:889–90.

———. 1975b. "An Equilibrium Model of the Business Cycle." *Journal of Political Economy* 83:1113–44.

————. 1976. "Econometric Policy Evaluation: A Critique." In *The Phillips Curve and Labor Markets*, edited by K. Brunner and A. H. Meltzer, pp. 19–46. Carnegie-Rochester Conference Series no. 1. New York: North-Holland.

————. 1977a. "Understanding Business Cycles." In *Stabilization of the Domestic and International Economy*, edited by K. Brunner and A. H. Meltzer, pp. 7–29. Carnegie-Rochester Conference Series on Public Policy, vol. 5. New York: North-Holland.

————. 1977b. "Some International Evidence on Output-Inflation Tradeoffs: Reply." *American Economic Review* 67:731.

Lucas, R. E., Jr., and Sargent, T. S. 1978. "After Keynesian Macroeconomics." In *After the Phillips Curve: Persistence of High Inflation and High Unemployment*, pp. 49–72. Conference Series no. 19. Boston: Federal Reserve Bank of Boston.

McCallum, B. T. 1979. "The Current State of the Policy-Ineffectiveness Debate." *American Economic Review* 69:240–45.

Phelps, E. S. 1967. "Phillips Curves, Expectations of Inflation, and Optimal Unemployment over Time." *Economica* 34:254–81.

Phelps, E. S., and Taylor, J. B. 1977. "Stabilizing Powers of Monetary Policy under Rational Expectations." *Journal of Political Economy* 85:163–90.

Sargent, T. J., and Wallace, N. 1975. " 'Rational' Expectations, the Optimal Monetary Instrument, and the Optimal Money Supply Rule." *Journal of Political Economy* 83:241–54.

————. 1976. "Rational Expectations and the Theory of Economic Policy." *Journal of Monetary Economics* 2:169–83.

Small, D. H. 1979. "A Comment on Robert Barro's 'Unanticipated Money Growth and Unemployment in the United States.' " *American Economic Review* 69, in press.

Taylor, J. B. 1979. "Estimation and Control of a Macroeconomic Model with Rational Expectations." *Econometrica* 47:1267–86.

2   Unanticipated Money and Economic Activity

Robert J. Barro and Mark Rush

This paper discusses ongoing research on the relation of money to economic activity in the post–World War II United States. As in previous work (Barro 1977, 1978), the stress is on the distinction between anticipated and unanticipated movements of money.

The first portion deals with annual data. Aside from updating and refinements of earlier analysis, the principal new results concern joint, cross-equation estimation and testing of the money growth, unemployment, output, and price level equations. The present findings raise doubts about the specification of the price equation, although the other relations receive further statistical support.

The second part applies the analysis to quarterly data. Despite the necessity of dealing with pronounced serial correlation of residuals in the equations for unemployment, output, and the price level, the main results are consistent with those obtained from annual data. Further, the quarterly estimates allow a detailed description of the lagged response of unemployment and output to money shocks. The estimates reveal some lack of robustness in the price equation, which again suggests some misspecification of this relation.

Results from Annual U.S. Data

Robert J. Barro

The first section of this paper summarizes and extends the results for annual U.S. data on money growth, unemployment, output, and the

This research was supported by a grant from the National Science Foundation. We have benefited from comments by Alan Blinder, Stanley Fischer, Robert King, Charles Plosser, and William Schwert.

price level (Barro 1977, 1978). The estimated money growth equation, which is used to divide observed growth rates into anticipated and unanticipated components, is

1941–77 sample (observations from 1941 to 1945 multiplied by 0.36):

(1) $$DM_t = .085 + .44DM_{t-1} + .18DM_{t-2} +$$
$$(.024)\quad (.14)\qquad\quad (.12)$$

$$+ .073FEDV_t + .027 \cdot \log(U/1 - U)_{t-1},$$
$$(.015)\qquad\quad (.008)$$

$\hat{\sigma}$ (for post–World War II sample) $= .0141,$

$D\text{-}W = 1.9,$[1]

where the money growth rate is $DM_t \equiv \log(M_t/M_{t-1})$, M_t is the annual average of the $M1$ concept of money,[2] real federal expenditure relative to "normal" is $FEDV_t \equiv \log(FED_t) - [\log(FED)]^*{}_t$, FED_t is total nominal federal expenditure divided by the GNP deflator, $[\log(FED)]^*{}_t$ is an exponentially declining distributed lag of $\log(FED)$ with current weight of 0.2, U is the unemployment rate in the total labor force, $\hat{\sigma}$ is the standard error of estimate, and $D\text{-}W$ is the Durbin-Watson statistic.

Using the residuals, DMR, from equation (1) to measure "unanticipated money growth," the estimated equations for the unemployment rate and output (real GNP) turn out to be

1949–77 sample:

(2) $$\log(U/1 - U)_t = -2.68 - 4.6DMR_t$$
$$(.04)\quad (1.6)$$

$$-10.9\ DMR_{t-1}$$
$$(1.6)$$

$$- 5.5DMR_{t-2} - 5.3MIL_t,$$
$$(1.6)\qquad\quad (0.6)$$

$$R^2 = .87, \hat{\sigma} = .113, D\text{-}W = 2.4$$

1. The Durbin h-statistic also shows no serial correlation of residuals for this equation. The weighting pattern accounts for a higher variance of the error term for observations prior to 1946. The value of 0.36 is determined from a maximum likelihood criterion (assuming normality for the errors).
2. A change from the previous money data involves an adjustment to the level of the money stock prior to 1947 by a factor of 1.013. See the notes to table 2.3.

1946–77 sample:

(3)
$$\log(y_t) = 2.93 + 0.99DMR_t + 1.18DMR_{t-1}$$
$$(.04) \quad (.22) \qquad (.22)$$

$$+ 0.37DMR_{t-2} + .0357 \cdot t + 0.54MIL_t,$$
$$(.19) \qquad\quad (.0004) \quad (.09)$$

$$R^2 = .998, \; \hat{\sigma} = .0159, \; D\text{-}W = 1.8,$$

where y is *GNP* in 1972 dollars, *MIL* is the military personnel/conscription variable that is discussed in Barro (1977), and t is a time trend.[3]

The unemployment rate equation (2) has been altered from that in my 1977 paper by dropping a minimum wage rate variable and omitting the 1946–48 observations. As discussed earlier (Barro 1979a), the estimated positive influence of the minimum wage variable turns out to be merely an imperfect attempt to account for the otherwise unexplained low values of the unemployment rate from 1946 to 1948. The variable is insignificant over the post-1949 sample (estimated coefficient of −0.1, standard error = 0.6 when added to equation (2)). Aside from a higher standard error of estimate, an unemployment rate equation estimated over a 1946–77 sample (with the minimum wage rate variable excluded) appears similar to that shown in equation (2).[4]

The estimated equation for the price level (GNP deflator), based on my previous analysis (Barro 1978) is

3. Estimation of equation (3) in first-difference form yields
$$Dlogy_t = .0350 + .80DDMR_t + .98DDMR_{t-1}$$
$$(.0038) \quad (.25) \qquad\quad (.27)$$

$$+ .19DDMR_{t-2} + .41DMIL_t,$$
$$(.24) \qquad\quad (.18)$$

$$R^2 = .52, \; \hat{\sigma} = .0208, \; D\text{-}W = 2.6,$$

where D is the difference operator. The robustness of the coefficient estimates to differencing—which turns out to apply here—is a useful check on the specification of the model. See Plosser and Schwert 1979.

4. The estimated equation over 1946–77 is
$$\log(U/1 - U)_t = -2.75 - 4.3DMR_t - 11.5DMR_{t-1}$$
$$(.05) \quad (2.1) \qquad (2.1)$$

$$- 5.3DMR_{t-2} - 4.6MIL_t,$$
$$(1.8) \qquad\quad (0.7)$$

$$R^2 = .76, \; \hat{\sigma} = .150, \; D\text{-}W = 1.7.$$

1948–77 sample:

(4) $$\log(P_t) = \log(M_t) - \underset{(0.2)}{4.4} - \underset{(.20)}{0.64DMR_t}$$

$$- \underset{(.23)}{1.52DMR_{t-1}} - \underset{(.28)}{1.80DMR_{t-2}}$$

$$- \underset{(.26)}{1.42DMR_{t-3}} - \underset{(.19)}{.73DMR_{t-4}}$$

$$- \underset{(.16)}{.37DMR_{t-5}} - \underset{(.0021)}{.0120 \cdot t}$$

$$+ \underset{(.16)}{.59(G/y)_t} + \underset{(1.1)}{4.3R_t,}$$

$$\hat{\sigma} = .0130, \, D\text{-}W = 1.6,$$

where G is real federal purchase of goods and services and R is the long-term interest rate (Aaa corporate bond rate). The inclusion of the G/y and R variables has been rationalized from their inverse influences on money demand (Barro 1978). Equation (4) is estimated using the lagged value R_{t-1} as an instrument for R_t. The coefficient of $log(M_t)$ in equation (4) is constrained to be unity (tests of this proposition are discussed in Barro 1978).[5]

Observations for 1946–47 are excluded from equation (4) because of the apparently strong persisting influence on reported prices of the World War II controls. The estimated negative effects of the DMR variables on the price level, as shown in equation (4), are substantially drawn out relative to the pattern of positive output effects shown in equation (3). An attempt to account for this discrepancy in terms of the dynamics of money demand has already been described (Barro 1978). It is worth stressing that this appearance of sluggish price adjustment does not correspond to the pattern of output and unemploy-

---

5. In an unconstrained regression the coefficient estimate for $log(M_t)$ is 1.01, *s.e.* $= .06$. The results with the $log(M_t)$ coefficient restricted or unrestricted are altered negligibly if $(G/\hat{y})_t$ is used as an instrument for $(G/y)_t$, where $\hat{y}_t$ is an estimated value of real GNP based on equation (3). OLS estimates differ from equation (4) mostly in the estimated coefficient of R_t, which becomes 3.1, *s.e.* $= 0.6$. OLS estimates of the price equation in first-difference form are

$$D\log P_t = \underset{(.0031)}{-.0082} + D\log M_t - \underset{(.20)}{.81DDMR_t} - \underset{(.28)}{1.30DDMR_{t-1}}$$

$$- \underset{(.32)}{1.43DDMR_{t-2}} - \underset{(.29)}{1.06DDMR_{t-3}} - \underset{(.25)}{.57DDMR_{t-4}}$$

$$- \underset{(.16)}{.21DDMR_{t-5}} + \underset{(.21)}{.38D(G/y)_t} + \underset{(0.8)}{2.5DR_t,}$$

$$\hat{\sigma} = .0143, \, D\text{-}W = 2.1.$$

Despite some reduction in the magnitude of the lagged *DMR* coefficients, the general results are robust to differencing; see n. 3, above.

ment persistence that appears in equations (2) and (3). Accordingly, explanations for price stickiness of the "disequilibrium" (Barro and Grossman 1976, chap. 2) or contracting variety (as in Taylor 1978) would not explain the results. These theories seem to account only for a pattern of price stickiness that corresponds to the patterns of output and unemployment stickiness.

The estimated elasticity of response of the price level to a contemporaneous money shock can be ascertained from equation (4) to be 1.00 (from $\log(M_t)$) plus -0.64 (from DMR_t) to be 0.36. The corresponding effect of this year's money shock on $\log(P_{t+1})$ can also be calculated, making use of equations (1) and (2) to determine the movement in $\log(M_{t+1})$, to be $-.020$. Therefore, the type of relative price variable stressed by Lucas and others, $\log(P_t) - \log(P_{t+1})^e$ (where the expectation of $\log(P_{t+1})$ includes all data generated up to date t), is estimated to respond with an elasticity of 0.56 to a contemporaneous money shock. Accordingly, the contemporaneous output response coefficient of 0.99 shown in equation (3) would require an elasticity of output supply with respect to this relative price variable of about 1.8.[6] Since this elasticity is of "plausible" size in the context of response to a temporary opportunity for high prices, it may be that this channel of effect from money shocks to contemporaneous output responses is more important empirically than I once thought (Barro 1978, p. 579). The earlier calculations neglected the effect of DMR_t on $\log(P_{t+1})^e$ and were also based on a larger magnitude coefficient estimate for DMR_t in the price equation.

My previous analyses involved a number of tests of the proposition that monetary influences on unemployment and output operate only in the form of unanticipated movements, $DMR \equiv DM - \widehat{DM}$, where $\widehat{DM}$ is estimated money growth from a relation of the form of equation (1). Tests were also carried out for the hypothesis that fully perceived changes in the level of money (shifts in M with the DMR's and R held fixed) imply a one-to-one, contemporaneous effect on the price level. The best way to test these hypotheses involves joint estimation of the money growth, unemployment, output, and price level equations. In particular, this joint estimation appropriately allows the estimation of coefficients in the money growth equation to take account of the effect on the fit of the other equations through the calculation of DMR values. In the two-part estimation procedure described in equations (1)–(4), the coefficient estimates reported in equation (1) consider only the fit of the money growth equation.[7]

Write the money growth equation as $DM_t = F(X_t) + DMR_t$, where X_t is a set of money growth predictors—in the present case, $F(X_t) =$

---

6. This calculation assumes no monetary wealth effect on supply.
7. See Leiderman 1979 for a discussion of this matter.

$\alpha_0 + \alpha_1 DM_{t-1} + \alpha_2 DM_{t-2} + \alpha_3 FEDV_t + \alpha_4 \log(U/1-U)_{t-1}$. The condition, $DMR_t \equiv DM_t - F(X_t)$, with corresponding substitutions for DMR_{t-1}, etc., can then be applied to the unemployment, output, and price level equations. The system can be estimated in an unrestricted manner by allowing separate coefficients on the variables— $DM_{t-1}, DM_{t-2}, \ldots$ —contained in $F(X_t)$, $F(X_{t-1})$, etc., in each of the equations. The underlying unanticipated money growth hypothesis, which amounts to a set of nonlinear coefficient restrictions across the equations, is that $F(X_t)$ in the unemployment, output, and price level equations corresponds to the coefficients in the money growth equation. A likelihood ratio test can be carried out to check whether the imposition of these restrictions on the joint estimation produces a statistically significant deterioration of the fit—in which case the underlying hypothesis would be rejected.

The joint estimates for the money growth, unemployment, and output equations that are subject to the restrictions implied by the unanticipated money growth hypothesis and which comprise the same sample periods and weighting scheme for the DM equation as shown above are[8]

(1')
$$DM_t = \underset{(.012)}{.074} + \underset{(.11)}{.36 DM_{t-1}} + \underset{(.09)}{.18 DM_{t-2}}$$
$$+ \underset{(.010)}{.079 FEDV_t} + \underset{(.004)}{.022 \cdot \log(U/1-U)_{t-1}},$$
$$\hat{\sigma} = .0133, \ D\text{-}W = 1.8,$$

(2')
$$\log(U/1-U)_t = \underset{(.06)}{-2.65} - \underset{(1.3)}{4.7 DMR_t}$$
$$- \underset{(1.3)}{10.8 DMR_{t-1}} - \underset{(1.6)}{5.0 DMR_{t-2}}$$
$$- \underset{(0.6)}{6.2 MIL_t},$$
$$\hat{\sigma} = .090, \ D\text{-}W = 2.6,$$

(3')
$$\log(y_t) = \underset{(.03)}{2.90} + \underset{(.18)}{1.00 DMR_t} + \underset{(.21)}{1.09 DMR_{t-1}}$$
$$+ \underset{(.19)}{.44 DMR_{t-2}} + \underset{(.0002)}{.0358 \cdot t} + \underset{(.10)}{.68 MIL_t},$$
$$\hat{\sigma} = .0129, \ D\text{-}W = 1.9,$$

where asymptotic standard errors are shown in parentheses. Note that these σ values are not adjusted for degrees of freedom and are there-

---

8. The estimation, carried out with the TSP regression package, includes contemporaneous covariances for the error terms across the equations. But the covariance of the money growth error term with that in the other equations is zero by construction.

fore not directly comparable to those shown in equations (1)–(3).[9] As would be expected, the fit of the unemployment and output equations is improved relative to that shown in equations (2) and (3)—the worsening in fit of the DM equation turns out to be minor. The only notable changes in coefficient estimates are in the DM equation: the estimated coefficient of DM_{t-1} is reduced and the estimated standard error of the lagged unemployment rate coefficient declines sharply.

The three equations have also been fitted with the relaxation of the cross-equation restrictions implied by the unanticipated money growth hypothesis. A comparison of the unrestricted and constrained results leads to the calculation of a value for $-2 \cdot log$(likelihood ratio) for a test of the cross-equation restrictions, which would be distributed asymptotically as a χ^2 variable with 16 degrees of freedom. The actual value of 16.3 is below the 5% critical value of 26.3. Therefore, the unanticipated money growth hypothesis is accepted by this joint test on the money growth, unemployment, and output equations.

The cross-equation restrictions associated with the unanticipated money hypothesis are not accepted when the price equation is included in the joint estimation. This conclusion applies to the four-equation system for (DM,U,y,P) and also for the system that comprises only the DM and P equations. The joint estimates for this last case that embody the cross-equation restrictions of the unanticipated money hypothesis are[10]

(1″)
$$DM_t = \underset{(.011)}{.098} + \underset{(.12)}{.44DM_{t-1}} + \underset{(.09)}{.16DM_{t-2}}$$
$$+ \underset{(.011)}{.061FEDV_t} + \underset{(.004)}{.031 \cdot log(U/1-U)_{t-1},}$$
$$\hat{\sigma} = .0134, D\text{-}W = 1.8,$$

(4″)
$$logP_t = logM_t - \underset{(.15)}{4.58} - \underset{(.12)}{.85DMR_t} - \underset{(.15)}{1.31DMR_{t-1}}$$
$$- \underset{(.18)}{1.36DMR_{t-2}} - \underset{(.17)}{.94DMR_{t-3}}$$
$$- \underset{(.12)}{.61DMR_{t-4}} - \underset{(.10)}{.16DMR_{t-5}}$$
$$+ \underset{(.15)}{.34(G/y)_t} + \underset{(0.5)}{2.9R_t} - \underset{(.0015)}{.0096 \cdot t,}$$
$$\hat{\sigma} = .0069, D\text{-}W = 2.2.$$

9. There is also a minor problem in that the presently used computer program allows for different numbers of observations across equations only by introducing some extra observations (for the U and y equations) that are then set to zero on both sides of the equations. This procedure inflates the apparent degrees of freedom and thereby leads to an underestimate of standard errors of coefficient estimates and disturbances.

10. This estimation does not use R_{t-1} as an instrument for R_t in the price equation. For the case of equation (4), OLS estimates differed mainly in the estimate of the R_t coefficient.

Unrestricted estimation of the two equations leads to the calculation of a value for $-2 \cdot \log$(likelihood ratio) for a test of the cross-equation restrictions. The actual value of 66.8 is well above the 5% χ^2 value with 14 degrees of freedom of 23.7. Similar results obtain for the four-equation system, where the actual value for $-2 \cdot \log$(likelihood ratio) of 122.2 exceeds the 5% χ^2 value with 30 degrees of freedom of 43.8.

A large part of the discrepancy in results seems to involve estimation of contemporaneous effects, specifically, the response of P_t to DM_t. The estimated coefficient of DM_t in the unrestricted form comparable to equation (4″) is -1.33, s.e. $= .12$, as compared with the restricted estimate (on DMR_t) of $-.85$, s.e. $= .12$. The estimation of this contemporaneous relation could involve a simultaneity problem, for example, if there were within-period feedback from P_t to DM_t. If the DMR_t variable (which would satisfy the usual properties of an error term) is omitted from the restricted price equation, and the DM_t, $FEDV_t$, and $\log(U/1 - U)_{t-1}$ variables are deleted from the unrestricted form, the value for $-2 \cdot \log$(likelihood ratio) associated with the unanticipated money hypothesis turns out to be 31.8, as compared with a 5% χ^2 value with 12 degrees of freedom of 21.0. Although the discrepancy is substantially reduced in this case, the unanticipated money hypothesis would still be rejected. It seems clear that there are some important unresolved questions about the specification of the price equation that will require further investigation. One possible source of difficulty would be feedback to money growth from the price level or interest rates, which were not included as explanatory variables in equation (1).

A number of people have raised reasonable doubts about the meaning of the military personnel/conscription variable MIL in the unemployment and output equations. The MIL variable was viewed initially as a draft pressure influence that would increase employment and reduce labor force participation. (In this context see Small 1979 and my reply 1979a.) I have noted some problems with the MIL variable that concerned its surprisingly strong output effect and insignificant price level influence (1978). Although the MIL variable is highly significant in unemployment and output equations, as in equations (2), (2′), (3) and (3′) above, it should be noted that this variable (see Barro 1977, table 2) does not exhibit major variations from 1951 to 1969, especially from 1955 to 1969. Mostly, the MIL variable shows a sharp increase from its 1949–50 values at the start of the Korean war, a mild decline from 1953 to 1958, a mild increase with the Vietnam war for 1967–69, and a sharp drop (to zero with the end of the selective, nonlottery draft) in 1970.

I have considered the possibility that the MIL variable is proxying for movements in real federal purchases of goods and services. In the case of output, a substitution of $\log(G)$ for MIL, where G is real federal purchases and the DMR values are the residuals from equation (1), yields (for the 1946–77 sample)

$$(5) \qquad \log(y_t) = \underset{(.05)}{2.92} + \underset{(.23)}{1.06 DMR_t} + \underset{(.24)}{1.08 DMR_{t-1}}$$
$$+ \underset{(.20)}{.07 DMR_{t-2}} + \underset{(.0004)}{.0330 \cdot t}$$
$$+ \underset{(.013)}{.070 \cdot \log(G_t)}$$
$$R^2 = .998, \ \hat{\sigma} = .0169, \ D\text{-}W = 1.5.$$

For the case of the unemployment rate, I have entered the ratio of G to y as an explanatory variable to obtain the estimated equation for the 1949–77 sample,[11]

$$(6) \qquad \log(U/1 - U)_t = \underset{(.12)}{-2.21} - \underset{(2.0)}{6.3 DMR_t}$$
$$\underset{(2.0)}{-10.5 DMR_{t-1}} - \underset{(2.0)}{1.9 DMR_{t-2}}$$
$$\underset{(1.0)}{- 6.7 (G/y)_t,}$$
$$\hat{\sigma} = .145, \ D\text{-}W = 1.6.$$

Lagged values of $\log(G)$ and G/y are insignificant when added to equations (5) and (6), respectively. The estimated equations do suggest an important expansionary effect of the contemporaneous amount of federal purchases. (Another result is the loss of significance of the DMR_{t-2} variable; that is, with $\log(G)$ or G/y substituted for MIL, the lagged effects from money shocks to output and unemployment are shorter than those estimated previously.) If the MIL variable is added to equations (5) and (6), however, its estimated coefficients are significant (0.4, $s.e. = 0.2$ for output; -5.2, $s.e. = 1.4$ for unemployment), while those on $\log(G)$ or G/y become insignificant (.01, $s.e. = .03$ for output; -0.2, $s.e. = 1.8$ for unemployment). Similar results obtain even if the samples are terminated in 1969, that is, if the period where the MIL variable drops to zero is omitted.

It may be worth noting that equation (2), which includes the MIL variable, and equation (6), which contains G/y, have similar implications for the time path of the natural unemployment rate. With all DMR variables and the error term set to zero, equation (2) implies an unemployment rate of 6.4% at the 1977 value of MIL (zero), and 4.5% for the values of MIL (.07 to .08) prevailing in the early 1960s. Equation (6) yields values for the unemployment rate of 6.2% at the 1977 value

---

11. The results differ negligibly if G/y is used as an instrument for $G/\hat{y}$, where $\hat{y}$ is an estimated value of real GNP based on equation (5).

of G/y (.076) and also about 4.5% for the values of G/y (around .125) that existed in the early 1960s. Conceivably, this pattern for the natural unemployment rate is approximately correct even if neither the *MIL* nor the G/y variables are the properly specified military/government purchases influence on unemployment.

Jointly estimated equations that include the federal purchases variables are

(1''')
$$DM_t = \underset{(.015)}{.086} + \underset{(.10)}{.41DM_{t-1}} + \underset{(.08)}{.15DM_{t-2}}$$
$$+ \underset{(.010)}{.079FEDV_t} + \underset{(.005)}{.027 \cdot \log(U/1 - U)_{t-1}},$$
$$\hat{\sigma} = .0132, \ D\text{-}W = 1.9,$$

(5''')
$$\log(y_t) = \underset{(.03)}{2.88} + \underset{(.19)}{1.00DMR_t} + \underset{(.22)}{1.03DMR_{t-1}}$$
$$+ \underset{(.17)}{.00DMR_{t-2}} + \underset{(.0005)}{.0329 \cdot t}$$
$$+ \underset{(.015)}{.081 \cdot \log(G_t)},$$
$$\hat{\sigma} = .0138, \ D\text{-}W = 1.6,$$

(6''')
$$\log(U/1 - U)_t = - \underset{(.13)}{2.19} - \underset{(1.7)}{6.0DMR_t}$$
$$- \underset{(1.7)}{10.7DMR_{t-1}} - \underset{(1.7)}{0.6DMR_{t-2}}$$
$$- \underset{(1.1)}{7.0(G/y)_t},$$
$$\hat{\sigma} = .117, \ D\text{-}W = 1.7.$$

In this case the test statistic for the cross-equation restrictions implied by the unanticipated money hypothesis turns out to be 26.0, which is slightly below the 5% χ^2 value with 16 degrees of freedom of 26.3.

Results from Quarterly U.S. Data

Robert J. Barro and Mark Rush

The second portion of this paper describes results from applying the preceding analysis to quarterly U.S. data.

Money Growth

An estimated equation for money growth, based on quarterly, seasonally adjusted observations, for the period 1941:I to 1978:I, and following the general form of equation (1) is

(7) $$DM_t = \underset{(.0048)}{.0149} + \underset{(.08)}{.54DM_{t-1}} - \underset{(.09)}{.05DM_{t-2}}$$

$$+ \underset{(.09)}{.03DM_{t-3}} + \underset{(.08)}{.09DM_{t-4}} - \underset{(.08)}{.01DM_{t-5}}$$

$$+ \underset{(.07)}{.13DM_{t-6}} + \underset{(.0030)}{.0104FEDV_t}$$

$$- \underset{(.005)}{.003} \cdot \log(U/1 - U)_{t-1}$$

$$+ \underset{(.007)}{.015} \cdot \log(U/1 - U)_{t-2}$$

$$- \underset{(.005)}{.007} \cdot \log(U/1 - U)_{t-3},$$

$$\hat{\sigma} = .0049, \quad D\text{-}W = 2.0,$$

where DM is measured at quarterly rates (see the notes to table 2.3 for data definitions), $FEDV$ is comparable to the annual variable discussed above but with an adjustment coefficient of .05 per quarter, and observations from 1941–46 have been weighted by 0.25. This weight was determined from a maximum likelihood criterion (under normally distributed errors).

The principal explanatory power from the past history of the money growth series appears in the first quarterly lag value, DM_{t-1}. Lags from quarters two through six are of marginal joint significance (the F-value for joint significance is 2.0, which is actually just below the 5% critical value of 2.3). The pattern of DM effects after the first lag is difficult to interpret and may well reflect some persistence that is induced by inappropriate seasonal adjustment procedures (which one would wish to filter out for the present analysis).

The reaction of money growth to lagged unemployment is primarily with a two-quarter lag; the first lag value is insignificant. There is some indication from the negative coefficient on the third lag that DM_t reacts positively to the change in unemployment from period t-3 to t-2 as well as to the level of unemployment at date t-2. Lagged values of the $FEDV$ variable (with $FEDV_t$ included) and additional lag values of the DM and $\log(U/1 - U)$ variables are insignificant when added to equation (7). A comparison of the quarterly and annual money growth equations is carried out in a later section.

Actual values of DM are shown in table 2.3 along with estimated values, $\widehat{DM}$, and residuals, DMR, from equation (7).

Output and Unemployment

The quarterly analysis of output, unemployment, and the price level uses the residuals from equation (7) to measure "unanticipated money growth," *DMR*. Since anticipated money growth is then conditioned on values of *DM* and *U* up to a one-quarter lag, the assumption is that the relevant information lag on these variables is no more than one quarter. We continue to use the contemporaneous value of the *FEDV* variable to generate anticipated money growth (see Barro 1977, p. 106), although a substitution of $FEDV_{t-1}$ has a negligible effect on the results.[12]

A quarterly ordinary least squares equation for output is shown in table 2.1, column 2. This equation includes as explanatory variables a contemporaneous and 10 quarterly lag values of the *DMR* variable, the contemporaneous *MIL* variable, and a time trend. Additional lag values of *DMR* are insignificant. The most interesting result is the precision in the estimates of the quarterly lag pattern for *DMR*, which involves a strong contemporaneous response, a peak effect with a 3–4 quarter lag, a strong persisting effect through two years, and no significant remaining effect after 10 quarters.

The *MIL* variable has a highly significant, positive effect. Lag values over 4 quarters are insignificant. The substitution of the $\log(G_t)$ variable for MIL_t (col. 3) produces only minor changes in the fit or in the estimated pattern of *DMR* coefficients; principally, there is some shortening in the lagged *DMR* effect, which is now significant for only 8 quarters. Lagged values of the $\log(G)$ variable are unimportant, although there is some indication of a negative effect for the first lag.

The estimated output equations show strong positive serial correlation of residuals with *D-W* values of 0.4 and 0.3 in columns 2 and 3, respectively. Estimation of the pattern of residual serial correlation turned out to require a second-order autoregressive form: $u_t = \rho_1 u_{t-1} + \rho_2 u_{t-2} + \epsilon_t$, where ϵ_t is serially independent. The estimated values (based on a maximum likelihood criterion under normally distributed errors) for ρ_1, ρ_2, as shown in column 4 of table 2.1 (which uses the *MIL* variable), are 1.20, *s.e.* $= .09$ and -0.37, *s.e.* $= .09$.[13] Similar results appear in column 5, which uses the $\log(G)$ variable. This pattern of

---

12. With $FEDV_{t-1}$ substituted for $FEDV_t$, the σ value for the *DM* equation rises from .00490 to .00496. The estimated coefficient of $FEDV_{t-1}$ is .0089, *s.e.* $= .0031$, as compared with .0104, *s.e.* $= .0030$ for $FEDV_t$ in equation (7). The other coefficient estimates and standard errors are changed negligibly from those shown in equation (7). The substitution of $FEDV_{t-1}$ for $FEDV_t$ in the *DM* equation is also inconsequential for the analysis of output, unemployment, and the price level.

13. The 95% confidence interval for the sum of the two residual serial correlation coefficient estimates, $(\widehat{\rho_1 + \rho_2})$, which was constructed by finding the restricted value for the sum that yielded the 5% critical value of the likelihood ratio, turns out to have an upper limit of .92, which is below the nonstationary region. In particular, the value of $-2 \cdot \log(\text{likelihood ratio})$ corresponding to the restriction $\rho_1 + \rho_2 = 1.0$ is 14.6, which exceeds the 5% critical value for the χ^2 distribution with 1 degree of freedom of 3.8. A difficulty with this test, however, is that the usual desirable asymptotic properties of the estimators do not hold in the region where $\rho_1 + \rho_2 \geq 1$. For the case of the unemployment rate

persistence for the error term implies strong positive serial correlation of residuals from quarter to quarter, but much weaker association from year to year.

The main impact of the residual serial correlation correction on the coefficient estimates of the output equations are, first, a reduction in the contemporaneous *DMR* effect, and second, a shortening of the overall lag response, which is now significant (in cols. 4 and 5 of table 2.1) for only 7 quarters. The pattern of output response to monetary shocks is now concentrated in the 1–5 quarter range. The coefficient estimates of the *MIL* or log(*G*) variables (and the time trend) are not materially altered from those in the *OLS* regressions. If the *MIL* and log(*G*) variables are entered simultaneously in the case where estimation of a second-order pattern of residual serial correlation is also carried out, the coefficient estimates are .16, *s.e.* = .16 for *MIL* and .060, *s.e.* = .027 for log(*G*). But the "relative significance" of these two variables is reversed in the unemployment rate equation (below).

Actual values of output growth, $DY_t \equiv \log(y_t/y_{t-1})$, are shown along with estimated values, $\widehat{DY}_t \equiv \widehat{\log(y_t)} - \log(y_{t-1})$, and residuals in table 2.3, where $\widehat{\log(y_t)}$ is calculated from the equation in table 2.1, column 4.

Results for the unemployment rate, shown in columns 6–9 of table 2.1, are basically similar to those for output. These equations involve a starting date in 1949 (corresponding to that for the annual data discussed above), although a shift to samples that begin in 1947 does not substantially alter the estimates. There is again a precisely estimated pattern of lag response to *DMR* values, with a shortened lag appearing in the equations (cols. 8 and 9) that contain a correction for second-order residual serial correlation. The peak response of the unemployment rate to *DMR* values in columns 8 and 9 of table 2.1 is at 2–5 quarter lag, which is slightly delayed relative to the response of output.

The unemployment rate equations shown in columns 6 and 8 use the *MIL* variable, while those in columns 7 and 9 use the variable $(G/y)_t$. (The use of $(G/\hat{y})_t$ as an instrument, where $\hat{y}_t$ is an estimated value for output calculated from the equations shown in cols. 2–5, produces a negligible change in results.) The estimated coefficients of the *MIL* or G/y variables are not sensitive to the correction for serial correlation of residuals. If the *MIL* and G/y variables are entered simultaneously in an equation that also includes correction for residual serial correlation,

---

equation (table 2.1, col. 8), a similar procedure yields a 95% confidence interval for $(\widehat{\rho_1 + \rho_2})$ with an upper limit of .85. The value of $-2 \cdot \log(\text{likelihood ratio})$ corresponding to $\rho_1 + \rho_2 = 1$ is 23.0 in this case. Finally, for the price level equation (table 2.2, col. 5), the upper limit of the 95% confidence interval for $(\widehat{\rho_1 + \rho_2})$ is .97 and the value of $-2 \cdot \log(\text{likelihood ratio})$ corresponding to $\rho_1 + \rho_2 = 1$ is 10.8.

Table 2.1 Quarterly Output and Unemployment Rate Equations

(1)	(2)	(3)	(4)	(5)	(6)	(7)	(8)	(9)
Dep. Var.	$\log(y_t)$	$\log(y_t)$	$\log(y_t)$	$\log(y_t)$	$\log(U/1-U)_t$	$\log(U/1-U)_t$	$\log(U/1-U)_t$	$\log(U/1-U)_t$
Sample	47:I–78:I	47:I–78:I	47:III–78:I	47:III–78:I	49:I–78:I	49:I–78:I	49:III–78:I	49:III–78:I
Constant	5.79(.01)	5.59(.03)	5.78(.03)	5.56(.07)	−2.70(.02)	−2.28(.06)	−2.69(.06)	−2.48(.17)
DMR_t	1.01(.35)	1.03(.36)	0.52(.18)	0.55(.18)	−3.7(2.8)	−4.4(3.3)	−4.1(1.7)	−4.0(1.9)
DMR_{t-1}	1.50(.35)	1.40(.36)	1.13(.27)	1.22(.27)	−6.2(2.8)	−6.5(3.3)	−7.2(2.5)	−7.1(2.7)
DMR_{t-2}	1.47(.34)	1.34(.35)	1.25(.32)	1.40(.32)	−11.3(2.8)	−11.7(3.3)	−12.2(2.9)	−11.8(3.2)
DMR_{t-3}	1.79(.32)	1.94(.33)	1.53(.34)	1.64(.34)	−11.9(2.7)	−12.8(3.3)	−13.6(2.9)	−13.0(3.3)
DMR_{t-4}	1.73(.31)	1.67(.32)	1.60(.34)	1.64(.34)	−14.6(2.7)	−16.3(3.3)	−15.2(2.9)	−14.7(3.3)
DMR_{t-5}	1.51(.31)	1.43(.32)	1.13(.31)	1.18(.31)	−14.5(2.7)	−14.6(3.3)	−12.2(2.8)	−11.6(3.2)
DMR_{t-6}	1.33(.30)	1.27(.32)	0.75(.25)	0.80(.25)	−14.6(2.7)	−14.0(3.3)	−8.4(2.5)	−8.1(2.7)
DMR_{t-7}	1.11(.30)	0.88(.32)	0.28(.16)	0.33(.15)	−13.3(2.7)	−11.2(3.2)	−4.0(1.7)	−4.0(1.8)
DMR_{t-8}	0.98(.30)	0.54(.32)			−10.3(2.7)	−7.5(3.2)		
DMR_{t-9}	0.82(.29)				−6.6(2.7)			
DMR_{t-10}	0.43(.29)				−5.4(2.7)			
MIL_t	0.35(.04)		0.36(.11)		−3.3(0.2)		−3.4(0.5)	
$\log(G_t)$		.066(.007)		.072(.017)				
$(G/y)_t$						−6.2(0.5)		−4.5(1.4)
t	.00897(.00006)	.00828(.00006)	.00897(.00019)	.00828(.00014)				
u_{t-1}			1.20(.09)	1.22(.09)			1.16(.09)	1.19(.09)
u_{t-2}			−0.37(.09)	−0.42(.09)			−0.41(.09)	−0.39(.09)
R^2	.997	.997	—	—	.82	.74	—	—
σ	.0179	.0187	.0092	.0090	.135	.161	.083	.089
D-W	0.4	0.3	2.1	2.1	0.5	0.4	2.2	2.1

the coefficient estimates are for MIL_t: -4.0, $s.e. = 1.1$, and for $(G/y)_t$: 1.4, $s.e. = 2.1$.

The pattern of serial correlation of residuals, $\rho_1 = 1.16$, $s.e. = .09$ and $\hat{\rho}_2 = -0.41$, $s.e. = .09$ in column 8, is similar to that found for output. Actual values of U are shown with estimated values and residuals from the column 8 equation in table 2.3.

Price Level

Quarterly price level estimates are shown in table 2.2. The *OLS* regression in column 2 of the table includes an unrestricted coefficient estimate for the $\log(M_t)$ variable, while the column 3 regression restricts this coefficient to equal unity. (Inclusion of R_{t-4} as an instrument for R_t affects principally the estimates of the R_t coefficient, which increase from those shown in cols. 2 and 3 of table 2.2.)

The estimated *DMR* coefficients in the equations shown in columns 2 and 3 are negative and individually significantly different from zero over a lag of 24 quarters. For example, in column 3, which sets the coefficient of $\log(M_t)$ to 1, the *DMR* pattern is remarkably flat and strongly negative for lags between 1 and 18–20 quarters. As with the annual data, the elongation of the *DMR* pattern relative to that revealed by the output equation is evident from these results.

Similar to the output and unemployment results, the quarterly price equation estimated by *OLS* exhibits strong positive serial correlation of residuals. Reestimation subject to a second-order autoregressive process for the error term is carried out in columns 4 and 5 of table 2.2. The estimated pattern: $\hat{\rho}_1 = 1.60$, $s.e. = .08$; $\hat{\rho}_2 = -0.67$, $s.e. = .07$, indicates that the serial correlation of residuals is even more pronounced than that found for the output and unemployment equations.

The estimated coefficient of $\log(M_t)$ in column 4, .93, $s.e. = .09$, differs insignificantly from 1. The pattern of *DMR* coefficients in this equation and in the column 5 equation that constrains the $\log(M_t)$ coefficient to equal 1 are substantially less drawn out than those shown in columns 2 and 3. Lagged values over 14 quarters are now significant, with the principal effects occurring in the 1–12 quarter range.

NOTES TO TABLE 2.1

The variables U, y, M, and G are seasonally adjusted. The dependent variable for cols. 2–5 is $\log(GNP)$, where GNP is in 1972 dollars. The dependent variable for cols. 6–9 is $\log(U/1 - U)$, where U is the unemployment rate in the total labor force. G is real federal purchases of goods and services, and t is a time trend. *MIL* is the military personnel variable discussed in the text. DMR_t is the residual from the money growth equation (7).

Cols. 4, 5, 8, and 9 involve estimation of a second-order autoregressive process for the error term, as described by the coefficients on u_{t-1} and u_{t-2}. Standard errors of coefficient estimates are shown in parentheses. $\hat{\sigma}$ is the standard error of estimate. *D-W* is the Durbin-Watson statistic.

Table 2.2 **Quarterly Price Level Equations**

(1)	(2)	(3)	(4)	(5)
Sample	48:I–78:I	48:I–78:I	48:III–78:I	48:III–78:I
Constant	−1.13(.10)	−0.79(.01)	−0.36(.40)	−0.64(.03)
$\log(M_t)$	1.08(.02)	1	0.93(.09)	1
DMR_t	−.42(.28)	−0.37(.30)	−0.64(.14)	−0.70(.11)
DMR_{t-1}	−1.02(.27)	−0.98(.28)	−1.04(.24)	−1.13(.20)
DMR_{t-2}	−1.25(.27)	−1.21(.28)	−1.08(.31)	−1.18(.28)
DMR_{t-3}	−1.38(.27)	−1.36(.28)	−0.96(.37)	−1.05(.33)
DMR_{t-4}	−1.47(.26)	−1.46(.28)	−0.92(.40)	−1.01(.37)
DMR_{t-5}	−1.68(.27)	−1.66(.28)	−0.88(.42)	−0.97(.39)
DMR_{t-6}	−1.87(.26)	−1.89(.28)	−1.08(.43)	−1.16(.40)
DMR_{t-7}	−2.06(.25)	−2.07(.27)	−1.03(.43)	−1.10(.40)
DMR_{t-8}	−2.16(.26)	−2.20(.27)	−1.01(.42)	−1.07(.40)
DMR_{t-9}	−2.09(.26)	−2.09(.27)	−0.97(.41)	−1.02(.39)
DMR_{t-10}	−1.88(.26)	−1.83(.27)	−0.78(.37)	−0.83(.36)
DMR_{t-11}	−1.85(.25)	−1.81(.26)	−0.90(.33)	−0.93(.32)
DMR_{t-12}	−1.79(.25)	−1.77(.26)	−0.84(.26)	−0.86(.26)
DMR_{t-13}	−1.58(.24)	−1.55(.25)	−0.51(.18)	−0.52(.18)
DMR_{t-14}	−1.50(.23)	−1.39(.24)	−0.31(.10)	−0.32(.09)
DMR_{t-15}	−1.09(.23)	−0.96(.24)		
DMR_{t-16}	−1.23(.23)	−1.05(.24)		
DMR_{t-17}	−1.13(.21)	−0.93(.21)		
DMR_{t-18}	−1.28(.21)	−1.08(.21)		
DMR_{t-19}	−1.12(.21)	−0.88(.21)		
DMR_{t-20}	−1.02(.20)	−0.82(.20)		
DMR_{t-21}	−0.90(.17)	−0.75(.18)		
DMR_{t-22}	−0.73(.17)	−0.61(.18)		
DMR_{t-23}	−0.57(.17)	−0.43(.18)		
DMR_{t-24}	−0.43(.17)	−0.32(.18)		
$(G/y)_t$	.62(.07)	.58(.07)	−0.32(.14)	−0.30(.15)
R_t	2.7(0.3)	3.0(0.3)	−0.2(0.3)	−0.2(0.3)
t	−.0028(.0002)	−.0023(.0002)	−.0005(.0009)	−.0011(.0003)
u_{t-1}			1.60(.08)	1.60(.08)
u_{t-2}			−0.67(.07)	−0.67(.07)
R^2	.999	.998	—	—
σ	.0123	.0130	.0052	.0051
D-W	0.4	0.4	2.2	2.2

NOTES
The dependent variable is $\log(P_t)$, where P is the seasonally adjusted *GNP* deflator (1972 = 1). M is the level of the seasonally adjusted $M1$ concept of the money stock. R is the Aaa corporate bond rate. See the notes to table 2.1 for other definitions.

The coefficient of $\log(M_t)$ is constrained to equal 1 in cols. 3 and 5. Estimation of a second-order autoregressive process for the error term is carried out in cols. 4 and 5.

The coefficients of the G/y, R, and t variables are not robust to the correction for serial correlation of residuals. In particular, the coefficient estimate for G/y changes sign, while that for R becomes insignificant. These results are indicative of some specification error in the price equation—a conclusion that also emerged from some hypothesis tests that were carried out above with the annual data.

We have not yet obtained any jointly estimated equations from quarterly data for systems involving the money growth and other equations.

Comparison of Annual and Quarterly Results

Correspondence between the annual and quarterly results constitutes an additional check on the statistical properties of a "dynamic" model. There does turn out to be a close correspondence in the results for the money growth, unemployment, and output equations, but not for the price equation.

Consider first the annual unemployment equation (2) (equation (2′) is similar) and the quarterly equation in column 8 of table 2.1, which includes the MIL variable and adjustment for serial correlation of residuals. The constant terms are virtually identical, so that both equations generate a "natural" unemployment rate of .064 at $MIL = 0$ and with all values of the DMR variables set to zero. Since the money growth rates are measured at quarterly rates in the quarterly equation, the overall level of estimated DMR coefficients in this equation should be roughly 4 times those shown in the annual equation. In fact, the sum of the magnitude of the DMR coefficients from the quarterly regression (table 2.1, col. 8) is 76.9, which is 3.7 times the sum (21.0) from the annual equation (2). Therefore, the two equations generate approximately the same response of the unemployment rate to a sustained DMR stimulus (which would, since DMR is constructed to be serially independent, be an unusual event). The quarterly estimates provide a much finer description of the dynamic response, although the peak effect at a four-quarter lag is consistent with the peak at a one-year lag in the annual data.

A discrepancy arises in the estimated MIL coefficients, which are -5.3, $s.e. = 0.6$ in the annual equation and -3.4, $s.e. = 0.5$ in the quarterly case. Similarly, when the G/y variable is substituted for MIL, the annual coefficient estimate in equation (6) is -6.7, $s.e. = 1.0$, while the quarterly estimate (table 2.1, col. 9) is -4.5, $s.e. = 1.4$.

The comparison of annual and quarterly results for output is basically similar. The sum of DMR coefficient magnitudes in the quarterly equation from table 2.1, column 4 is 8.2, which is 3.3 times the annual sum (3.5) from equation (3). The quarterly MIL coefficient is .33, $s.e. = .15$, which is below the annual estimate of .54, $s.e. = .09$. In

Table 2.3   Quarterly Values of Money Growth, Output Growth, and Unemployment

(1)	(2)	(3)	(4)	(5)	(6)	(7)	(8)	(9)	(10)
	DM	$\widehat{DM}$	DMR	Dy	$\widehat{Dy}$	DyR	U	$\widehat{U}$	UR
1941:I	.0553	.0452	.0101						
41:II	.0348	.0506	−.0158						
41:III	.0345	.0348	−.0003						
41:IV	.0168	.0396	−.0228						
42:I	.0470	.0339	.0131						
42:II	.0500	.0446	.0054						
42:III	.0693	.0584	.0109						
42:IV	.0774	.0543	.0231						
43:I	.0866	.0622	.0244						
43:II	.0457	.0640	−.0183						
43:III	.0752	.0431	.0321						
43:IV	.0108	.0649	−.0541						
44:I	.0373	.0337	.0036						
44:II	.0476	.0426	.0050						
44:III	.0345	.0458	−.0113						
44:IV	.0591	.0323	.0268						
1945:I	.0404	.0522	−.0118						
45:II	.0269	.0302	−.0033						
45:III	.0236	.0234	.0002						
45:IV	.0227	.0223	.0004						
46:I	−.0002	.0196	−.0198						
46:II	.0325	.0128	.0197						

Notes to table 2.3 are on p. 47.

Table 2.3 (Continued)

(1)	(2) DM	(3) $\widehat{DM}$	(4) DMR	(5) Dy	(6) $\widehat{Dy}$	(7) DyR	(8) U	(9) $\widehat{U}$	(10) UR
46:III	.0140	.0242	−.0102						
46:IV	.0036	.0098	−.0062						
47:I	−.0017	.0009	−.0026						
47:II	.0163	.0031	.0132						
47:III	.0089	.0061	.0028	.0011	.0070	−.0059			
47:IV	.0044	.0053	−.0009	.0121	.0128	−.0007			
48:I	.0000	.0019	−.0019	.0076	.0134	−.0058			
48:II	−.0089	−.0024	−.0065	.0181	.0094	.0087			
48:III	−.0009	−.0054	.0063	.0098	.0144	−.0046			
48:IV	−.0036	.0021	−.0057	.0103	.0077	.0026			
49:I	−.0054	−.0014	−.0040	−.0101	−.0011	−.0090			
49:II	.0018	−.0037	.0055	−.0041	.0050	−.0091			
49:III	−.0036	.0034	−.0070	.0092	.0098	+.0006	.065	.061	.004
49:IV	.0000	−.0005	.0005	−.0085	.0076	−.0161	.068	.065	.003
1950:I	.0090	.0047	.0043	.0446	.0158	.0288	.062	.066	−.004
50:II	.0151	.0072	.0079	.0262	.0279	−.0017	.055	.054	.001
50:III	.0105	.0069	.0036	.0324	.0194	.0130	.045	.050	−.005
50:IV	.0087	.0062	.0025	.0222	.0309	−.0087	.040	.036	.004
51:I	.0103	.0051	.0052	.0140	.0211	−.0071	.033	.035	−.002
51:II	.0093	.0084	.0009	.0190	.0162	.0028	.029	.030	−.001
51:III	.0126	.0079	.0047	.0199	.0131	.0068	.030	.027	.003
51:IV	.0182	.0105	.0077	.0017	.0134	−.0117	.032	.031	.001

Table 2.3 (Continued)

(1)	(2) DM	(3) $\widehat{DM}$	(4) DMR	(5) Dy	(6) $\widehat{Dy}$	(7) DyR	(8) U	(9) $\widehat{U}$	(10) UR
52:I	.0130	.0137	−.0007	.0095	.0061	.0034	.029	.032	−.003
52:II	.0081	.0119	−.0038	.0014	.0042	−.0028	.028	.028	.000
52:III	.0104	.0086	.0018	.0104	.0049	.0055	.030	.029	.001
52:IV	.0103	.0098	.0004	.0235	.0057	.0178	.026	.032	−.006
53:I	.0039	.0114	−.0075	.0157	.0012	.0145	.026	.028	−.002
53:II	.0063	.0057	.0006	.0064	.0003	.0061	.025	.029	−.004
53:III	.0016	.0076	−.0060	−.0061	−.0017	−.0044	.026	.029	−.003
53:IV	.0008	.0033	−.0025	−.0097	−.0100	.0003	.035	.030	.005
54:I	.0031	.0021	.0010	−.0136	−.0016	−.0120	.050	.043	.007
54:II	.0023	.0060	−.0037	−.0041	−.0003	−.0038	.055	.056	−.001
54:III	.0092	.0070	.0022	.0144	.0047	.0097	.057	.055	.002
54:IV	.0107	.0095	.0012	.0189	.0184	.0005	.050	.053	−.003
1955:I	.0113	.0096	.0017	.0237	.0143	.0094	.045	.044	.001
55:II	.0060	.0075	−.0015	.0150	.0122	.0028	.042	.043	−.001
55:III	.0045	.0054	−.0009	.0145	.0095	.0050	.039	.040	−.001
55:IV	.0015	.0047	−.0032	.0101	.0053	.0048	.040	.039	.001
1956:I	.0037	.0032	.0005	−.0044	.0030	−.0074	.038	.041	−.003
56:II	.0022	.0056	−.0034	.0051	−.0013	.0064	.040	.039	.001
56:III	.0007	.0033	−.0026	.0006	.0009	−.0003	.039	.043	−.004
56:IV	.0044	.0031	.0013	.0116	.0046	.0070	.039	.040	−.001
57:I	.0022	.0046	−.0024	.0069	.0083	−.0014	.037	.041	−.004
57:II	.0000	.0031	−.0031	.0007	.0040	−.0033	.039	.038	.001

Table 2.3 (Continued)

(1)	(2) DM	(3) $\widehat{DM}$	(4) DMR	(5) Dy	(6) $\widehat{Dy}$	(7) DyR	(8) U	(9) $\widehat{U}$	(10) UR
57:III	.0007	.0011	−.0004	.0069	.0066	.0003	.040	.042	−.002
57:IV	−.0059	.0029	−.0088	−.0132	.0030	−.0162	.047	.044	.003
58:I	−.0015	−.0015	.0000	−.0197	−.0015	−.0182	.061	.052	.009
58:II	.0117	.0034	.0083	.0072	.0124	−.0052	.071	.063	.008
58:III	.0101	.0125	−.0024	.0240	.0172	.0068	.070	.068	.002
58:IV	.0122	.0107	.0015	.0255	.0201	.0054	.062	.062	.000
59:I	.0134	.0113	.0021	.0122	.0275	−.0153	.056	.053	.003
59:II	.0084	.0104	−.0020	.0217	.0145	.0072	.049	.049	.000
59:III	.0049	.0078	−.0029	−.0107	.0126	−.0233	.051	.046	.005
59:IV	−.0062	.0067	−.0129	.0105	.0002	.0103	.054	.052	.002
1960:I	−.0042	.0017	−.0059	.0198	.0008	.0190	.049	.057	−.008
60:II	−.0014	.0042	−.0056	−.0024	.0062	−.0086	.050	.052	−.002
60:III	.0077	.0032	.0044	−.0043	.0028	−.0071	.053	.052	.001
60:IV	.0021	.0073	−.0052	−.0052	.0047	−.0099	.061	.058	.003
61:I	.0041	.0042	−.0001	.0064	.0097	−.0033	.066	.062	.004
61:II	.0083	.0063	.0020	.0167	.0211	−.0044	.068	.064	.004
61:III	.0061	.0094	−.0033	.0129	.0222	−.0093	.066	.062	.004
61:IV	.0095	.0079	.0016	.0237	.0199	.0038	.060	.058	.002
62:I	.0061	.0112	−.0051	.0143	.0213	−.0070	.054	.055	−.001
62:II	.0040	.0077	−.0037	.0129	.0086	.0043	.053	.050	.003
62:III	−.0020	.0060	−.0080	.0075	.0072	.0003	.054	.055	−.001
62:IV	.0060	.0041	.0019	.0019	.0080	−.0061	.053	.053	.000

Table 2.3 (Continued)

(1)	(2) DM	(3) $\widehat{DM}$	(4) DMR	(5) Dy	(6) $\widehat{Dy}$	(7) DyR	(8) U	(9) $\widehat{U}$	(10) UR
63:I	.0093	.0085	.0008	.0095	.0083	.0012	.056	.054	.002
63:II	.0098	.0091	.0007	.0125	.0126	−.0001	.055	.055	.000
63:III	.0097	.0096	.0001	.0182	.0154	.0028	.053	.053	.000
63:IV	.0103	.0096	.0007	.0096	.0188	−.0092	.054	.049	.005
64:I	.0057	.0088	−.0031	.0166	.0121	.0045	.053	.052	.001
64:II	.0095	.0080	.0015	.0126	.0140	−.0014	.050	.050	.000
64:III	.0162	.0102	.0060	.0097	.0145	−.0048	.048	.047	.001
64:IV	.0123	.0129	−.0006	.0038	.0101	−.0063	.048	.046	.002
1965:I	.0067	.0098	−.0031	.0214	.0065	.0149	.047	.047	.000
65:II	.0079	.0081	−.0002	.0147	.0146	.0001	.044	.046	−.002
65:III	.0114	.0090	.0024	.0172	.0112	.0060	.042	.042	−.000
65:IV	.0166	.0103	.0063	.0209	.0122	.0087	.039	.041	−.002
66:I	.0157	.0135	.0022	.0183	.0133	.0050	.037	.038	−.001
66:II	.0121	.0120	.0001	.0069	.0088	−.0019	.036	.036	.000
66:III	−.0017	.0098	−.0115	.0093	.0011	.0082	.036	.037	−.001
66:IV	.0011	.0033	−.0022	.0075	.0009	.0066	.035	.037	−.002
67:I	.0102	.0064	.0038	.0016	.0029	−.0013	.036	.038	−.002
67:II	.0146	.0105	.0041	.0069	−.0002	.0071	.036	.038	−.002
67:III	.0220	.0118	.0102	.0122	.0074	.0048	.036	.037	−.001
67:IV	.0146	.0154	−.0008	.0078	.0146	−.0068	.037	.036	.001
68:I	.0128	.0100	.0028	.0096	.0104	−.0008	.035	.035	.000
68:II	.0189	.0111	.0078	.0173	.0188	−.0015	.034	.033	.001

Table 2.3 (Continued)

(1)	(2)	(3)	(4)	(5)	(6)	(7)	(8)	(9)	(10)
	DM	$\widehat{DM}$	DMR	Dy	$\widehat{Dy}$	DyR	U	$\widehat{U}$	UR
68:III	.0206	.0150	.0056	.0117	.0162	−.0045	.033	.032	.001
68:IV	.0197	.0153	.0044	.0027	.0060	−.0033	.033	.033	.000
69:I	.0183	.0153	.0030	.0094	.0084	.0010	.033	.033	.000
69:II	.0107	.0143	−.0036	.0045	.0065	−.0020	.034	.033	.001
69:III	.0058	.0099	−.0041	.0035	.0006	.0029	.035	.036	−.001
69:IV	.0058	.0087	−.0029	−.0055	.0005	−.0060	.035	.037	−.002
1970:I	.0091	.0089	.0002	−.0036	−.0047	.0011	.039	.039	.000
70:II	.0128	.0096	.0032	.0005	−.0053	.0058	.046	.048	−.002
70:III	.0126	.0117	.0009	.0073	.0010	.0063	.050	.054	−.004
70:IV	.0133	.0120	.0013	−.0098	.0052	−.0150	.056	.054	.002
71:I	.0168	.0117	.0051	.0221	.0070	.0150	.063	.058	.005
71:II	.0249	.0147	.0102	.0073	.0206	−.0133	.056	.061	−.005
71:III	.0165	.0206	−.0041	.0070	.0090	−.0020	.058	.053	.005
71:IV	.0065	.0134	−.0069	.0085	.0023	.0062	.053	.058	−.005
72:I	.0178	.0109	.0069	.0183	.0100	.0083	.061	.052	.009
72:II	.0200	.0161	.0039	.0189	.0118	.0071	.054	.064	.010
72:III	.0208	.0190	.0018	.0128	.0036	.0092	.054	.052	.002
72:IV	.0220	.0175	.0045	.0203	.0084	.0119	.048	.055	−.007
73:I	.0184	.0192	−.0008	.0227	.0091	.0136	.053	.047	.006
73:II	.0158	.0137	.0021	.0011	.0051	−.0040	.047	.055	−.008
73:III	.0137	.0166	−.0029	.0042	−.0002	.0044	.047	.047	.000
73:IV	.0127	.0132	−.0005	.0051	−.0047	.0098	.043	.050	−.007

Table 2.3 (Continued)

(1)	(2) DM	(3) $\widehat{DM}$	(4) DMR	(5) Dy	(6) $\widehat{Dy}$	(7) DyR	(8) U	(9) $\widehat{U}$	(10) UR
74:I	.0148	.0138	.0010	−.0100	−.0029	−.0071	.054	.047	.007
74:II	.0138	.0127	.0011	−.0046	−.0029	−.0017	.056	.061	−.005
74:III	.0104	.0156	−.0052	−.0062	−.0029	−.0033	.054	.060	−.006
74:IV	.0100	.0124	−.0024	−.0142	.0002	−.0144	.060	.056	.004
1975:I	.0014	.0112	−.0098	−.0252	−.0019	−.0234	.080	.067	.013
75:II	.0182	.0077	.0105	.0156	.0040	.0116	.085	.085	.000
75:III	.0176	.0207	−.0031	.0270	.0208	.0062	.084	.086	−.002
75:IV	.0058	.0179	−.0121	.0074	.0095	−.0021	.083	.081	.002
76:I	.0071	.0101	−.0030	.0211	.0089	.0122	.074	.083	−.009
76:II	.0204	.0129	.0075	.0123	.0225	−.0102	.073	.068	.005
76:III	.0108	.0167	−.0058	.0096	.0063	.0033	.077	.074	.003
76:IV	.0162	.0127	.0035	.0029	.0095	−.0066	.077	.076	.001
77:I	.0178	.0173	.0005	.0182	.0157	.0025	.074	.075	−.001
77:II	.0194	.0169	.0025	.0149	.0153	−.0004	.067	.069	−.002
77:III	.0199	.0170	.0029	.0125	.0178	−.0053	.065	.062	.003
77:IV	.0178	.0184	−.0006	.0095	.0154	−.0059	.060	.061	−.001
78:I	.0124	.0165	−.0041	−.0010	.0055	−.0065	.061	.060	.001

contrast, the quarterly estimate of the $\log(G_t)$ coefficient is .072, $s.e. = .017$ (table 2.1, col. 5), which corresponds to the annual estimate from equation (5) of .070, $s.e. = .013$.

In the case of the money growth equations, it is possible to compare the pattern of effects from the past history of the series that is shown over 6 lags for the quarterly equation (7) with that estimated from two annual lag values in equation (1). The autoregressive form of the quarterly equation (7) can be expressed as a moving average of independent shocks to money growth.[14] Four adjacent quarterly values can then be added to get an implied moving average representation for annual money growth rates.[15] It is then possible to determine the implied coefficients for a second-order autoregression on annual data. (There is an approximation here in that the annual data are actually log differences of annual average money stocks, rather than log differences of quarterly average money stocks separated by 4 quarters.) The coefficients for the annual equation that correspond to the 6 quarterly lag coefficients shown in equation (7) turn out to be .45 on DM_{t-1} and .11 on DM_{t-2}, which correspond closely to the estimates shown in equation (1). Therefore, the quarterly and annual forms of the money growth equation display similar patterns of persistence. It also turns out

14. The sequence of coefficients turns out to be: 1, .54, .24, .13, .17, .13, .21, .19, .14, .10, .09, .08, ...

15. The sequence of coefficients is: 1, 1.54, 1.78, 1.92, 1.08, .67, .64, .70, .68, .65, .53, .42, .36, .33, .30, ...

NOTES TO TABLE 2.3

$DM_t \equiv \log(M_t/M_{t-1})$ where M_t is the quarterly average value of $M1$ as adjusted for seasonality by the Federal Reserve and by Friedman and Schwartz before 1946. Data since 1947 are from the *Federal Reserve Bulletin*, incorporating revisions through April 1978. Data before 1947 are from Friedman and Schwartz 1970, table 2. These values have been multiplied by 1.013 as an approximate correction for the omission of deposits due to foreign banks. These deposits were included in $M1$ retroactively to 1947 with the revision in the October 1960 *Federal Reserve Bulletin*.

$\widehat{DM}_t$ is the estimated value from equation (7).

$DMR_t \equiv DM_t - \widehat{DM}_t$.

y_t is the Commerce Department seasonally adjusted GNP in 1972 dollars.

$Dy_t \equiv \log(y_t/y_{t-1})$

$\widehat{Dy}_t \equiv \widehat{\log y}_t - \log y_{t-1}$, where $\widehat{\log y}_t$ is the estimated value from the equation in table 2.1, col. 4.

$DyR_t \equiv Dy_t - \widehat{Dy}_t$.

U is the seasonally adjusted unemployment rate in the total labor force, calculated from standard Bureau of Labor Statistics figures on numbers of unemployed and the total labor force.

$\widehat{U}$ is the estimated value based on the equation in table 2.2, col. 8.

$UR \equiv U - \widehat{U}$.

that the σ value shown in the quarterly equation (7) is consistent with that estimated for the annual equation (1).

With respect to the lagged unemployment effect on money growth, consider an increase in the $\log(U/1 - U)$ variable that persists over a full year. The effect on next year's money growth rate can be determined from the quarterly equation (7) by taking account of the direct effect of the lagged U variables and also of the persisting effect from the presence of past values of the DM series. The impact on the sum of the four quarterly DM values for the next year turns out to involve a response coefficient of .028, which corresponds to the coefficient estimate of .027 that was estimated from annual data in equation (1).

A similar calculation for the $FEDV$ variable indicates that a sustained, uniform increase in this variable would, according to the quarterly equation (7), affect contemporaneous annual money growth with a coefficient of .065. This effect compares with an estimated coefficient of .073 in the annual equation (1).[16]

Correspondence between annual and quarterly estimates does not hold in the case of the price equation. The sum of the magnitude of the DMR coefficients from the quarterly price equation in table 2.2, column 5 (with the coefficient of $\log(M_t)$ constrained to 1 and with adjustment for second-order residual serial correlation) is only 2.1 times that shown in the annual equation (4), as compared with a theoretical value of 4. Interestingly, the quarterly price equation without serial correlation correction (table 2.2, col. 3) displays a sum of DMR coefficient magnitudes that is 4.8 times that in equation (4). The sensitivity of the estimated coefficients in quarterly price level equations to serial correlation adjustment and the discrepancy between quarterly and annual coefficient estimates probably reflect a common source of misspecification.

The volatility of the coefficient estimates of the G/y, R, and t variables in quarterly price equations has already been noted. The estimated coefficients of these variables in a price equation that is estimated without serial correlation adjustment (table 2.2, col. 3) actually correspond well to those found in an annual price equation (under OLS estimation; see n. 5, above). However, the introduction of residual serial correlation adjustment (table 2.2, col. 5) drastically alters the quarterly coefficient estimates of these variables and thereby produces a discrepancy between the quarterly and annual estimates.

---

16. The calculated value of .065 is an underestimate of the annual effect because of the larger adjustment of "normal" federal expenditure to the contemporaneous value of federal spending in the annual equation. With this effect considered, the quarterly and annual estimates would correspond more closely.

Comment   Alan Blinder

> Through the night of doubt and sorrow
> Onward goes the pilgrim band,
> Singing songs of expectation,
> Marching to the promised land.
> —B. S. Ingemann, 1825

Preliminaries

One need only look around this room to realize that the only way to have any real effect at this conference is to say something unanticipated. Hence, I want to begin by heaping praise upon Robert Barro for his imaginative and important empirical work. Along with Robert Lucas's justly acclaimed critique of econometric policy evaluation (Lucas 1976), Barro's well-known paper in the 1977 *American Economic Review,* of which the paper under discussion is a direct descendant, is in my view one of the two truly indispensable pieces in the rational expectations literature.

Needless to say, ever since Barro's work began circulating in draft form, Keynesians have been searching for an obvious flaw in his methodology. That one has not been found suggests that the basic flaw, if indeed there is one, is far from obvious. One result of this fruitless search has been that Barro's work has moved our priors somewhat. A priori assertions that one finds implausible and uncongenial are always easy to rebut by other a priori assertions. Empirical results cannot be dismissed so cavalierly.

Still, like most Keynesians, I am not yet ready to throw in the towel. One regression is not enough to destroy impressions built up over many years and buttressed by theoretical, statistical, and casual empirical evidence. And there do seem to be a few flies in the Barro ointment. This comment is mainly about the flies. But before going into them in detail, I want to stress that each of the criticisms provides no more than a reason why Barro's crucial result—that only unanticipated money matters—*might* be wrong; nothing here purports to show that he is in fact wrong. Barro's results are impressive and provocative, and the joint estimates presented here make them all the more so, despite some nagging worries about the price equation.

Theoretical Matters

One thing that makes many people uneasy with Barro's results is that the "second generation" of macroeconomic models incorporating rational expectations has shown that the conclusion that only unanticipated changes in the money supply have real effects is *not* generally true under rational expectations. I am referring here to such papers as Phelps and Taylor (1977), Fischer (1977, 1979), Blinder and Fischer (1978), Taylor (1979), Blanchard (chap. 3 below); and I apologize to other authors whom I have omitted from this list.

In contrast to the original series of papers by Lucas (1973, 1976), Sargent and Wallace (1975), and Barro (1976), these more recent explorations of the implications of rational expectations generally find that even anticipated changes in the money supply (or, perhaps, in its growth rate) have real (albeit transitory) effects through one of two mechanisms: either there are elements of fixity in wages or prices so that not all markets clear instantly, or anticipated money affects the real interest rate through its effect on the expected rate of inflation. I am confident that both of these factors are operative in the real world. How important they are empirically is another question, however, and this is why we need empirical work like Barro's.

There is an irony here that must be pointed out, lest we think there is anything new under the sun. In the old "Keynes versus the classics" debate over the neutrality of money, much ink was spilled before it was realized that the real effects of monetary policy rested on two main pillars: interest rate effects on some component of aggregate demand (at the time, distinctions were not usually made between real and nominal interest rates), and nominal wage-price rigidities.[17] This was true long before rational expectations, even adaptive expectations, become popular. It now seems that we have come full circle. As we start to digest the meaning of the rational expectations revolution, we come once again to realize that the nonneutrality of money rests on one of these two foundations.

All of this is relevant to Barro's work because his equations explaining unemployment and output are reduced forms that leave us relatively uninformed about the structure from which they are derived. Barro suggests that a Lucas-Sargent-Wallace type model lies behind the results; but, as just noted, embellishments to these models generally lead to the conclusion that anticipated money does matter.[18]

An obvious question thus comes to mind: Why didn't Barro try to estimate the structure of one of these models, or more specifically, the Lucas supply function, which is at their heart? This seems quite feasible since the type of analysis he conducts could be used to generate a series on unanticipated inflation, which is the principal (only?) dependent

17. There was also a strain of thought, embodied in many textbooks and countless lectures to students, based on money illusion. This was always a bit of an embarrassment and has been effectively demolished by search-theoretic approaches to the Phillips curve in conjunction with rational expectations.

18. But not always; see McCallum 1977. Barro 1979a is also relevant.

variable in the Lucas supply function. There is at least one example of an estimated structural model based on the ideas of the rational expectations school—Sargent's "classical" econometric model (1976a). In some tests of its predictive ability, Ray Fair (1978, 1979) has found it wanting.

Robustness

Barro and Rush use what I will call a reaction function of the Federal Reserve to generate predictions of the growth rate of the money supply (called *DM*) and then use the residuals from this reaction function (called *DMR*) as empirical representations of the theoretical notion of "unanticipated money growth." Skeptics—a set which includes all but the true believers—will want to know if the finding that anticipated money doesn't matter is robust to different specifications of the money reaction function, which would lead to different *DMR* series.

While Barro's original specification looks pretty good by conventional criteria (standard error, Durbin-Watson, etc.), I can't help wondering why there is no apparent reaction of monetary policy to interest rates and inflation. We know, or at least I always thought we knew, that Federal Reserve policy was dominated by a desire to limit interest rate fluctuations during much of the postwar period. Yet no interest rate term appears in Barro's reaction function. Similarly, many economists have thought that the Fed is relatively more "inflation averse" than "unemployment averse"; yet, according to the estimated equation, the Fed fights unemployment, but not inflation. This is doubly puzzling since, as we know, if the Lucas-Sargent-Wallace-Barro view of the world is correct, any monetary *rule* (i.e., the anticipated part of monetary policy) can only be effective against inflation, not against unemployment. Doesn't the Fed have rational expectations?

I gather from some remarks made by Barro about problems with his price equation (p. 30) that he is somewhat sympathetic to the inclusion of interest rate and price targets in the reaction function. My guess is that the most important unanswered question for Barro-type tests of the rational expectationists' hypothesis is how they will stand up to alternative specifications of *DM* and *DMR*.[19]

Contemporaneous Feedback

The principal stabilization activity in Barro's reaction function has the Fed raising this period's money growth rate (DM_t) whenever last

19. Barro (private communication) reports no success with interest rates or inflation in his reaction function and little effect on the equations for output and unemployment.

period's unemployment rate (U_{t-1}) goes up. This is quite reasonable when the period of observation is very short (say, a month) but to deny contemporaneous feedback from U_t to DM_t when the period of observation is a year strains credulity. In fact, we need not rely on credulity at all. The Barro and Rush results on *quarterly* data imply a clear reaction of *annual DM* to unemployment in the *same* year. If I do my calculations correctly, a sustained increase in Barro's variable $\log(U/1 - U)$ of 1.0 beginning in the first quarter of a year (which is, to be sure, a huge change in unemployment) would raise the money growth rates for the four quarters of that year by 0, 0.3%, 1.0% and 1.1%, respectively, which translates to a 0.8% increase in the annual money growth rate.

Furthermore, this probably underestimates the degree of contemporaneous feedback because monetary policy can, and apparently does, react to economic events within the quarter. In a paper published several years ago, Richard Froyen (1974) tested for such a within-quarter feedback by using monthly data and found it to be present.

I want to stress that this is not a nitpicking point. Ordinary least squares estimation forces the residuals in the reaction function $(DMR's)$ to be orthogonal to the regressors in that equation. Were $\log(U_t/1 - U_t)$ included in addition to (or instead of) $\log(U_{t-1}/1 - U_{t-1})$, the resulting DMR series would have been orthogonal to $\log(U_t/1 - U_t)$. This makes me wonder how good a job DMR would have done in explaining $\log(U_t/1 - U_t)$.

Observational Equivalence and Identification

In an important paper, Sargent (1976*b*) pointed out the "observational equivalence" of Keynesian and new classical macroeconomic models. Barro acknowledged this point in an earlier paper (1977) and pointed out that a Keynesian model could fit the data equally well, albeit with a few odd-looking coefficients. At the conference, much attention was paid to the point that Barro must impose a priori identifying restrictions in order to reach his conclusion that only unanticipated money matters. This is true, and a little bit worrisome since a priori restrictions, by definition, are not tested. Yet I think this reed is too slim for a Keynesian to hide behind comfortably. *Any* estimation requires some identifying restrictions, some maintained hypothesis.

A related point that might be called "observational near-equivalence" was brought up by Stanley Fischer in his paper for this volume. Let M_t be the money supply (or its log) and $_{t-s}M_t$ be the (rational) expectation of M_t formulated at time $t - s$. To a computer asked to estimate regression coefficients, a time series on $M_t - _{t-1}M_t$ will look very much like a time series on $M_t - _{t-2}M_t$—so much alike that it will be virtually impossible to discriminate between the two variables. While very close empirically, these alternatives are miles apart theoretically; for the former implies the strong conclusions associated with the rational expectations school, whereas the latter implies that even anticipated policy has real effects (see, for example, Fischer 1977).

Why the Long Lags?

As already noted, Barro and Rush estimate only reduced forms, but interpret them as coming from a Lucas-Sargent-Wallace type of structural model in which monetary policy has real effects only to the extent that it confuses producers and/or workers between relative and absolute price movements.

If this is the underlying model, it is difficult to understand why the lag of output behind an unanticipated change in the money growth rate should last two years in the annual regression or 10 quarters in the quarterly regression. Certainly the information necessary to know the general price level or the money supply cannot spread that slowly. Lucas (1975) has presented an equilibrium model of the business cycle in which the misinformation gets embodied in the capital stock and hence, while the misinformation disappears quickly, its real effects do not. But Lucas himself is skeptical that variations in the capital stock take us very far in understanding cyclical fluctuations of short duration.

I would like to suggest an alternative explanation of persistence that seems capable of explaining these short-term fluctuations and also seems to be empirically important.[20] Fischer and I (1978) have argued on theoretical grounds that, when output is storable, the Lucas supply function should be amended to read:

$$\log y_t = k_t + \gamma(p_t - {}_{t-1}p_t) + \theta(N^*_t - N_{t-1}),$$

where ${}_{t-1}p_t$ is the (rational) expectation of the price level, N_{t-1} is the stock of inventories at the end of period $t-1$, and N^*_t is the desired stock of inventories. In such a case, since optimal behavior will imply that $0 < \theta < 1$, the partial adjustment of production decisions to inventory imbalances will make shocks persist despite rational expectations. I note in passing that if N^* is sensitive to the real interest rate, then anticipated money will also have effects on real output.

Treatment of the Natural Rate

Barro's equation for the unemployment rate can be used to generate annual (or even quarterly) estimates of the natural rate of unemploy-

---

20. Taylor (1979) has suggested that staggered wage contracts can serve the same purpose.

ment by setting all the *DMR*'s equal to zero. Given the slightly modified specification used in this paper (which drops the minimum wage variable), Barro's natural rate depends *only* on the military personnel/ conscription variable. I find this a somewhat astounding theory of the natural rate. At the very least, one would like to see some attention paid to the well-known shifts in labor force composition, which are generally agreed to have added about ½ to 1 percentage point to the natural rate.

It is also a bit curious that the concept of the natural rate plays no role in Barro's reaction function. If the Fed really cared about stabilizing employment, I assume it would have reacted to a 5% unemployment rate differently in the 1950s (when the natural rate was perhaps 4%) and in the 1970s (when the natural rate was perhaps 6%). Barro's form of the reaction function denies this and, as a consequence, seems to embody a "natural rate of inflation." Specifically, any time the natural rate of unemployment increases, Barro's money growth equation implies that the long-run money growth rate, and hence the steady state rate of inflation, increases as well. It is hard to understand why the Fed should want to do this.

Conclusion

To summarize briefly, I have two principal questions about Barro's work. First, as is always true of the reduced form approach, one is left uneasy (and uninformed) about the theoretical model that is supposed to be supported by the empirical evidence. The remedy for this is, as always, to spell out the structural model and try to estimate it. Second, one wonders about the robustness of the results to alternative specifications of the money reaction function. This is a straightforward question that can be answered by some further empirical work.

I will conclude by reiterating that we all should thank Robert Barro for starting to put some empirical content into a debate that had previously been based on competing a priori assertions. I hope the empirical debate that he started will continue, for the history of economic thought shows that empirical debates, unlike a priori theoretical debates, sometimes do get resolved.

Comment   Robert J. Gordon

Introduction

The point of departure for this empirical paper by Robert Barro and Mark Rush (and earlier papers by Barro) is the proposition, associated with the names of Lucas, Sargent, and Wallace (LSW), that real output is independent of predictable movements in the money supply.[21] The innovative and controversial feature of this hypothesis is *not* that money is neutral in the long run, for this proposition—"the natural rate" hypothesis (NRH)—was accepted by a substantial majority of economists by the time the LSW hypothesis was advanced. Instead, if it is to have any independent content, the LSW hypothesis must state that systematic monetary stabilization has no effect on output in the *short run*.

If valid, the LSW hypothesis would undermine much of the existing literature on stabilization policy. Regular countercyclical activist intervention, implemented as a predictable response to movements in output or unemployment, would be both futile and unnecessary.[22] The entire optimal control branch of the stabilization policy literature, and existing demonstrations that particular derivative or proportional feedback control formulae are more effective stabilizers than a constant growth rate rule, would be rendered irrelevant.[23] The concept of the political business cycle, and of the manipulation of the economy for electoral purposes, would be relegated to a museum for obsolete economic ideas (see Nordhaus 1975).

All formal statements of the LSW hypothesis are based on the underlying supply assumption that output deviates from its "natural" level

This research was supported by the National Science Foundation and is part of the NBER's research program in economic fluctuations. Any opinions expressed are those of the author and not those of the National Bureau of Economic Research.

21. The first half of the paper by Robert Barro and Mark Rush presents a summary and extensions of a previous paper (Barro 1978) based on annual data; the second half contains estimates of some of the same equations for quarterly data. Since the present paper does not contain an explicit statement of the hypotheses being tested, nor of the alternative hypotheses that are implicitly rejected, it is necessary to refer back to the earlier papers (Barro 1977, 1978). These comments treat together the combined results of the three papers.

22. Perfect price flexibility, necessary for the LSW hypothesis to be valid, would insulate real output from any anticipated shock. For instance, the 1974 quadrupling of the price of oil, while it would reduce the "natural" level of output, could have no effect on the gap between actual and "natural" output, once the price hike was announced.

23. This would include a series of papers by the conference organizer, e.g., Fischer and Cooper 1973.

only when economic agents are surprised. In the words of Sargent and Wallace, output depends on "productive capacity and the gap between the current price level and the public's prior expectation of the current price level" (1975, p. 243). If the Fed is to have any effect on real output, even in the short run, it cannot act in a predictable way, because to do so would fail to generate the required surprise.

Most modern economies are characterized by a continuum of markets for goods and services, ranging from the pure auction markets for wheat and pork bellies to the markets for Scripto pencils and Trident chewing gum, where retail prices are sufficiently inflexible actually to be printed on the package supplied by the manufacturer. The LSW approach would be important and valid if the entire economy behaved like the market for wheat, but in fact the presence of administered prices and "customer markets" saps the hypothesis of any relevance to most of the productive activities carried out in industrial economies of the real world.

Consider a change in nominal income, whether brought about by a change in government spending, a change in animal spirits, an anticipated change in nominal money, or an unanticipated change in nominal money. If this demand shock does not change relative prices, and if factor inputs are held constant, the economy's equilibrium or "natural" output level remains fixed, and so there is an instantaneous change in the "market-clearing" price level at which that level of output can be sold. To the extent that any significant portion of the average price level does not adjust instantly, an effective demand constraint forces agents off their notional labor and output supply curves, making totally irrelevant the level of output that agents *want* to sell at the going price.

In contrast, the LSW hypothesis requires for its validity a nation of price-taking yeoman farmers and fishermen moving along notional supply curves. The imperfect flexibility of prices invalidates (over the period of price adjustment) the LSW supply hypothesis and in its place validates the effective disequilibrium approach of Barro and Grossman (1976). In an economy with a gradual adjustment of prices (GAP), as opposed to a LSW economy, the Fed can control output even when the entire population knows *exactly* what it is doing, because it can manipulate the *effective* demand curves for labor and output. The unemployed multitudes of 1933 knew that nominal spending had fallen 50% in four years, but that knowledge didn't help a bit.

The LSW approach can be contrasted once again with the natural rate hypothesis. Let us all agree that a pure demand shock is neutral in the "long run," which might be defined in a sample survey of economists as anything between five and twenty years. To differ from NRH, the LSW proposition must claim that *anticipated* changes in money are neutral over a significantly shorter run than that. Yet knowledge about the size and growth rate of the money supply spreads rapidly, over a period of weeks or months. If we can show that the period of gradual adjustment of prices to demand shocks is *significantly longer* than the brief span needed to adjust one's estimate of the money supply to the weekly Wednesday figure, then we shall have demonstrated that, in the interim between the adjustment of anticipations about a monetary change and the full adjustment of prices to that change, output in our real economy, which combines gradual adjustment of prices with NRH (NRH-GAP), is ruled by an effective demand constraint which the Fed is fully capable of manipulating.

Basic Flaws in Barro's Empirical Tests

Because of the radical implications of the LSW hypothesis for the theory and practice of stabilization policy, it is understandable that macroeconomists should have eagerly awaited a convincing empirical verification. But it is surprising to me that the series of papers by Robert Barro would be regarded as providing any such empirical support,[24] *for the Barro papers provide no test at all of the short-run neutrality proposition of LSW that would distinguish it from the widely accepted long-run "natural rate" neutrality hypothesis.* Barro's papers fail to provide any support for the LSW hypothesis for three separate reasons:

1. There is no explicit empirical test of the leading competing NRH-GAP hypothesis upon which the orthodox stabilization literature rests its case. GAP combined with NRH implies that any permanent shift in the growth rate of nominal income is initially divided between faster growth in both output and prices, but that the inflation rate gradually but continuously accelerates whenever output exceeds its "natural" level, so that gradually the output stimulus vanishes until higher inflation has fully absorbed the entire nominal income acceleration.

2. Far from attempting to distinguish the LSW and NRH-GAP hypotheses, Barro compares as determinants of output on the one hand *unanticipated* money change and on the other hand *raw* money change. The statistical defeat of the latter appears to be the only evidence put forth to support the LSW hypothesis. But this is like setting up a

24. Thus I was startled to read in Blinder's comment, that "Keynesians have been searching for an obvious flaw in his [Barro's] methodology. That one has not been found suggests that the basic flaw, if indeed there is one, is far from obvious." The present comment argues that the flaw is patently obvious: Barro's equations are simply irrelevant in determining the role of anticipated changes in policy, because his specification cannot distingush the LSW hypothesis from the competing price inertia hypothesis on which the orthodox view of stabilization policy is based.

World Series between the Yankees and a team of geriatric invalids. The real Yankee-Dodger World Series for the output determination trophy pits unanticipated money change as one explanatory variable versus the deviation between actual money change and an adaptively adjusting expected price change as the competing variable. Barro's correlations between the output gap and *raw* money change make no contribution whatsoever to distinguishing the dubious LSW hypothesis from the widely accepted NRH, because any such long-run relation between a real variable (output) and a nominal variable (raw money change) would violate the NRH. We know that the acceleration of monetary growth between the 1950s and 1970s did not produce a "permanent economic high," but this fact does not by itself constitute evidence against the *short-run* potency of stabilization policy.

3. Not only do Barro's output and unemployment equations fail to provide any evidence *supporting* the LSW hypothesis, but, worse yet, his price equations strongly undermine the theoretical rationale of the LSW hypothesis by validating the competing NRH-GAP hypothesis. Barro estimates that the full adjustment of prices to changes in the money supply takes between four and six years, while the formation of anticipations about monetary changes takes only a single quarter.[25] For LSW to be valid, any fully anticipated monetary change that raises the anticipated level of nominal GNP must raise the price level *simultaneously* by exactly the same percentage as the increase in nominal GNP, since the hypothesis states that real output must remain unaffected.[26] Thus Barro's price equations fail to validate the one-quarter lag between *actual* money and the price level that would be necessary to confirm the required contemporaneous response of the price level to an anticipated money change. In the long interval between the single-quarter adjustment of expectations about monetary change, and the four to six years required for the full price response to occur, anticipated monetary

25. Table 2.2 of the quarterly Barro and Rush results exhibit a six-year adjustment lag in the price equation when no correction is made for serially correlated residuals and a four-year lag in the equations reestimated with an adjustment for second-order serial correlation.

26. If the influence of a monetary surprise on sales is instantaneous, but the extra sales are partly met by a temporary reduction in inventories, then the effect of the surprise on real GNP will be spread out over time. In this case, the sentence in the text should be qualified to read "any fully anticipated monetary change that raises the anticipated level of nominal GNP must raise the price level *simultaneously*, by exactly the same percentage as the increase in nominal GNP, holding constant the influence of past surprises." Thus, holding constant the effect of past surprises on current output and prices, any fully anticipated monetary change must have its entire effect on the price level and leave real output unaffected.

change can affect real output.[27] The net result of Barro's research on prices, with its finding of a 24-quarter time interval between a monetary change and the full adjustment of prices, seems to amount to little more than a reconfirmation of my earlier study (1975), which found a 28-quarter lag.[28] One comparison of the two sets of results is exhibited in table 2.4.

In order to appreciate the complete and profound contradiction between Barro's long lags and the LSW supply hypothesis, imagine an economy in an initial situation with actual and expected inflation equal and with output at its natural level. There occurs a 1% addition to the money stock. According to Barro's annual coefficients in table 2.4, after two years the price level is essentially unaffected, requiring an increase in real output equal to 1% (adjusted for any change in velocity that occurs). But this combination of a positive output change with a zero price change contradicts the LSW supply hypothesis, in which the aggregate price level must rise relative to expectations to induce the required confusion between relative and absolute prices.

The Identification Problem

Unfortunately, the entire battery of econometric tests used in the three papers is useless for the purposes of distinguishing the radical implications of the LSW model from the familiar conclusions that emerge from NRH-GAP models based on inertia in the adjustment of prices. This identification problem is pursued in table 2.5. The left-hand side displays a general money supply equation of Barro's form in equation (1), his output equation in (2), and his price equation in (3) and (4). On the right-hand side equation (1a) states that the expected rate of inflation depends on lagged inflation and other current and lagged variables, designated X'_L, for example, the presence of war, supply

27. Barro's text explicitly denies any connection between the long price adjustment lags and "explanations for price stickiness of the 'disequilibrium' or contracting variety." This denial appears to rest entirely on the discrepancy between the adjustment lags in the output and price equations. Yet there is another explanation of the inconsistent lags, namely, his misspecification of both the output and price equations (see below).

28. The Barro and Rush results thus provide the needed refutation of the erroneous criticism of my conclusions (1975) that appears in Barro 1978, p. 571: "The effect of anticipated money movements on the price level can be virtually instantaneous at the same time that unanticipated movements . . . affect the price level only with a long lag." Far from being instantaneous, the full response of prices to an anticipated monetary change in Barro and Rush requires a time span of 23 quarters.

Table 2.4   **Lag Distribution of Price Change behind Actual Monetary Change**

	Barro (1978a, p. 571)	Gordon (1975, p. 646)
Sample Period	1948–76	1954:II–1971:II
Observations	Annual	Quarterly
Lags		
t	0.17	0.18
$t - 1$	−0.31	0.10
$t - 2$	0.46	0.13
$t - 3$	0.51	0.20
$t - 4$	0.27	0.26
$t - 5$	0.00	0.26
$t - 6$	−0.03	0.15
$t - 7$	−0.03	....
$t - 8$	0.01	....
Sum of coefficients	1.05	1.28
Mean Lag	2.8	3.3

NOTE

Quarterly Gordon coefficients are obtained for the published equation 7.2 on p. 646 from unpublished printouts and are converted to an annual basis by treating quarters 0–3 as "t", 4–7 as "$t - 1$," etc.

shocks, or controls. Equation ($2a$) is the familiar expectational Phillips curve, which allows the inflation rate to differ from what is expected when real output deviates from its "natural" rate (Q^*), or when there is an "s" effect from controls or supply shocks. Equation ($3a$) uses the quantity identity to replace Q, and ($4a$) expresses the reduced form.

There is simply no way of knowing whether Barro's reduced form relation between prices, lagged money, and variables related to velocity (the interest rate, real government spending, and a time trend) represents a test of the left-hand model or the right-hand model, since the same variables appear in each. The only evident difference between (4) and ($4a$) is that lagged velocity terms appear in ($4a$), but this simply points out a mistake in Barro's representation of his own model. Nominal income growth is identical on one side of the quantity equation to the sum of money growth and velocity growth and on the other side to the sum of price and output change. When there is a change in velocity, due either to a shift in the money demand function or in government spending, this must come out by definition as either a change in output or a change in prices. Barro's price equation is derived from a money demand function, and so velocity appears as a determinant of prices. But velocity does not appear in equation (2), which is simply

Table 2.5   Identifying the LSW and NRH-GAP Approaches

Barro Version of LSW Approach	Alternative Approach
(1) $m^e = \alpha(m_L, X_L)$	(1a) $p^e = \beta(p_L, X'_L)$
(2) $Q = Q^* + \phi(m - m^e)$	(2a) $p = p^e + \theta(Q - Q^*) + s$
(3) $P \equiv M + V(Z) - Q$ $\quad = M + V(Z) - Q^* - \phi(m - \alpha(m_L, X_L))$	(3a) $p = p^e + \theta(M + V(Z) - P - Q^*) + s$
(4) $P = \gamma(M_L, Z, X_L, Q^*)$	(4a) $P = \mu(M_L, Z_L, X'_L, Q^*)$, where s becomes part of X'_L

NOTES

Upper case: logs of levels; lower case: percentage growth rates.
V = velocity; Q = real output; M = money; P = price deflator; X and Z = "other variables"; s = effect of controls and supply shocks.

misspecified. It cannot be the deviation between actual and expected *money* growth, which influences real output, as long as velocity can change, but rather the deviation between actual and expected *nominal income* growth, where the latter depends on expected money, expected government spending, expected exports, and any systematic component in the private investment cycle. Stated another way, Barro's use of money surprises rather than nominal income surprises in his output and unemployment equations implies that velocity surprises are always equal to zero. Barro's agents are thus assumed to be able to predict velocity with precise accuracy, while their uncanny predictive powers do not extend to perfect foresight about the money supply.

Barro's failure to obtain consistent lags in the output and price equations is at least partly due to the inconsistent treatment of velocity. All of the ink spilled over the MIL variable also reflects this problem; instead of having anything to do with changes in the natural rate of unemployment, squeezed inside the MIL variable, velocity is struggling to get out as a determinant of output changes. In the paper presented here the shift to government spending as a determinant of output and unemployment represents a belated attempt to patch up this problem. It is ironic that the Barro and Rush results support fiscal fine-tuning, in the form of an instant effect on output and unemployment of actual (not unexpected) government spending. In contrast the Sargent and Wallace paper (1975) specified an IS curve and treated money and nonmoney exogenous variables symmetrically.

A Suggestion for Future Research

The identification problem posed in table 2.5 echoes an important theme running through recent discussions of the short-run and long-run neutrality hypotheses—the difficulty of identifying the structure of an economic model from aggregative time series data, because several models may be compatible with a time series dependence of, for instance, nominal GNP growth on lagged monetary changes (Sargent 1976b). More informally, "you can't get a structure out of a time series."

Nevertheless, neither Sargent's "observational equivalence" conundrum nor the related identification problem of table 2.5 prevents an empirical investigation of the competing LSW and NRH-GAP hypotheses. Although both hypotheses implicitly make real output and price change a function of a distributed lag of past nominal GNP or monetary change, the LSW alternative requires for its validity strong restrictions that can be statistically tested. Since output is required to depend only on nominal GNP "surprises," then any fully anticipated change in nominal GNP must leave real output unaffected and therefore have its full influence on prices. In short, the LSW hypothesis requires that the statistically estimated elasticity on anticipated nominal GNP change in an equation for price change must be unity, and in an equation for real output must be zero, holding constant other variables.[29] The opposing NRH-GAP hypothesis would predict that inertia in the price setting process would prevent price change from responding to anticipated nominal income change with a unitary elasticity.

There is no explicit test in Barro's paper of these coefficient restrictions implied by the LSW hypothesis. His output equations never test the hypothesis that the response of output to anticipated monetary change is positive during the transitional period of price adjustment (i.e., he uses raw money change as a variable rather than money change minus a distributed lag of past price changes). Further, his poorly specified price equation tests whether the price *level* is unit-elastic with respect to the *level* of the money supply over the postwar period; that is, it tests whether money is neutral in the long run, not whether the elasticity of price *change* to anticipated monetary *change* is unity in the short-run. A test of the zero-one restrictions of the LSW hypothesis should be high on the agenda for future research in empirical macroeconomics.

Comment   Robert Weintraub

Barro and Rush are doing important work. Their research is truly exploratory, and, like all explorations, it creates excitement. Nonetheless, it does not succeed.

Barro and Rush are trying to make operational and test the Lucas-Sargent-Wallace hypotheses about the relationships between money supply and macroeconomic performance. In summary, they specify equations to decompose M1 growth (measured at annual and quarterly rates) into expected and unexpected components. The unexpected element is then used both in regression equations, whose purpose is to explain changes in output and unemployment, and in a regression of what appears to be a rearranged real money demand equation, which purports to explain inflation. This is a sensible methodology. Although they do not succeed, their effort is not in vain. It casts light on the pitfalls that await us when we try to put the LSW hypotheses into operational form

I am indebted to Robert Auerbach and John Hambor.

29. In the general case in which output depends not just on current nominal surprises but also on the past history of surprises, as in the recent inventory model developed by Blinder and Fischer 1978, these "other variables" include past surprises.

and test them. Future researchers who try, including, I hope, Barro and Rush, will find they have an easier job as a result.

Expected M1 Growth

Empirical decomposition of M1 growth into expected and unexpected elements is the essential first step in testing LSW propositions. If the decomposition statistics are weak, or if the logic behind the statistics is questionable, the test of the LSW propositions will be neither fair nor useful. The Barro and Rush decomposition statistics are weak, and the logic on which they base their decomposition is suspect.

The equations that were used to estimate annual M1 growth in the original version of the Barro and Rush paper generated a steady-state M1 growth/unemployment relationship substantially different from the Barro and Rush quarterly expected M1 growth equation. In the revised version, a new equation (7) is used to estimate expected quarterly M1 growth. Its steady-state properties are consistent with the annual equation, but the new quarterly equation (7) raises other questions.

Briefly, the weakness of the coefficients on the lagged DM terms (other than $t - 1$) raises doubts about using them as regressors. More important, the irregularity of the response of expected money growth to lagged unemployment, as well as the weakness of the unemployment coefficients, raises doubts about relating expected money growth to lagged unemployment to begin with.

The standard errors of the regressions of the annual expected M1 growth regressions are high. The smallest error, which is from the jointly estimated equation (1'), is .0133. The standard error of the regression of equation (1), which was estimated by OLS, is .0140. This is an improvement on the .0227 standard deviation of the mean of log (M_t/M_{t-1}) in the 1946–77 period, but, .0140 is not small. It is too large for the regression to be economically meaningful. It is 37.5% of the .0373 mean of $\log(M_t/M_{t-1})$ in the 1946–77 period. Expressed in probability terms, this error cautions us that there is a one in twenty chance that the true value of expected money growth is 2.80 percentage points above or 2.80 percentage points below the estimate generated by Barro's equation (1). Using equation (1'), the error is 35.7% of .0373, and there is a one in twenty chance that the true value of expected M1 growth is 2.66 percentage points above or below the regression estimate. Given this magnitude of potential error, it is hard to see how anyone can take seriously the decomposition of M1 growth into the expected and unexpected components implied by Barro's expected M1 growth regressions.

Those who do should ponder the fact that it is easy to conjure up other explanations of expected M1 growth that fit the annual data about as well as Barro's independently estimated equation (1). Two examples are provided below:

- A linear regression for the 1946–77 period (Barro weights 1941–45 observations) of $\log(M_t/M_{t-1})$ on the log of last year's U.S. population divided by the population the year before last has a standard error of .0146. For the record, using POP to denote population,[30] this regression, with standard errors in parentheses, is

$$\log(M_t/M_{t-1}) = \underset{(.968)}{10.020} \; - \underset{(.685)}{4.614} \log(POP_t/POP_{t-1})$$

- The linear regression for the 1957–77 period of $\log(M_t/M_{t-1})$ on itself lagged both one and two years plus the change in the federal funds rate last year from the year before last has a standard error of .0127. This is only 30.5% of the .0418 mean of $\log(M_t/M_{t-1})$ in the 1957–77 period.

With Ffr to denote the federal funds rate, the results of this regression are

$$\log(M_t/M_{t-1}) = \underset{(.635)}{.824} \; + \underset{(.180)}{.599} \log(M_{t-1}/M_{t-2})$$
$$+ \; \underset{(.181)}{.290} \log(M_{t-2}/M_{t-3})$$
$$- \; \underset{(.0016)}{.0054} \, (Ffr_{t-1} - Ffr_{t-2})$$

The coefficient on the funds rate is highly significant. Its sign is negative, which indicates that contracyclical M1 growth can be expected after a year's delay.

Strictly speaking, this regression is not comparable with Barro's regressions because it was run for the subperiod 1957–77. The regression was fitted for this period because the Ffr data series dates back only to 1955. Moreover, interest rate data for the 1940s and early 1950s cannot be used to estimate how M1 growth responds to lagged interest rate changes because during those years interest rates were continuously pegged. A fair test of how well Barro's equation (1) estimates expected money growth compared with intuitive explanations that use interest rates as arguments must be made with post-Accord data. My bet is that the standard error of the mean of expected M1 growth from Barro's equation (1), estimated for the 1957–77 period, is not significantly less than .0127.

Barro's expected M1 growth equations are suspect for logical as well as statistical reasons. Specifically, the unemployment rate would not

---

30. The source of the population data used in this regression is the 1978 *Economic Report*, p. 287. In this regard, in computing the 1950/1949 ratio, it was necessary to adjust the reported 1950 population to exclude residents of Hawaii and Alaska because the series excludes them prior to 1950.

appear to be an appropriate variable for estimating expected M1 growth in a rational world. Here's why.

If M1 growth is expected to increase in response to an observed prior rise in unemployment, and if unexpected M1 growth is required to reduce unemployment, then, the Federal Reserve authorities cannot allow M1 growth to react to unemployment as the public expects if they want to reduce unemployment. They must target unexpected M1 growth because expected M1 growth is dissipated in inflation, and differences between actual and expected M1 growth that are due to the Federal Reserve's under- or overshooting targeted M1 growth are as likely to be minus as plus, and hence as likely to increase as to decrease unemployment. If, however, the Federal Reserve pursues M1 growth policies in response to lagged unemployment that are different from what the public expects, then Barro's method of separating unexpected and expected M1 growth is inappropriate. The historical relationship that Barro observed between lagged unemployment and M1 growth cannot be interpreted as a relationship between lagged unemployment and *expected* M1 growth. Barro's measure of the response of M1 growth to lagged unemployment would have emerged from policies designed to fool the public. In a rational world the public would know this and would not bet on the stability of the observed relationship between lagged unemployment and M1 growth. Put otherwise, if at any time after 1941 the Federal Reserve authorities had thought the public expected M1 growth to conform to Barro's regression results (which he interprets as what the public has expected all along), then, assuming the Federal Reserve authorities wanted to affect unemployment and knew that only unanticipated M1 growth would affect it, they would have made sure that those results turned out differently. Hence, Barro's results shed no light on the relationship between *expected* M1 growth and lagged unemployment.

More generally, logic would appear to rule out using unemployment in estimating expected M1 growth in the first place, except under the assumption that the Federal Reserve authorities don't know what they are doing or how the economy works. If the Federal Reserve authorities know that only unexpected M1 growth can affect the real economy, they are not likely to react to changes in real economic variables including unemployment in any systematic way, and any observed response of M1 growth to lagged unemployment rationally must be regarded as accidental.[31]

---

31. Stanley Fischer has pointed out to me in a letter dated 14 November 1978 that some may have difficulty seeing what I am driving at in this section. He asked whether I might put it a bit differently. Happily, in the same letter he did the job for me. He wrote: "My understanding is that you're saying the Fed must either

Inflation

Barro's inflation equations (4) and (4″) are overdrawn. Each includes the value of the long-term Aaa corporate bond index interest rate in the current year as an explanatory variable. It is used to capture inflation expectations. A rise, Barro explained in his original paper, with a caveat, "reflects a shift in anticipated inflation—but, one that is *unsatisfactorily* treated as exogenous in the present framework" (emphasis added).[32]

Nevertheless, Barro was and continues to be willing to use interest rate changes to capture shifts in inflation expectations. Apparently, he believes that such changes are not very important for explaining U.S. post–World War II inflation experience. In his original paper Barro recognized that, using the 3.8 coefficient on R_t from regression equation (4″), as originally reported, the rise in the long-term Aaa rate from .0744 to .0857 between 1973 and 1974 "accounts for .043 of the total estimated value for the 1974 inflation rate of .104." However, this did not seem to disturb him because he stated, "the interest rate change is not as important for 1975—accounting for only .010 of the total

---

itself have been irrational to have changed the money growth rate in response to unemployment (if Barro's theory is right) in a predictable way, or else that until recently Barro's theory can't have applied. The other possibility is that the Fed thought it could affect the unemployment rate and acted as the equation says it did, even though in fact it was only shadow boxing. This may be equivalent to its being irrational."

The only way I would modify Fischer's interpretation is by changing "until recently Barro's theory can't have applied" to "Barro's theory can't apply," i.e., his coefficients can't shed light on the expected M1 growth–lagged unemployment relationship if the Fed wants to affect unemployment and knows that only unexpected M1 growth will affect it.

Still another way of putting my point was suggested by Robert Solow in a letter dated 12 January 1979. He wrote: "Barro proceeds as if the Fed is a kind of passive machine-plus-random-disturbance which the public can learn about. But the whole point of view suggests that the Fed ought to be as smart as the public, in which case the situation becomes a kind of 2-person game. But then, as you point out, the Barro method is inappropriate."

Finally, Barro, in a letter dated 8 January 1979, urges that "Your discussion of the logic of the lagged unemployment rate as a DM predictor repeats a point from my 1977 paper (p. 114)." There he wrote: "'This observation raises questions concerning the rationality of the countercyclical policy response that appears in equation (2). One possibility is that the reaction of money to lagged unemployment reflects optimal public finance considerations."

It is clear that Barro knows that his approach is inappropriate. His reference to "optimal public finance considerations" does not rescue his methodology. The flaw is fatal.

32. This quotation and those that follow are taken from Barro's original paper before it was revised for publication.

1975 inflation estimate of .082." I concluded that Barro should have checked in other years. Following are the contributions to inflation as per his original equation (4″) of changes in the Aaa bond rate from the prior year in years since the Korean war when the rate rose and inflation, as measured by the log of the ratio of the value of the GNP deflator this year to last year's value, exceeded .020.

Year	Contribution	Inflation
1955	.006	.021
1956	.012	.031
1957	.020	.033
1959	.023	.022
1965	.003	.022
1966	.024	.032
1967	.014	.029
1968	.025	.044
1969	.032	.049
1970	.038	.052
1973	.009	.056
1974	.043	.096
1975	.010	.089

The record shows that in nine of the thirteen years since 1953 when the Aaa bond rate rose and inflation exceeded .020, the rise in the Aaa bond rate plays a major role in Barro's explanation of inflation.

In his letter of 8 January 1979, Barro stated that "I exaggerate the explanatory role of the interest rate variable." In this regard it should be noted that the results from equation (4″) in the current version of the Barro and Rush paper differ substantially from the equation (4″) results as they appeared in the paper delivered at the conference. The two equations are reproduced below.

$$(Conf.) \ \log P_t = \log(M_t) - \underset{(0.1)}{4.5} - \underset{(.12)}{.81 DMR}$$

$$- \underset{(.15)}{1.40 DMR_{t-1}} - \underset{(.18)}{1.45 DMR_{t-2}}$$

$$- \underset{(.14)}{1.08 DMR_{t-3}} - \underset{(.11)}{.79 DMR_{t-4}}$$

$$- \underset{(.09)}{.27 DMR_{t-5}} - \underset{(.0010)}{.0109 \cdot t}$$

$$+ \underset{(.11)}{.45 (G/y)_t} + \underset{(.4)}{3.8 R_t}$$

$$(Current)\ \log P_t = \log(M_t) - 4.58 - .85DMR_t$$
$$(.15)\quad (.12)$$

$$- 1.31DMR_{t-1} - 1.36DMR_{t-2}$$
$$(.15)\qquad\qquad (.18)$$

$$- .94DMR_{t-3} - .61DMR_{t-4}$$
$$(.17)\qquad\qquad (.12)$$

$$- .16DMR_{t-5} - .0096 \cdot t$$
$$(.10)\qquad\qquad (.0015)$$

$$+ .34(G/y) + 2.9R_t$$
$$(.15)\qquad (.5)$$

The conference equation was estimated jointly with the other three equations of Barro's four-equation system (DM,U,y,P). The current results were obtained from joint estimates "that embody the cross-equation restrictions of the unanticipated money hypothesis." Barro also notes that the current estimation "does not use R_{t-1} as an instrument for R_t," as did the estimation whose results were presented at the conference. This switch raises doubts about the reliability of the new coefficient on R_t (2.9) compared with the old (3.8).

Using the new coefficient on R_t requires modifying the inflation contributions of R_t tabulated above by .76. Definitely this is an improvement on the conference paper. However, the adjusted contributions are still unacceptably high. Though Barro might be appalled, the fact is that institutionalists who stress "cost-push" explanations of inflation will find his results, whether as reported at the conference or here, supportive of their arguments. As far as I am concerned, they are useless.

Another View

We advance our knowledge of the world in successive approximations. Most economists would now agree, I think, that familiar monetarist propositions approximate reality in the long run. The LSW hypotheses are intended to explain year-to-year or even shorter events. Barro and Rush have tried to test these hypotheses but what they have done is helpful only in pointing out some pitfalls that await those who attempt to make operational and test LSW hypotheses. It is not a fair test. Until they, or other researchers, do better, we will have to make do with the familiar monetarist propositions that, over the long haul, unemployment is invariant with respect to M1 growth while inflation and interest rates are closely and positively related to the rate of M1 growth. This does not mean that M1 growth changes will not temporarily affect output and unemployment, and the larger such shocks are the more lasting the real effects will be, as in the 1930s. But, with the mag-

Table 2.6   Unemployment, Inflation, Money Growth, and Interest Rates in Nonoverlapping Three-Year Periods, 1954–77

Period	Unemployment Rate	Inflation (CPI) Rate	Money Supply Growth Rate	Three-month T-bill rate
1954–56	4.7	0.5	2.0	1.8
1957–59	5.5	2.4	1.8	2.8
1960–62	5.9	1.3	1.4	2.7
1963–65	5.1	1.4	3.7	3.6
1966–68	3.7	3.3	5.3	4.9
1969–71	4.8	5.2	5.5	5.8
1972–74	5.3	6.9	6.7	6.3
1975–77	7.7	7.1	5.5	5.4
1955–57	4.3	1.5	1.6	2.6
1958–60	5.9	1.7	1.6	2.7
1961–63	6.0	1.2	2.4	2.8
1964–66	4.5	2.0	4.3	4.1
1967–69	3.6	4.1	5.7	5.5
1970–72	5.5	4.5	5.9	5.0
1973–75	6.3	8.8	5.7	6.9
1976–77	7.4	6.1	6.1	5.1
1956–58	5.1	2.5	1.0	2.6
1959–61	5.9	1.2	1.9	2.9
1962–64	5.5	1.3	3.0	3.2
1965–67	4.1	2.5	4.3	4.4
1968–70	4.0	5.2	5.7	6.2
1971–73	5.5	4.6	7.1	5.2
1974–76	7.3	8.6	4.9	6.2
1977	7.0	6.5	7.2	5.3

nitude of M1 growth changes that the U.S. has experienced during the post–Korean war years, it appears to take only three or at most six years for changes in M1 growth to be fully reflected (and dissipated) in changes in the rate of inflation and rates of interest. During the post–Korean war period, no relationship is observed between three year averages of M1 growth and unemployment. The relevant data are assembled for *nonoverlapping* three-year periods beginning, alternatively, 1954–56, 1955–57 and 1956–58 in table 2.6.

General Discussion

Robert Barro responded to several of the discussants' comments. He was not himself satisfied with the role of the unemployment rate in the Fed reaction function, since it implied some irrationality on the part of the

Fed. He was not sure on theoretical grounds how the interest rate should enter the reaction function but thought the issue worth further empirical exploration. He felt that the best approach to testing his hypothesis was the examination of the implied cross-equation coefficient restrictions. He agreed that increased government spending could increase output and did not see anything in natural rate theory to contradict this. Finally, he agreed that more than information confusions were needed to explain the serial correlation of output but did not see any reason to reject the role of information confusions on that account.

Robert Hall said that the novelty in Barro's work was not testable: there is no test that will distinguish the effects of anticipated from unanticipated money. If one substituted from Barro's reaction function into his output equation, one then had an equation in which current and lagged growth rates of money, and other factors, particularly a fiscal variable and lagged unemployment, affected current output. What Barro is actually testing is whether fiscal variables matter, as in the Saint Louis equation. In further discussion it was pointed out that Barro had addressed this issue (Barro 1977) and suggested that this point had also been made by Thomas Sargent (1976b).

Charles Nelson said that the power of Barro's test depended on how strongly the other variables—in this case the fiscal variable—entered the reaction function. In the Barro and Rush paper the t-statistics on the fiscal variable are reasonably high, so that the test is reasonably powerful.

Benjamin Friedman suggested that in thinking about the reaction function we should consider the Fed's operating procedures. In the short term the Fed sets interest rates, and the money stock is determined by money demand at that interest rate. Barro's reaction function looked like the reduced form resulting from that process. It would therefore be useful to view the Barro reaction function explicitly as a reduced form and try to identify the structural coefficients in the true reaction function.

Neil Wallace remarked that Barro's procedure derived identifying restrictions on the reaction function from elements that were not central to the theory that was being tested. The obvious way to test the hypothesis Barro was interested in was to look for periods in which money supply processes differed, as suggested in Sargent's observational equivalence paper.

Robert Barro thought the emphasis on the shift of regimes exaggerated. One could interpret the nonmoney variables in his supply function as representing changes in regime. He also suggested that you could achieve identification by noting the implications of the reaction function for the coefficients on other variables that would enter the reduced form. For instance, when the reaction function was substituted into the output equation in his current paper, it was implied that current and lagged values of the federal expenditure variable reduced current output. Some competing theories imply that federal spending would, if anything, enter with a positive coefficient, and they could therefore be rejected.

References

Barro, R. J. 1976. "Rational Expectations and the Role of Monetary Policy." *Journal of Monetary Economics* 2:1–32.
———. 1977. "Unanticipated Money Growth and Unemployment in the United States." *American Economic Review* 67:101–15.
———. 1978. "Unanticipated Money, Output, and the Price Level in the United States." *Journal of Political Economy* 86:549–80.
———. 1979a. "More on Unanticipated Money Growth." *American Economic Review*, forthcoming.
———. 1979b. "A Capital Market in an Equilibrium Business Cycle Model." *Econometrica*, forthcoming.
Barro, R. J., and Grossman, H. I. 1976. *Money, Employment, and Inflation*. Cambridge: Cambridge University Press.
Blinder, A. S., and Fischer, S. 1978. "Inventories, Rational Expectations, and the Business Cycle." Unpublished.
Fair, R. C. 1978. "An Analysis of the Accuracy of Four Macroeconometric Models." Unpublished.
———. 1979. "On Modeling the Effects of Government Policies." *American Economic Review*, forthcoming.
Fischer, S. 1977. "Long-term Contracts, Rational Expectations, and the Optimal Money Supply Rule." *Journal of Political Economy* 85:191–206.
———. 1979. "Anticipations and the Non-Neutrality of Money." *Journal of Political Economy* 87:225–52.
Fischer, S., and Cooper, J. P. 1973. "Stabilization Policy and Lags." *Journal of Political Economy* 81:847–77.
Friedman, M., and Schwartz, A. J. 1970. *Monetary Statistics of the United States*. Studies in Business Cycles no. 20. New York: National Bureau of Economic Research.
Froyen, R. T. 1974. "A Test of the Endogeneity of Monetary Policy." *Journal of Econometrics* 2:175–88.
Gordon, R. J. 1975. "The Impact of Aggregate Demand on Prices." *Brookings Papers on Economic Activity* 6:613–62.
Leiderman, L. 1979. "Macroeconometric Testing of the Rational Expectations and Structural Neutrality Hypotheses for the United States." *Journal of Monetary Economics*, forthcoming.

Lucas, R. E., Jr. 1973. "Some International Evidence on Output-Inflation Tradeoffs." *American Economic Review* 63:326–34.

―――. 1975. "An Equilibrium Model of the Business Cycle." *Journal of Political Economy* 83:1113–44.

―――. 1976. "Econometric Policy Evaluation: A Critique." In *The Phillips Curve and Labor Markets*, edited by K. Brunner and A. H. Meltzer, pp. 19–46. Carnegie-Rochester Conference Series no. 1. New York: North-Holland.

McCallum, B. T. 1977. "Price-Level Stickiness and the Feasibility of Monetary Stabilization Policy with Rational Expectations." *Journal of Political Economy* 86:627–34.

Nordhaus, W. D. 1975. "The Political Business Cycle." *Review of Economic Studies* 42:169–90.

Phelps, E. S., and Taylor, J. B. 1977. "Stabilizing Powers of Monetary Policy under Rational Expectations." *Journal of Political Economy* 85:163–90.

Plosser, C. I., and Schwert, G. W. 1979. "Money, Income, and Sunspots: Measuring Economic Relationships and the Effects of Differencing." *Journal of Monetary Economics*, forthcoming.

Sargent, T. J. 1976a. "A Classical Macroeconometric Model for the United States." *Journal of Political Economy* 84:207–37.

―――. 1976b. "The Observational Equivalence of Natural and Unnatural Rate Theories of Macroeconomics." *Journal of Political Economy* 84:631–40.

Sargent, T. J., and Wallace, N. 1975. " 'Rational' Expectations, the Optimal Monetary Instrument, and the Optimal Money Supply Rule." *Journal of Political Economy* 83:241–54.

Small, D. H. 1979. "A Comment on Robert Barro's Unanticipated Money Growth and Unemployment in the United States." *American Economic Review*, forthcoming.

Taylor, J. B. 1979. "Aggregate Dynamics and Staggered Contracts." *American Economic Review* 69:108–13.

3   The Monetary Mechanism in the Light of Rational Expectations

Olivier Jean Blanchard

This paper uses a structural empirical model to examine the effects of anticipated and unanticipated monetary policy under the assumption of rational expectations. In particular, it characterizes the effects of such a policy on output, the short-term real interest rate, and the stock market.

Existing macroeconometric models provide us with a description of the transmission mechanism, but they assume implicitly that the way agents form their expectations is invariant to policy and, as emphasized by Lucas (1976), this casts serious doubts on the usefulness of their answer. Furthermore, because they do not explicitly specify the role of expectations, their defects cannot be easily remedied; in effect a new model has to be set up and estimated.

The model used here extends the analytical model presented in an earlier paper (Blanchard 1978). It consists of two parts, aggregate demand and aggregate supply. The model of aggregate demand treats expectations explicitly and thus its structure should be approximately invariant to changes in policy. It has been estimated by Blanchard and Wyplosz (1978). The model of aggregate supply is not estimated but postulated; this reflects my belief that there may not be enough information in past data to obtain the exact specification of aggregate supply; the model has characteristics that are both desirable theoretically and in accordance with recent empirical evidence (Barro 1978b in particular).

The complete model is used to look at a very simple policy, namely, a decrease in the nominal money stock, starting from steady state. The

I thank Stanley Fischer and Francesco Giavazzi for useful discussions and Charles Wyplosz and Jeff Zax for excellent research assistance. The paper has benefited from the comments of Bennett McCallum, Michael Parkin, and David Lindsey. This research was supported by the National Bureau of Economic Research and the Alfred P. Sloan Foundation.

paper is organized as follows: Section 1 presents the model of aggregate demand. Section 2 describes the model of aggregate supply. Section 3 characterizes the steady state and the dynamic behavior of the complete model. Section 4 characterizes the effects of anticipated and unanticipated monetary policy with exogenous prices. The purpose of this section is to give a better understanding of the behavior of aggregate demand, independent of the particular formalization of aggregate supply. Section 5 presents the effects of the same policy with endogenous prices.

1. Aggregate Demand

Aggregate demand is defined as the value of output that equilibrates goods and assets markets given past, current, and anticipated values of the price level.[1] The structure follows the model of Metzler (1951) and emphasizes the interaction between wealth, spending, and output.

In the goods market, wealth determines private spending; private and public spending determine output. Human wealth and stock market wealth in turn are the present discounted values of anticipated labor and capital income; they therefore depend on the sequence of anticipated output.

The model is a quarterly model. Stock and flow variables are in intensive form, divided by physical capital K.[2] They will therefore be constant if the corresponding levels grow at the same rate as capital. (They are denoted by lower-case letters; corresponding upper-case letters will be used to denote their levels when convenient).

The following symbols are used:

$_t z_{t+1}$	the expectation of z_{t+1}, held at time t
q	the real value of a share which is the title to a unit of physical capital
h	the real (shadow) value of a unit of labor (in efficiency units)
p	the logarithm of the price level
i, r	the short-term nominal and (ex ante) real rates
m	the logarithm of the nominal money stock
b	the real value of government bonds
w	the real value of nonhuman wealth
y	output
yd	disposable income

1. This section summarizes Blanchard and Wyplosz 1978, to which the reader is referred for more detail about definitions of variables, specification, and estimation of the equations.

2. Note that the variables are divided by K, not by L, as is usual in growth models.

π	profit
L	the total labor force (in efficiency units)
c, in	consumption and investment
x	the sum of inventory investment, net exports, and government spending

The model was estimated with data from the period 1953:I to 1976:IV. Means and standard deviations of these variables for that period are given in table 3.1.

Each equation was estimated by two-stage least squares with first-order serial correlation correction. The instruments used for estimation were first tested for statistical exogeneity. Lag structures were left unconstrained. Each equation was tested for partial adjustment versus serial correlation and for subsample stability. The reported estimated coefficients are individually significant at the 90% confidence level.[3]

The equations are as follows:

Goods market

$$(1) \qquad c_t = .389\, h_t + (.028\, w_t + .041\, w_{t-1})$$
$$+ (.250\, yd_t + .117\, yd_{t-1})$$

$$(2) \qquad w_t \equiv q_t + b_t$$

$$(3) \qquad yd_t = .461 + .33\, y_t$$

$$(4) \qquad in_t = -.093 + (.003\, q_t + .025\, q_{t-1}$$
$$+ .019\, q_{t-2} + .021\, q_{t-3})$$
$$+ (.144\, y_t + .044\, y_{t-1})$$

$$y_t = c_t + in_t + x_t =>$$

$$(5) \qquad y_t = .097 + .107\, y_{t-1} + 1.29\, x_t + .502\, h_t$$
$$+ .040\, q_t + .085\, q_{t-1}$$
$$+ .025\, q_{t-2} + .027\, q_{t-3}$$
$$+ .036\, b_t + .053\, b_{t-1}$$

Asset markets

$$(6) \qquad m_t - p_t = (.543 - .193\, \ln K_t) + .590\, (m_{t-1} - p_{t-1})$$
$$+ .179\, y_t - 1.001\, i_t$$

$$(7) \qquad r_t \equiv i_t - 4\, (_t p_{t+1} - p_t)$$

---

3. Two coefficients are not individually significant at the 90% confidence level: current wealth (w_t) in the consumption equation with a t-statistic of 1.46 and current q in the investment equation with a t-statistic of .23.

Table 3.1   **Sample Means and Standard Deviations, 1953:I to 1976:IV**

	Mean	Standard Deviation	1976:IV Value
q	.823	.143	.690
h	1.[a]	—	—
i	3.99%	1.84%	6.11%
r	.91%[b]	—	—
b	.776	.151	.608
$m - p$	−1.073	.230	−1.497
ω	1.589	.189	1.299
y	1.370	.066	1.282
yd	.916	.023	.897
c	.838	.025	.836
in	.202	.021	.168
π	.067	.011	.062
x	.338	.040	.271
K	675.2	188.4	1004.1

NOTES

a. This variable is unobservable. Its mean is normalized to be unity, by the choice of units for labor.

b. This variable, the ex ante real rate, is unobservable. This is the mean ex post real rate defined as the nominal rate minus actual inflation.

(8)
$$q_t = \frac{1}{r_t + .075} \left(4 \left({}_t q_{t+1} - q_t \right) + 1.04\,\pi_t \right)$$

(9)
$$\pi_t = -.091 + .226\,y_t - .054\,y_{t-1} - .055\,y_{t-2}$$

(10)
$$h_t = \frac{1}{r_t + .075} \left(4 \left({}_t h_{t+1} - h_t \right) + .093\,yd_t \right)$$

(11)
$$yd_t = .461 + .33\,y_t$$

Equations (1)–(3) characterize consumption as a function of wealth —human and nonhuman—and income. Given that wealth is included, disposable income is not a proxy for wealth but indicates the effect of liquidity constraints on current consumption. Nonhuman wealth is defined as the sum of stock market wealth and government bonds. This definition does not, however, imply that the level of government bonds affects consumption: anticipated tax liabilities needed to pay interest on the debt will decrease either q or h (or both), possibly offsetting the effect of b (see Barro 1978a). Real money balances are excluded from wealth: outside money is very small compared with the other components.[4] (Equation (1) presents an estimation problem because h, the

4. As noted in Sargent 1976, the presence of outside money in wealth—the direct Pigou effect—leads to nonneutrality of anticipated monetary policy. Removing it from wealth removes therefore this nonneutrality, which is empirically unimportant. (Fischer reaches a similar conclusion; see chap. 7.)

present discounted value of expected labor income, is unobservable. Thus, in order to estimate (1), an assumption must be made about how agents formed their expectations of future labor income during the sample period. Estimation was done assuming static expectations for h.[5] If h was in fact correlated with w and yd, as is likely, the estimated coefficients on w and yd are likely to be biased upwards).

Equation (4) characterizes fixed investment. It depends on the valuation of capital, q. Empirically, investment depends significantly on output which is thus included, although theoretical reasons for its presence are not clear.

Equation (5) characterizes goods market equilibrium and is obtained by replacing equations (1)–(4) in the equilibrium equation. Components of spending other than consumption and fixed investment are unexplained at this stage and will therefore be taken as exogenous in simulations. Equation (5) gives output as a function of the different components of wealth and exogenous spending. The direct effect of the past on current y_t is small: the coefficient on y_{t-1} is .107. The direct short-run multiplier is 1.29: it does not, however, indicate the complete effect of exogenous spending because movements in x_t will usually affect the values of the different components of wealth. The long-run elasticities of y with respect to q and h are of 12% and 41% approximately.

In the assets markets, tradable nonmoney assets such as bonds and shares are assumed perfect substitutes. Equilibrium is thus characterized by equilibrium in the money market and the arbitrage equations between nonmoney assets.

Equation (6) characterizes equilibrium in the money market. This determines the nominal short-term interest rate, given y.[6] The implied elasticities of money demand using 1976:IV values for y and i are .23 and .061, respectively, in the short run, .56 and .148 in the long run. K_t enters equation (6) because, with the less than unitary elasticity with respect to income, the demand for money is not homogenous in K.

Equation (7) defines the ex ante real rate of interest. The presence of 4 comes from the measurement of interest at annual rates, whereas the time unit of the model is the quarter. $(_tp_{t+1} - p_t)$ is the logarithmic approximation to the expected rate of inflation.

5. Estimation under the assumption of rational expectations is intended.

6. The estimated demand for money depends on two interest rates, the three-month Treasury bill rate and the time deposit rate, j. The equation used here assumes that the time deposit rate follows:

$$j = .5 \ (.033) + .5 \ (i)$$
.033 is the sample mean of j.

Because of the presence of interest rate ceilings, the behavior of j is more the result of the Fed policy than unconstrained profit maximization by banks. Thus the above relation may be interpreted as a policy rule of the Fed.

Equation (8) is derived from the arbitrage condition between shares and short-term bonds. The expected return on shares—which is the sum of two components, profit income and capital gain (or loss)—must be equal to the expected return on short-term bonds plus a fixed premium β.

$$(8') \qquad \frac{\pi_t}{q_t} + 4\left(\frac{{}_t q_{t+1} - q_t}{q_t}\right) = r_t + \beta.$$

The arbitrage condition equivalently follows from the statement that q_t is the present discounted value of expected profit:

$$q_t = \sum_{\tau=0}^{\infty} {}_t\pi_{t+\tau}\left(\prod_{i=0}^{\tau}\left(1 + \frac{{}_t r_{t+i} + \beta}{4}\right)^{-1}\right).$$

The only coefficient to be estimated in equation (8′) is the premium; it is estimated by the difference between the sample mean return on shares and short-term treasury bills, which is approximately equal to 7.5%. Equation (8) is obtained by replacing β by its numerical value, making a minor adjustment for consistency of the q and π series, multiplying the π series by 1.04, and rearranging the above arbitrage equation (8′). Equation (9) gives profit income as a function of output.

Human wealth is the present discounted value of labor income but is not tradable; it is assumed that the relevant discount rate is the same as for stock market wealth, so that the value of a unit of labor is given by:

$$(10') \qquad h_t = \sum_{\tau=0}^{\infty} \frac{{}_t YL_{t+\tau}}{\overline{L}_{t+\tau}}\left(\prod_{i=0}^{\tau}\left(1 + \frac{{}_t r_{t+i} + \beta}{4}\right)^{-1}\right),$$

where YL_t denotes labor income and $\overline{L}_t$ denotes the total number of (efficiency) units of labor at time t. In the simulation, agents will be assumed to have rational expectations. If agents have rational expectations, equation (10′) implies that h_t follows an "arbitrage-like" equation:[7]

$$\left(\frac{K}{\overline{L}}\right)_t \frac{yl_t}{h_t} + 4\left(\frac{{}_t h_{t+1} - h_t}{h_t}\right) = r_t + \beta.$$

The first term is labor income per unit of labor, divided by the shadow value of a unit of labor. The presence of $\left(\dfrac{K}{\overline{L}}\right)_t$ is due to the fact that yl_t is labor income divided by physical capital: it must therefore be multiplied by capital and divided by labor to give labor income per unit of labor. The second term is the expected "capital gain" or loss.

---

7. This is derived as follows: Lead (10′) once and take conditional expectations as of time t on both sides. Multiply both sides by $(1 + ({}_t r_t + \beta)/4)^{-1}$ and subtract from (10′).

The simulations will assume physical capital and the labor force to be growing at the same constant rate, so that $\left(\dfrac{K}{L}\right)_t$ will be constant and equal to $\left(\dfrac{K}{L}\right)$. The value of $\left(\dfrac{K}{L}\right)$ depends on the choice of units for labor. They are chosen such that the value of one unit of labor is unity in steady state; this determines $\dfrac{K}{L} = .093$. Equation (10) is obtained by rearranging the above "arbitrage like" equation. Disposable income, yd_t is used rather than labor income yl_t, because of the poor quality of data on yl_t. Equation (11) gives the relation of disposable income to output.

Therefore in the assets markets, output and nominal money determine the short-term nominal rate, given prices. Given the anticipated rate of inflation, this determines the short-term real rate. Arbitrage equations determine the value of q_t and h_t given the anticipations $_tq_{t+1}$ and $_th_{t+1}$.

Because the effect of expectations on spending is treated explicitly in this model, through the presence of the different components of wealth, the coefficients of this model should be approximately invariant to policy: they should, abstracting from aggregation problems, depend mainly on coefficients reflecting institutional arrangements, tastes, and technology. Thus the model of aggregate demand, together with a model of aggregate supply can be used to examine the effects of changes in policy.

2. Aggregate Supply

Most economists agree that the behavior of the price level is such that, at least as a first approximation, nominal disturbances have no long-run effect on output. There is also a wide agreement that the short-run real effects of such disturbances, if any, coincide with deviations of the price level from its anticipated value, however defined. There is, however, little knowledge of the precise relation between price level deviations and output. There is little hope of obtaining a precise specification from empirical evidence: it is, for example, very hard to determine the separate effects of the predictions of today's price level made one year and two years ago. (This point is made empirically by Fischer chap. 7.) Thus, an aggregate supply equation can only be estimated by imposing strong specification restrictions, with little guidance by the theory. (An interesting attempt is made by Taylor 1978.)

The model of price level behavior used here is therefore not estimated but postulated; its characteristics and implications are in accordance with the available empirical evidence. Its structure is extremely simple: the price level adjusts toward the price that would equate aggregate supply and aggregate demand. When it differs from this price, production is determined by aggregate demand.[8]

1. If markets were auction markets and there was perfect information about the current state of the world, then, as shown by many authors (Sargent and Wallace 1975, for example), changes in money, both current or anticipated, would have no effect on real variables[9] such as output, the real interest rate, and the values of one unit of physical or human capital. The goods market equilibrium equation (5) and the arbitrage equations (8) and (10) would always be satisfied with y, r, q, h equal to their steady state values denoted $\bar{y}, \bar{r}, \bar{q}, \bar{h}$, respectively. The price level would therefore be such as to maintain portfolio balance. Define for simplicity

(12) $$a(t) \equiv .135 - .048 \ln K_t + .045 \, \bar{y} - 1.001 \, \bar{r}.$$

Denote the price level in this case by p^*. It would follow, from equations (6) and (7):

(13) $$({}_tp^*_{t+1} - p^*_t) = a(t) - .250 \, (m_t - p^*_t)$$
$$+ .147 \, (m_{t-1} - p^*_{t-1}).$$

This equation states that the expected rate of inflation must be such that agents are satisfied with their real money balances. It is, except for the presence of lagged money, similar to the equilibrium condition of the model of Cagan (1956). The behavior of the price level satisfying this condition and rational expectations has been studied by Sargent and Wallace (1973). It is useful to characterize this behavior in two cases, the case of an unanticipated change and the case of an anticipated change in nominal money.

"Unanticipated" and "anticipated" must first be defined. A change is unanticipated if the announcement and implementation of the change are simultaneous. It is anticipated if the announcement precedes the implementation. In both cases, the change is assumed to be known when it is implemented.

If a change in nominal money is unanticipated, and if it is assumed to be permanent, the price level will change at the time of the implementation and in the same proportion as nominal money. If it is anticipated, the price level will start to change at the time of the announcement: if it did not change until the implementation, agents would expect

8. Aggregate demand is assumed to determine sales. Because inventory behavior is unexplained at this stage, it also determines production. Relaxing the equality between production and sales would clearly be desirable.

9. This statement disregards various sources of nonneutrality (Tobin, Pigou effects), which are not present in the model of aggregate demand.

a large capital gain or loss on real money balances. The equilibrium path of the price level between the announcement and implementation must be such that agents are satisfied with their real money balances given the expected rate of change of the price level. The important implication, for our purposes, is that the price level will change before the actual change in nominal money if the change is anticipated.

2. The actual price level, p_t, will be assumed to adjust partially toward the "desired" level p^*_t in the following way:

$$(14) \qquad p_t = \gamma p^*_t + (1 - \gamma)\, p_{t-1},$$

$$\gamma \in [0,1],$$

where p^*_t is given by (13).

Prices would be perfectly flexible and nominal disturbances would have no real effect if $\gamma = 1$; they would be fixed for $\gamma = 0$. What are the characteristics of price level behavior if γ is between 0 and 1? Consider again a permanent change in nominal money.

If it is unanticipated, p^* adjusts immediately to its new equilibrium value and p adjusts gradually over time. After n periods, the proportional difference between them is $(1 - \gamma)^n$. Over time p converges to p^*, and there is no long-run effect of the change of money.

If the change was anticipated, both p^* and p change after the announcement. The longer the period between the announcement and the implementation, the smaller the initial change in p^*, the closer p will be to p^* and the smaller the real effects of a change in money. (This will be shown later.) Thus the longer a change in nominal money has been anticipated, the less real effect it has. If it has been anticipated "forever," it will have no real effect at all.

The only parameter to be chosen is γ. Recent empirical evidence by Barro shows that unanticipated nominal disturbances[10] affect prices over a period of four years. This suggests a value of γ between .1 and .2 approximately.[11] When $\gamma = .2$, the increase in the real money stock is .16 of the initial nominal increase after two years, .02 after four years. When $\gamma = .1$, these numbers are .43 and .18. The value of .2 will be used for most simulations in section 5.

Although equation (14) has desirable properties, it must be slightly changed if the nominal money stock is growing, so that p^* is also growing, say at rate λ. In this case if p followed (14), it would never equal p^*. The natural extension is then:

10. What Barro calls "unanticipated" would in this paper be called "anticipated for less than one year."

11. Another finding of Barro is that the effect of unanticipated money on prices has a hump-shaped lag structure. This cannot be captured adequately by the simple partial adjustment postulated in (14).

(15) $p_t = \gamma p^*_t + (1 - \gamma)(p_{t-1} + \lambda).$

This formalization implies that changes in the nominal money stock from trend, that is, temporary changes in the rate of growth of money, will have no effect in the long run, or no effect at all if fully anticipated.

Because the policies considered in the following sections will be temporary changes in the rate of growth of money, aggregate supply will be characterized by (13) and (15).

3. Steady State and Dynamics

The system is described by equations (1) to (11) and (13) and (15). I first characterize its steady state, then study its stability under the assumption of rational expectations; finally the exact policy experiment considered in the following sections is described.

The Steady State

The absence of an estimated supply equation does not allow one to determine from the model the steady state values for output and the real interest rate. If the system was approximately in steady state during the sample period, the sample values for the ratio of output to physical capital and the real (ex post) interest rate should be close to the steady state values. Values of 1.377 for $\bar{y}$, and of 1% for $\bar{r}$ are chosen as steady state values. This implies values of .847 for the real value of a unit of physical capital $\bar{q}$, 1.003 for the real value of a unit of labor $\bar{h}$, from the arbitrage equations.[12]

Values of .361 and .776 are chosen for $\bar{x}$ and $\bar{b}$, respectively. (It is clear that a constant value for b implies that government debt is growing at the same rate as capital; this was not true of the sample period.)

The demand for money is not homogenous in capital. Thus a constant ratio of real money to physical capital would lead to an excess supply of real money given the interest rate; equivalently, the ratio of real money to physical capital must decrease to maintain the same interest rate. If a steady state is a state in which the ratios of all real flows and stocks to physical capital are constant, this system has no steady state. For simplicity, this effect is removed by assuming $\ln K_t$ to be constant in the demand for money equation; this implies that the elasticity of the demand for money is less than one with respect to deviations of output from steady state and one with respect to steady state increase. The value of $\ln K_t$ will be taken to be 6.911, its 1976:IV value. In this case, the rate of inflation is equal in steady state to the

---

12. This is close to the mean sample value of q, which is .823. The fact that this sample value is less than one is a well-known puzzle. (The time series for q is taken from von Furstenberg 1977.)

rate of growth of money minus the rate of growth of output. This rate of inflation will be assumed to be equal to 4% at an annual rate. This implies a real money stock of 1.404 for equilibrium in the money market.

The Dynamics

The main conclusion here is that the system, linearized around its steady state, is stable under rational expectations with either exogenous or endogenous prices. "Stability" means that if the exogenous variables follow linear stationary processes, the endogenous variables will also follow linear stationary processes.

Consider first the case where prices are assumed to be exogenous and growing at the steady state rate of inflation. The system is then the aggregate demand system, composed of equations (1)–(11). This system is nonlinear in its two arbitrage equations and must first be linearized around the steady state values of $\bar{q}$, $\bar{h}$, and $\bar{r}$ in order to be solved for rational expectations. It can then be reduced to a system of seven variables. Define

$$z_t \equiv y_{t-1} \; ; z1_t \equiv z_{t-1} \text{ and}$$

$$q1_t \equiv q_{t-1} \; ; q2_t \equiv q_{t-2} \; ; q3_t \equiv q_{t-3}.$$

Then the system can be written as:

$$
(16) \qquad
\begin{bmatrix}
z_{t+1} \\
z1_{t+1} \\
q1_{t+1} \\
q2_{t+1} \\
q3_{t+1} \\
\cdots \\
{}_t h_{t+1} \\
{}_t q_{t+1}
\end{bmatrix}
=
\underset{(7 \times 7)}{A}
\begin{bmatrix}
z_t \\
z1_t \\
q1_t \\
q2_t \\
q3_t \\
\cdots \\
h_t \\
q_t
\end{bmatrix}
+ \Omega \xi_t,
$$

where ξ_t is a vector of exogenous variables and Ω is a matrix of required dimension.

Although this system resembles a first-order system, it cannot be solved in the usual way. Heuristically, at time t, a variable such as z_{t+1} "depends" on $z_t, z1_t, \ldots$, whereas a variable such as h_t "depends" on ${}_t h_{t+1}, {}_t q_{t+1}$.

A more precise statement is that the first five variables are predetermined at time t, whereas the last two, h_t and q_t, are not. Because of the absence of initial conditions for h_t and q_t, there is clearly an infinity of solutions to the system (16).

It may, however, be argued that variables such as h_t and q_t should not depend on the past, except through its effect on the currently predetermined variables, namely, $y_{t-1}, y_{t-2}, q_{t-1}, q_{t-2},$ and q_{t-3}. If such an argument is accepted, a unique solution satisfies this condition; this is the solution usually chosen in models with rational expectations and is referred to as the "forward" or "forward-looking" solution.

The forward solution to systems such as (16), together with its stability condition have been derived in another paper (Blanchard 1980). The stability condition is that the matrix A must be such that the number of roots inside the unit circle must be equal to the number of predetermined variables, namely five in this case. The roots of A are:

$$-.170$$
$$-.059 + .178\,i$$
$$-.059 - .178\,i$$
$$.196 + .151\,i$$
$$.196 - .151\,i$$
$$1.0212$$
$$1.0431$$

Thus this system is stable with exogenous prices.

The appendix gives the solution of the system, that is, the current values of the endogenous variables as a function of the past, current, and anticipated future exogenous variables. The five roots inside the unit circle determine heuristically the "weight" of the past in determining the current equilibrium (this is made clear by equations A1 and A2 in the appendix): their small absolute value indicates that the current equilibrium does not depend very much on the past. The inverse of the roots outside the circle determine the "weight" of the anticipated future; the fact that their value is close to unity indicates that the current equilibrium depends largely on these anticipations. These heuristical statements will help in understanding the results of the next two sections.

Consider now the full system of aggregate demand and aggregate supply. It can be reduced to a system of ten variables including the variables above plus p^*_t, $p1^*_t \equiv p^*_{t-1}$, and $p1_t \equiv p_{t-1}$. Both $p1^*_t$ and $p1_t$ are predetermined at time t. The system has the form:

$$(17) \quad
\begin{bmatrix}
z_{t+1} \\
z1_{t+1} \\
q1_{t+1} \\
q2_{t+1} \\
q3_{t+1} \\
p1_{t+1} \\
p^*1_{t+1} \\
\cdots \\
{}_tp^*_{t+1} \\
{}_th_{t+1} \\
{}_tq_{t+1}
\end{bmatrix}
=
\underset{(10 \times 10)}{\bar{A}}
\begin{bmatrix}
z_t \\
z1_t \\
q1_t \\
q2_t \\
q3_t \\
p1_t \\
p^*1_t \\
\cdots \\
p^*_t \\
h_t \\
q_t
\end{bmatrix}
+ \Omega \xi_t.$$

The stability condition is that the system must have seven roots inside the unit circle. This condition is satisfied. The system has the same roots as the aggregate demand system plus three roots which are:

$$.131$$
$$1 - \gamma$$
$$1.117$$

Thus if prices adjust rapidly, that is, if γ is large, all the roots inside the circle are again small and the past is relatively unimportant. If γ is small, prices adjust slowly and the current equilibrium depends more on the past, through prices.

The stability of the system is not just a happy accident. The property that the system has the same number of roots inside the unit circle as predetermined variables is called the "strict saddle point" property. Growth models with many assets have been shown to have this property usually and the present model has a structure similar to these theoretical models.

It is interesting to contrast this stability result with the instability of the MPS model with endogenous prices (the dynamic properties of this model have been studied by Corrado 1976). Except for the treatment of expectations, this model and the MPS have a similar structure. The MPS also emphasizes the role of wealth in spending decisions. Our model, however, assumes rational expectations, whereas the implicit expectations formation mechanism of the MPS is closer to an adaptive expectation mechanism. If we now consider the much simpler Cagan model, we find that it is stable under rational expectations but unstable under adaptive expectations if expectations adapt "too fast." For the same reason, our model is stable and the MPS is unstable.

Although, in principle, the current equilibrium depends on all anticipated future values of the exogenous variables, agents are assumed in the simulations to have a horizon of only (!) 200 quarters. A simulation must therefore specify at any time the anticipations for all future values for all exogenous variables for the following 200 quarters.

The Policy Experiment

The experiment will consist of a decrease in nominal money of 5%, announced n periods in advance. This experiment is shown graphically in figure 3.1. The number of periods, n, between the announcement and implementation, will be taken to be either zero (in which case the policy is unanticipated), five, or fifteen quarters.

Two simplifying assumptions will be made: If the decrease in money is realized through an open market operation, the increase in government bonds may have an effect on spending. It will be assumed that

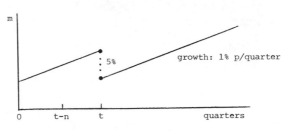

Fig. 3.1   The behavior of nominal money

in this case the increase in wealth in the form of government bonds is exactly offset by the increase in tax liabilities and has no effect on spending. Thus, for simplicity, the real value of bonds (divided by physical capital) and structure of anticipated taxes will remain unchanged in the simulation. Capital will be assumed to grow at a constant steady state rate. Thus, the effects of changes in investment spending on capital accumulation will not be taken into account.

4.   Monetary Policy with Exogenous Prices

In this section, prices are assumed to be exogenous and growing at the steady state rate of inflation, 4%. The decrease in nominal money of 5% in one quarter implies here a permanent decrease in real money of 5%.

It is clear that the "steady state" of this section is not a true steady state, for output may be permanently different from its normal level. This section is, however, useful to characterize the dynamics of aggregate demand, independent of the particular formalization of aggregate supply; in particular it shows clearly the interaction between the stock market, output, and the real short-term rate of interest.

The "Steady State"

Given prices, the steady state is characterized by two relations; first, wealth determines output. From equation (5), in steady state (deleting the symbol t):

$$y = .687 + .562\,h + .198\,q.$$

Second, output determines profit and labor income and the real interest rate together with the real money stock; this in turn determines wealth:

$$q = \frac{\pi}{r + .075} = \frac{-.095 + .117\,y}{-.410\,(m - p) - .675 + 179\,y}$$

$$h = \frac{yd}{r + .075} = \frac{.043 + .030\,y}{-.410\,(m - p) - .675 + 179\,y}$$

A lower real money stock leads to both higher interest and lower profit, thus lower wealth and output. A 5% decrease in real money decreases y by 6.2%, q by 20%, h by 10%; the real short-term rate increases by 50%, from 1% to 1.499%.

The Dynamic Effects of an Unanticipated Decrease in Real Money

The results of an unanticipated decrease in real money are reported in table 3.2. The main conclusion is that, in this case, the adjustment is *very fast*: 65% of the adjustment in output takes place in the first quarter; the adjustment is nearly complete in four quarters.

This fast adjustment differs drastically from the effects of a similar change in nominal money in existing models (see again Corrado 1976 for the effects of a similar policy in the MPS with exogenous prices): these models indicate a slow adjustment of the economy to a change in nominal money. There are probably three main reasons for this difference. The first is the assumption about expectations and is probably the most important one. The second comes from the fact that a decrease in the money stock in this and, say, the MPS model may in fact correspond to two different experiments. The fast adjustment is obtained here under the assumptions that the decrease in money is both unanticipated and believed to be permanent. It is possible, for example, that the decrease in money considered in the MPS is of a different nature (implicitly, for the model does not distinguish between anticipated and unanticipated, permanent and temporary). The underlying assumptions may, for example, be that the decrease is initially thought of as temporary by agents and that only over time do agents think of it as being

Table 3.2	**The Effect of an Unanticipated Decrease in the Nominal Money Stock of 5% with Prices Exogenous, Announced and Implemented in the First Quarter.**

Quarters	y	r	π	q	
0	1.377	1.000%	.070	.847	
1	1.319	3.947	.057	.666	Announcement/Implementation
2	1.302	1.691	.056	.674	
3	1.296	1.593	.059	.675	
4	1.291	1.503	.059	.676	
5	1.291	1.498	.059	.676	
6	1.291	1.499	.060	.676	

permanent; this may partially explain the difference between the models.

The third reason is that inventories are taken as exogenous in this model, whereas they are endogenous in the MPS. Intuition (supplemented by the study of the effects of inventory behavior in Blinder and Fischer 1978) suggests that the endogeneity of inventories may lead to a smaller initial response and a slower adjustment process.

Consider now the dynamics of output, wealth and the short-term rate: After the decrease in money, agents anticipate both a higher sequence of interest rates and a lower sequence of profit and labor income. Both effects decrease wealth immediately. The stock market drops by as much as 21%. This in turn decreases spending and output over time, decreasing income and validating the initial anticipations of lower profit and labor income.

Over time the decrease in output reduces the demand for money, leading to a decrease in the interest rate. The decrease in profit is initially large because profit depends both on the level and the rate of change of output. After the first quarter, output decreases but at a slower rate; this affects profit in opposite directions. The combined decrease in the relevant sequence of discount rates and the approximately constant sequence of profits lead to a slight increase in q over time. Initially q decreases by more than its long-run change and after that increases slightly.

Therefore, not only the speed but the qualitative behavior of this model is different from the behavior of existing models; rather than slowly adjusting over time to the higher short-term real rate, the stock market reacts immediately and strongly to the decrease in money.

The Dynamic Effects of a Decrease in Real Money, Announced in Quarter 1 and Implemented in Quarter 6

Table 3.3 presents the behavior of output, the real interest rate, profit, and the stock market.

The announcement is itself contractionary. The stock market drops by 18% in the quarter of the announcement. This is due to anticipations of both higher interest rates and lower profits. This leads to a rapid decrease in output: 52% of the long-run change takes place in the first quarter and the decrease in output between the announcement and the implementation is larger than its long-run change. Over time, between the announcement and the actual implementation, output is decreasing but the real money stock is still constant. Because of the lower transaction demand for money, the short-term rate decreases. Thus the stock market and the short rate move in opposite directions.

As the actual implementation becomes closer in time, the sequence of higher short-term rates also becomes closer, explaining the further

Table 3.3		The Effect of a Decrease in the Nominal Money Stock of 5% with Prices Exogenous, Announced in Quarter 1 and Implemented in the Sixth Quarter.			
Quarters	y	r	π	q	
0	1.377	1.000%	.070	.847	
1	1.332	.183	.060	.687	Announcement
2	1.311	−.179	.058	.684	
3	1.303	−.334	.059	.681	
4	1.295	−.474	.059	.678	
5	1.291	−.544	.059	.674	
6	1.287	4.382	.059	.670	Implementation
7	1.290	1.495	.060	.676	
8	1.291	1.497	.060	.676	
9	1.291	1.499	.060	.676	
10	1.291	1.499	.060	.676	

decline of wealth and thus output. These capital losses are expected; note, however, that they are relatively small compared with the initial unexpected drop; they are equal to less than 1% per quarter.

At the time of the implementation, the real money stock decreases, leading to a very large increase in the short-term rate. Because this change was expected, however, little else happens: output and the stock market are already close to their equilibrium values; output even increases slightly after the decrease in real money.

The results of this section have been derived under the assumption of exogenous prices and thus of the possibility that output may be permanently different from its long-run value. This assumption is now relaxed.

5. Monetary Policy with Endogenous Prices

Prices are now endogenous and their behavior is described by equations (13) and (15). The value of γ is .20, unless otherwise indicated: 20% of the desired adjustment of prices takes place during a quarter.

A change in nominal money has no effect in the long run as prices adjust, leaving real money unchanged. Thus only the dynamics of adjustment are of interest.

The Dynamic Effects of an Unanticipated Decrease in Nominal Money

Figure 3.2 gives the behavior of y, q, r, and π in response to an unanticipated decrease in nominal money.

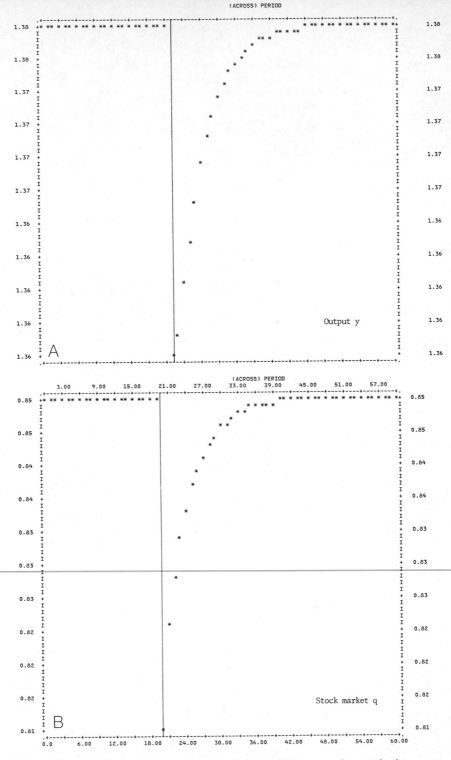

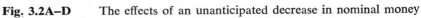

Fig. 3.2A–D   The effects of an unanticipated decrease in nominal money

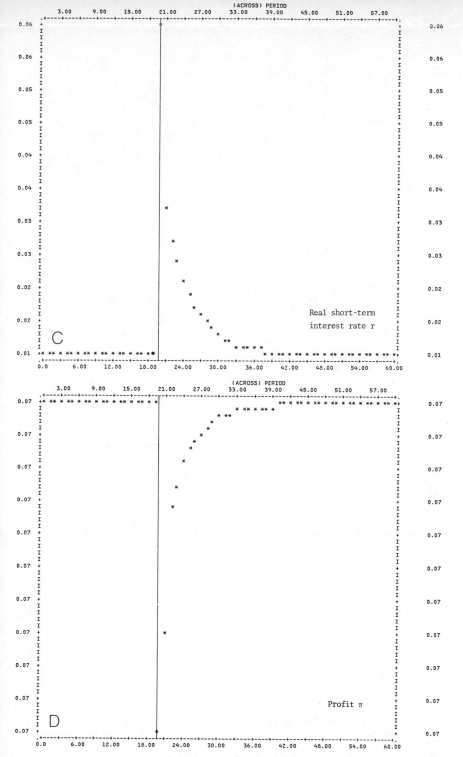

Real short-term
interest rate r

C

Profit π

D

What is the initial impact of the decrease in money? Again, the combination of lower anticipated profits and higher real rates decreases wealth; the stock market drops but since the economy is expected to return to steady state, profits and interest rates are expected to return to their steady state values; the drop is thus only 5% in the quarter of the policy change compared with 21%, in the exogenous price case. The behavior of y and q in both cases is given in columns 1, 2, 5, and 6 in table 3.4.

The smaller drop in the stock market and in output must be contrasted with the increase of the short-term real rate, which is *larger* than in the exogenous price case: the short-term real rate increases to 6.311% compared with 3.497%. The reason is the presence of the Mundell effect: in addition to the decrease in real money, which increases the nominal rate, there is expected lower inflation, which, given the nominal rate, increases the real rate. This higher short-term real rate, however, is not expected to remain: real rates are expected to be lower in the future than in the exogenous price case. This explains why the decrease in wealth is smaller than in the exogenous price case.

Over time, both the real money stock and the real rate return to their steady state values; wealth increases. There are initially two opposite effects on output: the initial decrease in wealth tends to decrease it; the following increase tends to increase it. The second effect is more powerful for $\gamma = .20$, but, as shown in table 3.4, the first effect dominates initially for $\gamma = .10$: output decreases in the first two quarters before it increases again.

Most of the effect of the policy on real variables has disappeared after 10 quarters: although prices are still 10% away from their steady state value, output is less than 2% away from its steady state value.

The Dynamic Effects of a Decrease in Nominal Money, Announced in Quarter 1 and Implemented in Quarter 6

Figure 3.3 gives the behavior of y, q, r, and π in response to a decrease in money anticipated 5 quarters in advance. The results may be compared with the results of the exogenous price case presented in table 3.3. There are two mechanisms at work: the first one is the one described in the exogenous price case, the second one is the behavior of desired and actual prices. Through the first one, the announcement leads to an anticipated recession and thus a decrease in wealth at the time of the announcement; this implies a rapid decrease in output. There are contradictory effects on the stock market between the announcement and implementation: the higher sequence of anticipated profit tends to increase it but the relevant sequence of discount rates changes over time in a complex way, as can be seen in figure 3.3. In

Table 3.4   **The Effects of an Unanticipated Decrease in Nominal Money in the First Quarter: the first five quarters.**

	1	2	3	4	5	6
	$\gamma = 0$ (fixed prices)		$\gamma = .10$		$\gamma = .20$	
Quarter						
	y	q	y	q	y	q
0	1.377	.847	1.377	.847	1.377	.847
1	1.319	.666	1.350	.799	1.356	.812
2	1.302	.674	1.348	.809	1.357	.824
3	1.296	.675	1.350	.814	1.360	.830
4	1.291	.676	1.351	.817	1.363	.833
5	1.291	.676	1.354	.821	1.366	.836
6	1.291	.676	1.356	.824	1.368	.839

this case, the net effect is to increase wealth slightly between the first quarter and the sixth.

The implementation again has no noticeable effect, except on the short-term real rate. After that, wealth and output increase slowly back to their steady state value.

The second mechanism is through prices: after the announcement, the desired price adjusts to its lower level; this leads in turn to an adjustment of the actual price (see above). When nominal money decreases, the actual price has already decreased (compared with its trend) and this leads to a smaller decrease in real money. This reduces the effect of nominal money on output: when unanticipated, the policy led to a maximum decrease in output of 1.5%; when it is anticipated five quarters in advance, the maximum decrease in output is only 1.1%.

The Dynamic Effects of a Decrease in Nominal Money, Announced in Quarter 1 and Implemented in Quarter 16

If a decrease in nominal money is anticipated so long in advance, we would not expect it to have much effect. This is the reason for considering this case. The results are given in figure 3.4.

The effects on y and q are indeed very small. The maximum decrease in output, which takes place at the time of the actual implementation in quarter 16, is of .7%.

The complexity of the different effects of anticipated interest rates and anticipated profit income on the stock market is clearly indicated by the behavior of the stock market between the announcement and the implementation. The rest of the effect is otherwise qualitatively similar to the case of a decrease anticipated five quarters in advance.

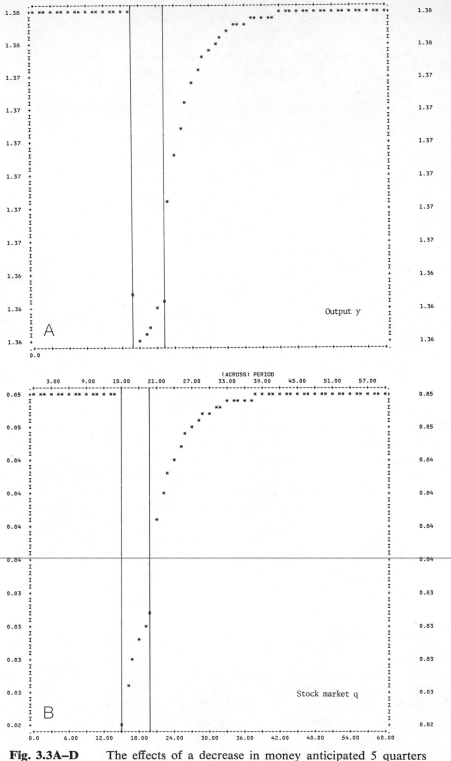

Fig. 3.3A–D   The effects of a decrease in money anticipated 5 quarters in advance. (The first vertical line indicates the quarter in which the decrease is announced. The second vertical line indicates the quarter in which it is implemented.)

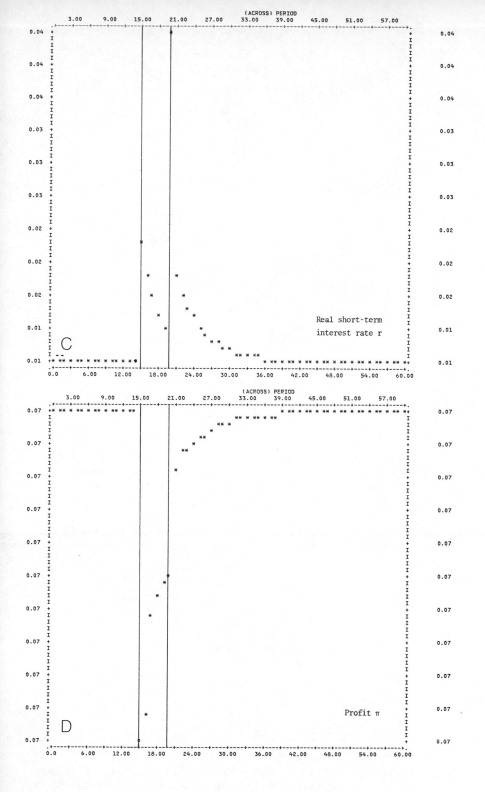

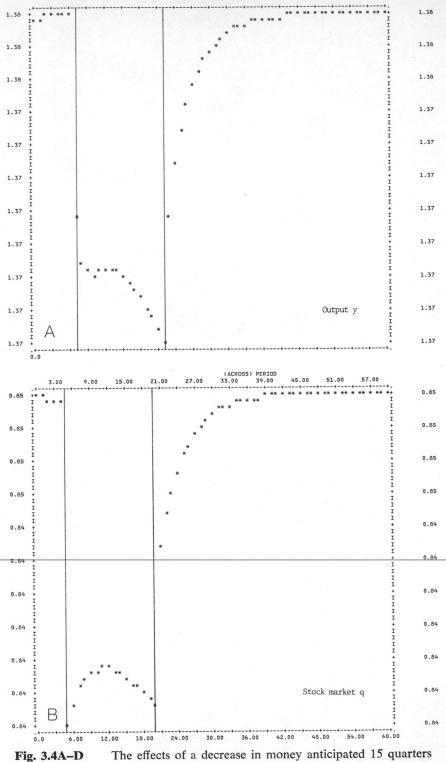

Fig. 3.4A–D   The effects of a decrease in money anticipated 15 quarters in advance. (The first vertical line indicates the quarter in which the decrease is announced. The second vertical line indicates the quarter in which it is implemented.)

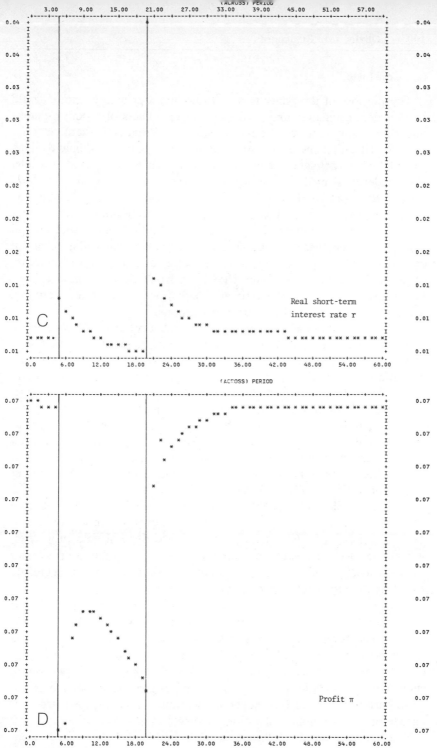

6.   Conclusion

The purpose of the paper was to show that a structural model could be specified, estimated, and used to study the effects of a policy change under the assumption of rational expectations. What is the verdict?

1. Specification and estimation of a model of aggregate demand which should be approximately invariant to policy rules does seem possible. The model used in this paper stresses the role of observable variables, such as the stock market, which contains information about agents' expectations; the result of such a specification is to minimize the number of parameters to estimate in equations with unobservable expectational variables. Given that, estimation does not present particular technical difficulties. A serious problem—not directly related to the assumption of rational expectations—comes, however, from the dubious identification status of some of the estimated equations: few of the potential instruments seem to be statistically exogenous.

It is, in fact, impossible to specify a model involving only observable variables. Because there is no market for human wealth, assumptions about expectations must be made to estimate the effect of human wealth on consumption spending. In the same way, the specification and estimation of inventory investment, which is not explained at this stage, would require the use of unobservable variables such as sales expectations and, thus, an assumption about the formation of these expectations in the sample period. Specification of such relations does not present particular problems and if rational expectations are assumed, the implied cross-equation constraints should help rather than hinder estimation (Wallis 1977 or Sargent 1978).

Even a detailed and reliable model of aggregate demand is of little use without a model of aggregate supply. Although the model of supply used here has both theoretically and empirically desirable properties, it is neither derived from theory nor estimated. The question of whether we can specify and estimate a policy invariant model of aggregate supply is therefore not answered by this paper.

2. Once a model is specified and estimated, the technical problems involved in obtaining policy simulations under the assumption of rational expectations are easily solved. A policy simulation requires the specification for all simulation periods of all current expectations for all future values of all exogenous variables. Although this implies more cumbersome simulations than those in existing models which only require current values of the exogenous variables, this is a logical consequence of the assumption of rational expectations.

The policies considered here are both simple and deterministic but there are no conceptual or technical problems in considering feedback or stochastic rules or both.

3. Although it would be unwise to take the exact quantitative results of the simulations too literally, the following qualitative features of the adjustment process after a change in nominal money are probably fairly robust:

If prices were exogenous, the adjustment of the real variables to their new equilibrium level would be fast, in response to a permanent change in money. With endogenous prices, an unanticipated change in nominal money, assumed to be permanent, has its largest effect on output and the stock market at or shortly after the implementation; there is no slow transmission from short- to long-term rates, to the stock market, and finally to output.

When a policy is anticipated, the announcement itself has a large effect on the stock market and on output; the actual implementation affects the short-term interest rate but has little noticeable effect on the path of output and wealth. Finally, the longer a change in nominal money has been anticipated, the smaller are its effects on real variables.

Appendix

Systems (16) and (17) are of the form:

$$\begin{bmatrix} \mathbf{X}_{t+1} \\ {}_t\mathbf{Y}_{t+1} \end{bmatrix} = \mathbf{A} \begin{bmatrix} \mathbf{X}_t \\ \mathbf{Y}_t \end{bmatrix} + \Omega\, \xi_t,$$

where

$\mathbf{X}$ is a vector of n variables predetermined at t
$\mathbf{Y}$ is a vector of m variables not predetermined at t
ξ is a vector of k exogenous variables
$\mathbf{X} = \mathbf{X}_0$ at time t_0
$\mathbf{A}, \Omega$ are $((n+m) \times (n+m))$ and $((n+m) \times k)$, respectively.

First decompose this system $\mathbf{A}$ and Ω as follows:

$$\begin{bmatrix} \mathbf{X}_{t+1} \\ {}_t\mathbf{Y}_{t+1} \end{bmatrix} = \begin{bmatrix} \mathbf{A}_{11} & \mathbf{A}_{12} \\ {}_{(n \times n)} & {}_{(n \times m)} \\ \mathbf{A}_{21} & \mathbf{A}_{22} \\ {}_{(m \times n)} & {}_{(m \times m)} \end{bmatrix} \begin{bmatrix} \mathbf{X}_t \\ \mathbf{Y}_t \end{bmatrix} + \begin{bmatrix} \Omega_1 \\ {}_{(n \times k)} \\ \Omega_2 \\ {}_{(m \times k)} \end{bmatrix} \xi_t.$$

$\mathbf{A}$ is similar to a diagonal matrix Λ: $\mathbf{A} = \mathbf{B}\,\Lambda\,\mathbf{B}^{-1}$
Λ is ordered by increasing absolute value of the characteristic roots
$\mathbf{B}$ and Λ are partitioned as follows:

$$B = \begin{bmatrix} B_{11} & B_{12} \\ {\scriptstyle(n \times n)} & {\scriptstyle(n \times m)} \\ B_{21} & B_{22} \\ {\scriptstyle(m \times n)} & {\scriptstyle(m \times m)} \end{bmatrix} ; \quad B^{-1} = \begin{bmatrix} C_{11} & C_{12} \\ {\scriptstyle(n \times n)} & {\scriptstyle(n \times m)} \\ C_{21} & C_{22} \\ {\scriptstyle(m \times n)} & {\scriptstyle(m \times m)} \end{bmatrix} ;$$

$$\Lambda = \begin{bmatrix} \Lambda_1 & 0 \\ {\scriptstyle(n \times n)} & \\ 0 & \Lambda_2 \\ & {\scriptstyle(m \times m)} \end{bmatrix} .$$

For these systems to be stable, Λ_1 must include all the roots inside the unit circle, and Λ_2 include all the roots outside.

Then for $t > t_0$ (see Blanchard 1980).

(A1)
$$X_t = B_{11}\Lambda_1 B_{11}^{-1} X_{t-1} + \Omega_1 \xi_{t-1}$$

$$- A_{12}C_{22}^{-1} \sum_{i=0}^{\infty} \Lambda_2^{-i-1}(C_{21}\Omega_1$$

$$+ C_{22}\Omega_2)_{t-1}\xi_{t-1+i}$$

and

(A2)
$$Y_t = - C_{22}^{-1}C_{21}X_t$$

$$- C_{22}^{-1} \sum_{i=0}^{\infty} \Lambda_2^{-i-1}(C_{21}\Omega_1 + C_{22}\Omega_2)_t \xi_{t+i}.$$

An algorithm giving the values for X_t and Y_t given the sequence of actual and anticipated ξ_t's is available upon request.

Comment   Bennett T. McCallum

The basic purpose of Blanchard's study is to specify and estimate a macroeconometric model that can be used for valid policy simulations— that is, simulations that are not open to Lucas's (1976) fundamental critique. It seems clear that this would be, if successful, a very useful project. There are a few such models in existence (Barro 1978, Sargent 1976a, and Taylor 1979b, for example), but Blanchard's aggregate demand sector is specified with considerably more detail than in any of these others.[13] Let us then consider whether his approach seems likely to prove successful.

I shall begin by noting the way in which Blanchard has attempted to build policy-invariance into the model's structure. The main step—

I am indebted to Robert Flood and Peter Garber for helpful discussions and to the National Science Foundation for financial support (SOC 76-81422).

13. Of course the Barro and Sargent models are ones in which the choice among systematic policy feedback rules has no effect on output or unemployment processes. Taylor's, like Blanchard's, leaves more scope for activist stabilization policy.

in conjunction with the adoption of the rational expectations hypothesis —is to make h_t and q_t (the present values of expected future real wage and real profit streams) the principal determinants of consumption and investment demand, respectively. Policy changes should then bring about changes in expected future wage and profit variables and consequently, by way of h_t and q_t, current consumption and investment. While one could quibble over details, this general approach seems reasonably satisfactory in principle,[14] so the issue becomes one of empirical implementation. I shall therefore devote some attention to the model's estimation, which is described in a separate paper by Blanchard and Wyplosz (1978).[15]

In any analysis in which one adopts the rational expectations hypothesis, and accordingly abstains from the use of distributed-lag "proxies" for expectational variables, estimation will necessarily involve some technique that is not entirely "standard" in macroeconomics. In trying to discern how Blanchard has proceeded in this regard, one gradually becomes aware that a significant part of his strategy is to design the model so that unobservable expectational variables appear in very few places. In fact, they appear only in the arbitrage equations, those designated (8) and (10). Furthermore, these equations include a minimal number of parameters—and the values 1.04 in (8) and 0.093 in (10) are simply unit-of-measurement conversion factors that do not need to be obtained by estimation. Thus the *only* parameter estimated in either (8) or (10) is the risk premium, denoted β. The value was estimated as 0.075 in (8) and assumed to be applicable in (10) as well. This strategy for minimizing the number of parameters in equations with expectational variables must be regarded as highly ingenious.

The procedure actually used to estimate β does not, however, strike me as desirable. Blanchard and Wyplosz in effect by writing

$$(1) \qquad \beta = \frac{4(_tq_{t+1} - q_t) + 1.04\pi_t}{q_t} - r_t,$$

---

14. This statement refers only to the aggregate demand portion of the model. I shall have more to say about aggregate supply below. In addition, it should be mentioned that the current version of the model does not include tax rate variables in several places in which they would be necessary for fiscal policy simulations. Indeed, estimation has probably suffered from these omissions since tax schedules were altered during the sample period. But Blanchard is fully aware of this problem and will no doubt be eliminating it in future versions.

15. I have little to say about the numerical results of the estimation. Two items should, however, be mentioned. First, the estimates of the autoregressive parameters in the structural equations estimated by Fair's (1970) procedure are very high: 0.83 to 0.96. Second, current income variables enter strongly in both the investment and consumption functions, despite their absence from the theoretical model.

where $\pi_t = $ profit per unit of capital, $r_t = $ *expected* real rate of return on Treasury bills, and $_tq_{t+1} = $ the value of "Tobin's q" (as calculated by von Furstenberg 1977) for period $t + 1$ expected as of period t. Next they delete the capital gains term $(_tq_{t+1} - q_t)/q_t$, arguing that its sample average should be small, adopt Nordhaus's (1974) estimate of the mean value of π_t for 1953–73, and compute sample period mean values for q_t and r_t, using for the latter the ex post real rate $i_t - (p_{t+1} - p_t)$ instead of $i_t - (_tp_{t+1} - p_t)$. Finally, they substitute these three mean values into expression (1) and use the resulting number as their estimate, β. This use of the ex post real rate and the deletion of the capital gains term are perhaps justifiable, given the rational expectations condition, so β may be statistically consistent. But since the estimation procedure ignores period-to-period interactions among the various terms of (1), it would appear to be unusually inefficient.[16] In addition, it does not permit the calculation of a standard error for β. Thus there is no way of telling, from the Blanchard and Wyplosz paper, whether their estimate is significantly different from zero—or, for that matter, from unity.

The most serious problem with the model's estimation pertains, however, to the consumption function. The source of the problem is that h_t is unobservable in the following specification:

$$c_t = a_1 h_t + a_2 w_t + a_3 w_{t-1} + a_4 y d_t$$
$$+ a_5 y d_{t-1} + \epsilon_t.$$

How, then, is estimation effected? In fact, the procedure is to choose units of measurement so that the sample mean value of the unobservable h_t must be 1.0, and then simply estimate

$$c_t = a_1 + a_2 w_t + a_3 w_{t-1} + a_4 y d_t$$
$$+ a_5 y d_{t-1} + \epsilon_t,$$

using the resulting constant term as an estimate of the slope parameter for h_t. Clearly, this procedure must be inconsistent, because of the omitted variable. And the omission seems particularly inappropriate in the context of a study focusing upon aggregate demand: the consumption function is estimated by a procedure that pretends that its main driving variable is not a variable at all. Blanchard and Wyplosz express the intention of using a more satisfactory procedure in the future, however.

A few words should perhaps be added about identification. I have found rather persuasive the contention of Sims (1979) that the appro-

---

16. There is, of course, no attempt to exploit or test cross-equation restrictions implied by the rational expectations hypothesis. On this subject, see Wallis 1977.

priate identification criterion for dynamic macroeconometric models is the one developed by Hatanaka (1975), which does *not* assume that distributed-lag lengths and serial correlation properties are known a priori. Also hard to resist is Sims's argument that statistical exogeneity tests should be passed by variables classified as exogenous for purposes of estimation and identification. In fact, Blanchard and Wyplosz carry out such tests for variables used as exogenous instruments (i.e., first-stage regressors) in estimation, a step that should be widely regarded as commendable. But the set of instrumental variables ultimately used is not reassuring. There are six in this set, but two[17] actually fail the exogeneity tests and, of the remaining four, one is the federal profit tax rate while another is the total profit tax rate—which would hardly seem to qualify as distinct variables. Furthermore, the final two in the set are government spending and exports. But in Blanchard's model these apparently enter only in the expenditure equation (5), where they are additive components of the variable x_t. Perhaps one of the two should appear in some additional equation that is not listed explicitly as part of the model.[18] But, if not, these two variables can only count as one for the purpose of identification. Consequently, the system contains only two or perhaps three truly exogenous variables. But the consumption function includes four endogenous variables (counting h_t), even with the current real interest rate excluded, so its identification status should be regarded as dubious.[19] This argument should not be taken as a criticism of Blanchard, whose practice is more conscientious than is usually found in empirical work,[20] but as an indication of the inherent difficulty of reliably identifying structural equations.

My final point concerns the aggregate supply specification in Blanchard's model.[21] At first glance, it appears similar to one that I have used (McCallum 1978), for mine includes a price adjustment equation exactly like Blanchard's (14),

$$p_t - p_{t-1} = \gamma(p^*_t - p_{t-1})$$

$$0 \leq \gamma \leq 1,$$

17. The federal personal tax rate and the actual (realized) required reserve ratio.

18. That there must be some such equations is evident from the list of variables tested as potential instruments, as most of these do not appear at all in Blanchard's equations (1) to (11).

19. The same is true (as Blanchard and Wyplosz point out) for the money demand function.

20. Also commendable is the practice of testing for parameter constancy across sample subperiods.

21. The following comments do not distinguish between the three versions of Blanchard's supply function.

with p^*_t defined as the (log of the) price level that would equate aggregate demand and supply. But my model is one in which monetary policy can affect output only by creating monetary surprises—despite the slow price adjustments that take place with small values of γ—while Blanchard's simultations show output effects without monetary surprises. So the specifications must differ in some important way.

The main difference, it turns out, is that under my specification, aggregate demand is a distinct variable from aggregate supply or output.[22] In most periods the two will differ in value, with inventory holdings fluctuating as a result. In Blanchard's model, by contrast, the same symbol (y_t) denotes both output and quantity demanded, so the two are always equal. They can both differ from their common steady state value, but not from each other.

Now it would seem that, if one is going to construct a model in which price level stickiness leads to discrepancies between aggregate demand and supply in *some* sense, he would want to permit output to differ from quantity demanded. These are, after all, supposed to be determined by different agents (to some extent) and in response to different stimuli. But having said this, I must add that my model, like Blanchard's, has not been justified by any explicit profit-maximizing analysis of inventory-holding producer behavior. Such an analysis has recently been worked out, however, by Blinder and Fischer (1978). Their model features profit-maximizing responses of output and inventory holdings—and therefore prices—to changes in aggregate demand.[23] It would seem that an aggregate supply function based on this sort of analysis would be preferable to the one used by Blanchard. In particular, it should be more likely to be invariant to policy choices than the one used in his simulations.

In summary, then, I have definite reservations about Blanchard's supply specification, his model's identifiability, and some of the estimation procedures. Consequently, it appears that his project has not yet been brought to a successful conclusion. Nevertheless, the model in its present form represents an imaginative and interesting beginning. Studying Blanchard's paper was, for me, a pleasure.

22. With output a distinct variable, another behavioral relation is needed to close the model. In my paper, output is determined by a Lucas-type supply function. Accordingly, even with (14), systematic monetary policy cannot affect output.

23. In the first version of the Blinder-Fischer model, monetary policy has no effects on output. They also present a version in which there are "non-neutralities," but these seem to reflect effects on the "full-employment" output level, rather than the discrepancy between actual and full employment levels. Thus the Blinder-Fischer nonneutralities do not provide theoretical support for activist *stabilization* policy.

Comment   Michael Parkin

Blanchard's paper is a useful, compact summary of two other papers (Blanchard 1978, Blanchard and Wyplosz 1978). It sets out the structure, together with numerical parameter estimates, of the aggregate demand side of a macroeconomic model with five markets—goods, money, bonds, equity, and labor. The model is "completed" by adding an ad hoc aggregate supply assumption that the price level gradually adjusts toward its equilibrium level. Simulation experiments are conducted which take account of the policy regime on the expectations of agents, thereby overcoming the Lucas problem. Attention is focused on the stock market and real output responses.

It is possible to get a better feel for how the model hangs together and how it works by looking at Blanchard's earlier paper. The basic structural equations describing the goods market may be summarized as

$$(1)\qquad \dot{y} = \sigma(aq - by + g),$$

where y = real output, q = the stock market price of capital, and g = government expenditures, less tax receipts; $\sigma, a, b > 0$. This is a dynamic version of the IS curve of a standard macroeconomic model. The term in parentheses $(aq - by + g)$ is simply the excess of expenditure plans over current receipts. The term aq can be thought of as investment and by as savings, with g representing the net injection of government purchases. Thus equation (1) simply says that output will rise proportionately to the excess of current expenditure plans over current receipts.

Asset equilibrium is summarized by

$$(2)\qquad r = cy - h(m - p),$$

where r = the nominal rate of interest, m = the logarithm of the money supply, and p = the logarithm of the price level. This is simply the LM curve. It has no inherent dynamics.

Next there is perfect arbitrage between bonds and equities so that

$$(3)\qquad r = \frac{\dot{q}^e}{q} + \frac{\alpha_0 + \alpha_1 y}{q},$$

where the superscript e denotes the expectation of the relevant variable. The second term in this equation $(\alpha_0 + \alpha_1 y)/q$ represents the rate of profit, which is postulated to be an increasing function of output. This simply says that the rate of profit plus the expected rate of capital gain (or loss) on equities must equal the current rate on bonds. Expectations are rational so that

$$(4)\qquad \dot{q}^e = \dot{q}.$$

These four equations constitute the aggregate demand system.

The model is completed by adding a fifth equation, namely,

(5) $\qquad \dot{p} = \gamma(p^* - p),$

where p^* is the equilibrium (logarithm) of the price level.

The model is most simply analyzed if we consider first the case where $\gamma = 0$ and therefore where the price level is stuck at its existing value. In this case the subsystem of equations (1), (2), (3), and (4) determines the level of output, the interest rate, and the stock market value of the capital stock for a given g, m, and p. Figure 3.5 summarizes this model. Equation (1) can be plotted as the IS curve for $\dot{y} = 0$ and equations (2), (3), and (4) used to eliminate the interest rate and $\dot{q}^e$ and plotted for $\dot{q} = 0$. (There are in fact two cases of the $\dot{q} = 0$ locus depending on whether a rise in the profit rate raises or lowers the interest rate in equilibrium. The case we work with is that which the empirical results correspond to.) The only expectational variable in this model is the stock market value of the capital stock. There is no uncertainty explicitly introduced, and therefore we have the deterministic analogue of rational expectations, namely, perfect foresight. All the paths of adjustment of this economy turn out to be perfect foresight paths. However, if we impose the usual terminal conditions to achieve uniqueness, the economy will travel along an arm such as aa', achieving a steady state at E.

If this economy is disturbed by say a rise in the money stock, then the $\dot{q} = 0$ locus shifts (fig. 3.6) from that marked $M = M_0$ to that marked $M = M_1$. The initial equilibrium was point E and the new equilibrium is B. How the economy moves from E to B depends on the timing of the announcement and the implementation of the change in the money stock. Blanchard analyzes several cases. The most simple and

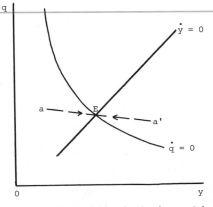

Fig. 3.5   Dynamic adjustment in the basic model

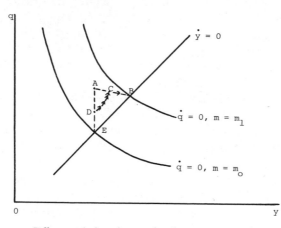

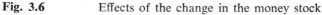

Fig. 3.6   Effects of the change in the money stock

direct is that of a previously unanticipated rise in the money stock. Up to some date, the money stock was at M_0. At the date of shock the money stock is increased to M_1, and it is known that it will be permanently held at M_1 thereafter. At that instant the economy jumps to A and thereafter follows the trajectory marked from A to B. If the rise in the money stock is announced ahead of time, at the moment of announcement the stock market will jump to a position such as D, and in the transition between the announcement and the implementation of the money stock change the economy will follow the trajectory DC. The money stock actually rises to M_1 at point C and thereafter the economy follows the trajectory CB. The further ahead the money supply increase is announced relative to its implementation, the closer will the economy move to traveling along the IS curve. In the limit of an announcement an infinite amount of time ahead of the change the economy would simply gradually track up the IS curve and, at the moment when the money stock was increased, the economy would be at point B.

Blanchard's numerical simulations based on alternative assumptions about the lead time of the anticipation illustrate the differences that arise in the alternative cases. It is clear that the more abrupt a policy change is, the more overshooting we would expect to observe in the stock market, with stock market expectations being regressive once the economy is on the stable arm following the actual change in the policy variable.

In all this discussion the price level has been held constant. It is of some importance to analyze the effects of allowing the price level to change simultaneously with the movements of output in the stock market index. Analytically it is easier to get a feel for what is going on if we examine the special case of $\gamma = \infty$ (equivalent to the $\gamma = 1$ in the discrete time case used in the explicit numerical analysis of Blanchard).

Figure 3.7 illustrates the economy in full equilibrium with output at its equilibrium level y^*. The stock market equilibrium value q^* is determined by the point at which the $\dot{y} = 0$ locus cuts the full employment line. The LM cum arbitrage condition determines the price level, which ensures the the $\dot{q} = 0$ locus is compatible with q^* and y^*. Now let there be an unanticipated change in the money stock. Recall, however, that once the money stock has changed it is understood that it is now at a different level forever. What does this do to the equilibrium displayed in figure 3.7? The answer clearly is nothing. The rise in the money stock would shift the LM arbitrage $\dot{q} = 0$ condition to the northeast. The rise in the price level would, however, bring it back to its original position. There would thus be no dynamics at all to investigate.

In between the extreme cases of no price adjustment and perfect price adjustment, if the price level is permitted to move gradually (and Blanchard allows it to close the equilibrium gap by ⅕ each quarter), then the dynamics become somewhat complicated to deal with analytically. There are, however, some strong and persistent real effects following a monetary shock that occur in the numerical simulations presented.

It is clear that the source of these real effects is the specified aggregate supply assumption. Blanchard's view is that the data are inadequate to discriminate amongst alternative aggregate supply formulations and therefore the ad hoc assumption used is justified. This may turn out to be correct. At the same time it should be noted that the key persistence results arise from ad hoc, and therefore the most unsatisfactory, aspect of Blanchard's model. Were it not for sluggish price adjustment, the model would produce very different price, output, and stock market dynamics. Furthermore, it is interesting to note that the rational ex-

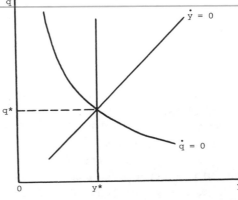

Fig. 3.7   The determination of long-run equilibrium

pectations content of this model bears no relation at all to the standard rational expectations models of price and output determination. The expectations dynamics in Blanchard's analysis concern the stock market price and not the general price level. In fact expectations of the general price level play virtually no role in the analysis at all.

The main virtue of Blanchard's work is in showing how in principle we can develop models that contain rational expectations and yet use those models for policy simulation purposes, taking full account of the effects of the change in the policy regime on the particular expectations formed. Its substantive contribution to the policy debate is limited by virtue of the unsatisfactorily ad hoc and untested assumptions employed on the aggregate supply side. It is in this area that the major research effort is required.

Comment   David E. Lindsey*

I was encouraged by Blanchard's paper, particularly by its emphasis upon adjustment of interest rates and stock prices on the basis of rational expectations of the future course of economic variables. While Bennett McCallum noted that expected—as opposed to observed—variables directly enter only in the arbitrage equations, he would not deny that the demand equations include variables which are functions of expected variables. For example, q is a function of expected paths of dividend streams and real discount rates. The profession has been tardy in focusing macroeconomic rational expectations theory on financial markets and can, in fact, go considerably further in this area than this paper does. I shall return to this point later. First, let me clear away some minor underbrush.

The first point has to do with q, which in Blanchard's paper is defined as the real value of a unit of physical capital in the stock market, or the nominal price of stocks divided by the price of goods. His arbitrage equation equalizes the real bond rate plus a premium with the dividend-price ratio plus the expected capital gains in this real stock price, q. But, his empirical estimates use Tobin's q in the consumption and investment functions. Tobin's q is defined as the value of capital in the stock market divided by its replacement cost, or—if a stock is a claim on one unit of capital—the nominal price of stocks divided by the nominal price of capital goods.

*The views expressed herein are entirely mine and do not necessarily represent the opinions of the Board of Governors of the Federal Reserve System.

Unlike the one good economy of Blanchard's theory, in the real world the price of capital goods and the average price of all goods are not identical and do not move together. Thus, Blanchard's q in the real capital gains part of the arbitrage equations represents a concept different from Tobin's q in the estimated demand equations. If the model were to be simulated over the sample period or for policy purposes over an actual post-sample period, this inconsistency would cause the model's forecasts to go astray. As it is, Blanchard's simulations are over hypothetical periods, and it is implicitly assumed that capital prices and all goods prices are identical.

A related problem in my view is that in Blanchard's simulations, which introduce disturbances to the steady state of the economy, the steady state value of Tobin's q is assumed to be .85. This implies that in the steady state, in which capital is growing, firms are continually issuing 85 cents worth of stock to finance $1 purchases of capital goods, a not very profitable operation. It is a bit hard to accept this description of the steady state, where adjustment costs do not play a role.

On a more important matter, the aggregate supply sector of the model—determining price behavior—is unworthy of the name, since, as McCallum noted, the price level is consistent with any aggregate quantity supplied, which is passively determined by aggregate demand. Given money growth, the path of the price level in this recursive model is determined independently of movements in real income and interest rates, which are then solved for in the demand sector of the model, given expected price levels. While the partial adjustment of prices adds realism to the model, I would have preferred to see it appended to a Lucas-type aggregate supply function—distinguishing between aggregate supply and aggregate demand—so that all the variables could be simultaneously determined. I wonder whether the dynamic properties of the model—involving rapid adjustments of real variables which constitute the paper's main contribution—would not be significantly altered by such an alternative specification.

Another extension of the model that would greatly enhance its realism would be to make the money stock endogenous via a central bank reaction function. Such behavior plays a crucial role in current operations of financial markets. Very short term interest rates and the nominal money stock can be usefully viewed as determined by the interaction of a money demand function and an upward sloping rate setting function of the Federal Reserve, dependent on the observed money stock and other variables, as discussed in Shiller's paper. Thus, as confirmed by Blanchard's statistical causality tests, reserves and high-powered money are in fact endogenous. These variables are adjusted by the Federal Reserve in response to short-run changes in either money demand or the multiplier in order to maintain the desired Federal funds rate (determined by the reaction function).

Market participants essentially forecast the future points of intersection of the money demand and Federal Reserve reaction functions, which imply an expected future path of short-term rates. Then, as is implicit in Blanchard's model, the term structure of rates used in discounting expected stock dividends is determined. Unexpected movements in the stock of money affect market participants' perceptions of future short-term rates and thus affect longer-term rates and stock prices.

There is evidence from studies using weekly data that market participants view the money demand function as being more unstable than the Federal Reserve reaction function. The portion of weekly changes in the money stock that is unexpected gives rise to immediate movements in one-month and longer interest rates in the same direction and immediate movements in stock prices in an opposite direction. That is, when announcements of weekly money stock changes are higher than expected by the market, the market believes that a future increase in the funds rate operating target is then more likely. Hence, all rates tend to move up a bit. Similar estimates of the magnitude of this effect in the 1970s have been found in studies that use different measures of the weekly innovation in the money stock. Each $1 billion innovation in M1 announced at 4:10 P.M. on Thursday is associated, on average, with a 1 to 3 basis point change of the same sign in levels of short and long rates from the close on Thursday to the opening on Friday. This effect is quite significant statistically.

This kind of behavior could be captured in a model like Blanchard's that incorporated the Federal Reserve's reaction function, as well as stochastic effects. Identification problems in the estimation of such a function, however, are severe, as Shiller noted. Incidentally, such problems plague Blanchard's estimated money demand equation, as he is aware.

General Discussion

In responding to comments, Blanchard stated that the main purpose of his paper was to build a structural model that could meet the Lucas challenge, and be used in policy simulations. It became clear very quickly that the data are not powerful enough to distinguish among different aggregate supply specifications. He believed the characteristics of the aggregate supply specification he had chosen were reasonable.

Blanchard said it was difficult to find variables that are exogenous with respect to aggregate demand. He thought that the lack of instruments might be a problem mainly for the demand for money function. He added that he did not think the fact that the steady state value of q in his model was less than one was of great significance, since the level might well be improperly measured.

Robert Hall commented that the conference was not really about rational expectations at all, but rather about market clearing. The Blanchard paper accepts rational expectations and uses it in a clear way but is something of a throwback in not specifying the basis for predetermined prices. He did not see why prices should be predetermined and thought that contract theory did not justify any such assumption. Setting price and letting the buyer determine quantity is not rational. He felt that we are neglecting a key link by merely assuming sticky wages and prices.

Edmund Phelps responded that the Calvo and Phelps paper (1977) tries to explain rigid wages—in Phelps's view, with some success.

Alan Blinder noted that there were nonneutralities of money other than those arising from sticky prices. For instance, real interest rate effects on investment would allow monetary changes to affect output. He felt that the Blanchard paper was missing inventories and their effects on production. He also remarked that the government budget constraint is violated in the paper.

Robert Gordon agreed that there was no good theory of rigid prices. He believed that the required theory would build on the heterogeneity of goods and factors, as well as markets. For instance, there is no time to conduct a separate auction for every item in a supermarket; similarly it is optimal to keep prices of airline seats fixed in the short run. He was not himself sure that labor markets deserved the central role they had been given.

Robert Solow felt there was a tendency to believe there must be a single reason for wage and price inflexibility, whereas there are in fact probably ten or eleven. He added that he saw nothing bad in Blanchard's strategy of elaborating on the demand side of his model and assuming a slow adjustment process on the supply side.

In summing up, Blanchard remarked that the aggregate demand side of a model had to be specified, whatever was done about aggregate supply. He had tried to incorporate inventories, but so far without much empirical success.

References

Barro, R. J. 1978a. "Public Debt and Taxes." Unpublished.

―――. 1978b. "Unanticipated Money, Output, and the Price Level in the United States." *Journal of Political Economy* 86:549–80.

Blanchard, O. J. 1978. "Output, the Stock Market, and Interest Rates." Unpublished.

―――. 1980. "The Solution of Linear Difference Models under Rational Expectations." *Econometrica*, forthcoming.

Blanchard, O. J., and Wyplosz, C. 1978. "An Empirical Structural Model of Aggregate Demand." Unpublished.

Blinder, A., and Fischer, S. 1978. "Inventories, Rational Expectations, and the Business Cycle." Unpublished.

Cagan, P. 1956. "The Monetary Dynamics of Hyperinflation." In *Studies in the Quantity Theory of Money*, edited by M. Friedman. Chicago: University of Chicago Press.

Calvo, G., and Phelps, E. S. 1977. "Appendix: Employment-Contingent Wage Contracts." In *Stabilization of the Domestic and International Economy*, edited by K. Brunner and A. H. Meltzer, pp. 160–68. Carnegie-Rochester Conference Series on Public Policy, vol. 5. New York: North-Holland.

Corrado, C. 1976. "The Steady State and Stability Properties of the MIT-Penn-SSRC Model." Ph.D. thesis, University of Pennsylvania.

Fair, R. C. 1970. "The Estimation of Simultaneous Equation Models with Lagged Endogenous Variables and First Order Serially Correlated Errors." *Econometrica* 38:507–16.

Furstenberg, G. M. von. 1977. "Corporate Investment: Does Market Valuation Matter in the Aggregate?" *Brookings Papers on Economic Activity* 2:347–408.

Hatanaka, M. 1975. "On the Global Identification of the Dynamic Simultaneous Equations Model with Stationary Disturbances." *International Economic Review* 16:545–54.

Lucas, R. E., Jr. 1976. "Econometric Policy Evaluation: A Critique." In *The Phillips Curve and Labor Markets*, edited by K. Brunner and A. H. Meltzer, pp. 19–46. Carnegie-Rochester Conference Series no. 1. New York: North-Holland.

McCallum, B. T. 1978. "Price Level Adjustments and the Rational Expectations Approach to Macroeconomic Stabilization Policy." *Journal of Money, Credit, and Banking* 10:418–36.

Metzler, L. 1951. "Wealth, Saving, and the Rate of Interest." *Journal of Political Economy* 59:93–116.

Nordhaus, W. 1974. "The Falling Share of Profits." *Brookings Papers on Economic Activity* 1:169–208.

Sargent, T. J. 1976a. "A Classical Macroeconometric Model for the United States." *Journal of Political Economy* 84:207–37.

———. 1976b. "Interest Rates and Expected Inflation: A Selected Summary of Recent Research." *Explorations in Economic Research* 3:303–25.

———. 1978. "Rational Expectations, Econometric Exogeneity, and Consumption." *Journal of Political Economy* 86:673–700.

Sargent, T. J., and Wallace, N. 1973. "The Stability of Models of Money and Growth with Perfect Foresight." *Econometrica* 41:1043–48.

———. 1975. "Rational Expectations, the Optimal Monetary Instrument, and the Optimal Money Supply Rule." *Journal of Political Economy* 83:241–54.

Sims, C. A. 1979. "Macroeconomics and Reality." *Econometrica* 47, in press.

Taylor, J. B. 1979a. "Aggregate Dynamics and Staggered Contracts." *American Economic Review* 69:108–13.

———. 1979b. "Estimation and Control of a Macroeconomic Model with Rational Expectations." *Econometrica* 47, in press.

Wallis, K. F. 1977. "Econometric Implications of the Rational Expectations Hypothesis." Unpublished.

4   Can the Fed Control Real Interest Rates?

Robert J. Shiller

Introduction

One contribution that the recent literature on "rational expectations" in macroeconomic models[1] has to make to the older literature on the neutrality of money is to suggest a definition of the real interest rate in a stochastic environment and to suggest senses in which it may or may not be controllable by the monetary authority (or "Fed"). The new definition takes the "rationally expected real rate of interest" as the nominal or "money" interest rate (as quoted in financial markets or perhaps as an after-tax interest rate) minus the *optimally forecasted* inflation rate. The senses in which it may or may not be controlled are described in terms of the nature of the influence of chosen parameters of the Fed *policy rule* on the stochastic properties (and relation to other variables) of the real rate so defined.

There are at least three distinct hypotheses concerning the Fed's influence over rationally expected real interest rates that seem to be suggested in recent discussions of monetary policy. We will give a brief statement of them here subject to clarification below. We will disregard at this point whether we wish to use an "after-tax real rate." It is assumed throughout that Fed policy takes the form only of open market operations and that the interest rate is a short-term one. In order of decreasing stringency and testability, these nested hypotheses are:

This research was supported by the Federal Reserve Bank of Philadelphia, and the National Science Foundation under grant #SOC 77-26798. The views expressed here are the author's and do not necessarily represent the views of the supporting agencies.

The author is indebted to Leslie Appleton for research assistance. Data was kindly supplied by Eugene Fama.

1. This literature is surveyed by Poole 1976 and Shiller 1978.

Hypothesis 1. The form the Fed policy rule takes, whether deterministic or random, has no effect on the behavior of rationally expected real interest rates. That is, the Fed has no ability to shock rationally expected real interest rates at all in the short run or long run. This hypothesis has apparently never been asserted outright in the published literature but does seem implicit in many discussions. The hypothesis seems to be suggested by those who would try to explain interest rates in terms of inflationary expectations without apparent regard to the form monetary policy has taken. Fama, in his well-known article on interest rates as predictors of inflation (1975), seems to suggest this hypothesis when he extends his own hypothesis that one-month real rates are constant to periods when the Fed apparently caused a credit crunch, but at another point he also appears to deny explicitly that the Fed has no influence at all over real interest rates.[2]

Hypothesis 2. The Fed can shock rationally expected real interest rates, but only by taking policy actions other than the actions the public supposes they are taking. That is, if Fed policy on a particular day is known by the public on that day, it will have no effect on real rates.

Hypothesis 2 has some important implications. First, it implies that the Fed's ability to affect real interest rates relies essentially on secrecy. If the Fed opened up all of its internal discussion to public scrutiny without time lag, it would then lose any ability to affect real interest rates. Second, the hypothesis implies that even if the Fed is allowed to maintain secrecy, then still the *systematic* (i.e., nonrandom) part of its policy rule is without effect on real interest rates. That is, if the Fed attempts consistently to pursue any "sensible" or "purposeful" policy then its policy behavior will bear some consistent relation to business conditions and will become predictable by economic agents outside the Fed. This assumes that the Fed has no secrets about business conditions, that is, does not have any "information advantage" over the public.

Hypothesis 2 would appear to be suggested by many models that incorporate the Lucas-Sargent-Wallace aggregate supply relation (see, for example, Lucas 1973), or variations on it, and is specifically an implication of the macroeconomic model of Sargent and Wallace (1975).

Hypothesis 3. Any policy action by the Fed that is known by the public sufficiently far in advance will have no effect on rationally expected real interest rates. That is, we could in principle identify a "policy effectiveness interval," which might be as short as a few days or as long as many years. If the Fed policy rule depends only on information known

---

2. Data before 1951 is not usable, Fama (1975) said, because "in effect a rich and obstinate investor (i.e., the Fed) saw to it that Treasury bill rates did not adjust to predictable changes in inflation rates."

earlier by this time interval, then the form the rule takes will have no effect on the behavior of real interest rates.

The implications of hypothesis 3 depend on the length of the policy effectiveness interval. If the interval is years long, then the Fed may have substantial scope for systematic countercyclical monetary policy. Since the business "cycle" is not rigidly periodic, it cannot be forecasted years in advance, and so even if the Fed policy rule follows a consistent or systematic relation to business conditions, the public will still not have enough advance notice of the policy to react in such a way that real rates become uncontrollable. But if the interval is very short, then there may not be an important difference between hypothesis 3 and hypothesis 2. We will speak of this hypothesis as implying generally a policy effectiveness interval of, say, at least a number of months, but less than a number of years.

Hypothesis 3 seems to be suggested in many discussions. It is specifically a consequence of a model by Phelps and Taylor (1977) and would appear to be implied (though not explicitly in his model) by Fischer (1977). These models connected the policy effectiveness interval with the length of time prices are rigid (Phelps and Taylor) or the length of time labor contracts run (Fischer).[3]

All of our hypotheses are meant to characterize economies in "expectations equilibria," and in the literature that suggested them, "rational expectations equilibria." By an expectations equilibrium we mean merely a situation in which economic agents have *unchanging* subjective probability distributions for all stochastic variables in the economy. If this equilibrium is rational, these subjective distributions are correct. In such an equilibrium, then, economic agents have a correct understanding, to the extent that it will ever be understandable, of the Fed policy rule. What economic agents do not understand is represented as a stochastic term with known properties. Our hypotheses 2 and 3 concern comparative expectations equilibria, that is, what changes in the behavior of economic variables will occur when the parameters of the policy rule are changed *after* the public fully appreciates the systematic nature of the change. In understanding hypotheses 2 or 3, it is particularly important to bear this in mind. If the Fed changes its policy rule (e.g., changes the way the money growth rate responds to unemployment), then there will no doubt be a transition period before a new rational

---

3. In Phelps and Taylor 1977, prices are assumed to be fixed by firms one period in advance and the money supply fixed by the Fed based on information *not* known one period in advance. If Fed policy were known one period in advance, then taking expectations of their expression (8) based on information known at time $t-1$ and using their expression (6), one finds that the money stock drops out of the real part of their model altogether.

expectations equilibrium is reached.[4] The length of this transition period is not to be confused with the policy effectiveness interval.

These hypotheses would seem in principle to be subject to some form of empirical verification. The concepts of a "rationally expected real interest rate" and of a "Federal Reserve policy rule" and changes thereof are sufficiently slippery, however, to make it difficult to bring empirical evidence to bear on *any* of these hypotheses, as we shall discuss in the next section of this paper. It is perhaps for this reason that the literature relating to these hypotheses is almost exclusively theoretical. Empirical literature on the real interest rate (e.g., the Fama 1975 article mentioned above), while perhaps relevant to our evaluation of these hypotheses, does not explicitly consider them.

At the same time, there are some who have asserted, on the basis of their observations of real world phenomena, that certain of these hypotheses are highly "implausible." It is apparently a useful exercise, therefore, to discuss ways in which empirical evidence (qualitative as well as quantitative) might be brought to bear on them, if at all.

Our purpose in this paper is (*a*) to discuss the definitions of "rationally expected real interest rates" and "Fed policy rule" and the meaning of the three hypotheses described above, (*b*) to discuss the kind of subjective beliefs that must be added before these hypotheses have any testable implications, and (*c*) to look at the data and empirical literature in monetary economics to see if there are any clues to the plausibility of the hypotheses when they are given "reasonable" interpretations.

Some will perhaps argue that the abstract models that yielded these hypotheses are not to be taken literally, that they are intended as abstract possibilities that suggest a change in our methods of monetary policy evaluation. Nonetheless, people *have* applied them to discussions of historical experience and will no doubt be inclined to do so in the future. We think, then, that it is not premature to discuss whether these hypotheses might be considered useful in understanding historical experience. Needless to say, our examination of these hypotheses should not be interpreted as an evaluation of the contribution to the history of economic thought of the abstract models that gave rise to them.

Definition and Measurement of Real Interest Rates and Fed Policy Rule

The Real Rate of Interest

A number of different definitions have been applied to the term "real interest rate." For simplicity, we will at this point disregard tax considerations in defining them.

4. The economy may never reach a new rational expectations equilibrium, or may never be in one. These are important theoretical possibilities that lessen the appeal of models that assume rational expectations equilibria (see Shiller 1978).

First, the m-period real interest rate at time t has been defined as the money or "nominal" interest rate (the usual rate quoted at time t in financial markets) minus the actual inflation rate from time t to time $t + m$.[5] Since the inflation rate is not known with certainty, the real interest rate by this definition is not known at time t, and hence we will refer to this as the ex post real interest rate. By this definition the real interest rate is readily measured ex post, at least insofar as inflation can be measured.

Second, the m-period real interest rate at time t has been defined as the nominal interest rate minus the average inflation rate forecast by professional forecasters as quoted in the news media. Readers of business periodicals are regularly supplied with inflation forecasts by the major consulting firms that specialize in macroeconomic forecasting. It has been argued that, realistically, no one in the public has any significant information advantage over these professional forecasters and that it would seem rational to base decision making on these forecasts. These consensus forecasts, while not market determined, are the result of intense discussion in a sort of intellectual "marketplace," especially in more recent years. We will call this the *consensus* real interest rate. The consensus real interest rate is readily measured with a slight lag, which is a publication lag. Since inflation forecasts usually move slowly, this lag is generally not important, but is *potentially* important in some hypothetical circumstances.

Third, the m-period real interest rate at time t has been defined as the rate quoted at time t on an m-period index bond. An m-period index bond is a bond whose coupons or principal due at maturity at time $t + m$ are guaranteed in *real* terms, that is, they are escalated by a price index. We will call this the *market* real interest rate. The market real interest rate is readily measurable at time t, since it is a rate quoted on financial markets. Unfortunately, a market for such index bonds does not yet exist in the United States.

We will digress for a moment to consider whether the Fed might control the real interest rate by any of these definitions. The ex post real rate is obviously not fully controllable, since inflation cannot be fully forecasted. Clearly, however, the Fed can always control the consensus real interest rate as it desires (so long, at least, as this is consistent with a positive nominal rate) if it is willing to accept the economic consequences of the control. The Fed can choose a real interest rate, add to that the latest consensus inflation forecast, and then "peg" the nominal rate at their sum. If we abstract from current institutional details, the

5. Slight variations in the definition arise because of different ways of handling compounding. For example, we might define the real interest rate as one plus the nominal rate divided by one plus the rate of inflation. We disregard the differences among these definitions in what follows.

owner of the "printing press" could announce that it stands ready to borrow and lend unlimited amounts at this nominal rate, and then no one would borrow from another person at a higher rate nor would one lend to another at a lower rate. If the Fed can print nominal bonds as well as money in unlimited amounts, there is no limit to its ability to do this (or to repay the principal on the nominal bonds when they come due). One might question, however, whether it is really of interest that the Fed can do this. If the Fed, in its control of consensus real interest rates, were to cause rapid economic changes, then the publication lag might make the consensus forecast unimportant to economic decisions. Should markets not all clear, the inflation rate based on quoted prices might become less relevant to economic decision making. A hyperinflation might ensue if the Fed tried to peg rates too low or if it consistently followed certain policy rules which would ultimately cause money to be abandoned as the medium of exchange. A deflation might ensue if the Fed tried to peg rates too high; this might cause nominal rates to hit zero, ending the Fed's latitude for control.

It would seem highly plausible a priori that at any moment of time there is nonzero range over which the Fed can influence consensus real interest rates. Efforts to peg such real interest rates do not create unlimited riskless profit opportunities. In contrast, suppose (to take a simple extreme example) the Fed tried to establish different borrowing and lending (nominal) rates and offered to lend, say, at 3% and borrow at an incrementally higher rate. It would thereby create an unlimited riskless profit opportunity. Individuals would borrow from the Fed and use the proceeds to lend to the Fed and would reap a profit with certainty. It is realistic to suppose that if the Fed really announced this, however small the increment, it would quickly find an infinite supply of both lenders and borrowers. If, however, the Fed announced a reduction of the consensus real interest rate from 2%, say, to 1%, it seems hard to imagine that anything really dramatic would happen and historical experience appears to confirm this. The question, then, is how far and for how long it can reduce or raise the consensus real interest rate.

The Fed would seem to have the same sort of potential control over market real interest rates with one modification. It could announce a market real interest rate and offer to buy unlimited quantities of index bonds at this rate, but it cannot sell unlimited quantities of index bonds. While it can promise to deliver unlimited quantities of money in the future, it cannot promise to deliver unlimited quantities of real goods in the future. There are limits to the Fed's ability to command real resources through inflationary finance. Hence it would seem that the Fed could *depress* market real interest rates as it pleases, but there are limits to its ability to elevate them. A hyperinflation is, of course, a possible consequence of depressing the market real interest rates too far or for too long.

The *m*-period *rationally expected* real interest rate at time *t*, which is defined as the *m*-period nominal rate quoted at time *t* minus the optimal forecast of the inflation between time *t* and time $t + m$, is not so readily observed either ex ante or ex post. The rationally expected real rate of interest is not necessarily equal to the consensus real rate of interest or market real rate of interest. In fact, the rationally expected real rate of interest is undefined unless economic variables are stochastic processes whose random properties are given. Such a definition thus makes sense only when the Fed's behavior itself can be described as a stochastic process or policy rule related to other economic variables. The question then is, can the Fed, in deciding on its policy rule, choose a rational expectations equilibrium characterized by a desired behavior of the rationally expected real interest rate?

Such a definition of the real rate of interest is inherently academic, and at the same time a rather elusive concept. It is academic because in a world that is enormously complex and constantly changing, there is no way to define an optimal forecast without some assertion of faith in a model of some sort. Economic agents clearly have diverse models and forecasts. We can estimate empirical forecasting equations, but these will differ depending on the structure we assume, the explanatory variables we include, and the sample period we choose. The concept is also elusive when applied to the present issue for a couple of reasons. First, monetary authorities do not think of themselves as outcomes of stochastic processes and tend to think of themselves as exercising free will. If they must be described in terms of a reaction function, it would be logical to ask whether they can even choose parameters of this function. Second, it is no longer possible to speak of the Fed as defining its policy rule as a function of an observed real interest rate or observed expected rate of inflation, since these depend on the policy rule. That is, the Fed cannot announce that it will buy and sell bonds at 2% plus the optimally forecasted rate of inflation, since it does not know what this will become upon announcement. A rational expectations theorist might be able, given a complete model of the economy, to find an "inflationary expectation" as a function of observable variables predetermined at time *t*, so that if the Fed pegs nominal rates at the desired real rate plus this inflationary expectation, then this inflationary expectation will be an optimal forecast of the resulting inflation. But it is not obvious that we know the model that might enable rational expectations theorists to do this. It is also conceivable that no such rational expectations equilibrium at the desired real rate of interest exists or that, even if it might exist, there may be no path of economic variables that makes a transition from the present equilibrium to the alternative equilibrium. It may be, for example, that an announced policy of pegging the real yield of an index bond may not cause the economy to converge on a rational expectations equilibrium at all, because the price level may explode to infinity.

In this sense, then, models in which the indefinite fixing of market real yields at some announced function of state variables will result in unstable price behavior might be described as models in which the rationally expected real rate is absolutely uncontrollable.

Given the difficulties with the concept of a rationally expected real rate of interest, a practical control theorist might conclude that there is no point even in considering the concept. One might wish to define the structure of the economy in terms of observable variables. Yet it may be, as rational expectations theorists have argued, that the true structure of the economy is not comprehensible unless such variables are included in our model.

Tax Law and the Definitions of the Real Interest Rate

For an individual or corporation in marginal income or corporate profits tax bracket τ the after-tax ex post real rate of interest is found by subtracting the inflation rate from $(1 - \tau)$ times the nominal rate. This is the rate of increase in real after-tax buying power. Definitions of consensus real rates and rationally expected real rates may also be put on after-tax basis by replacing the nominal rate in the definition by $(1 - \tau)$ times the nominal rate. Now, we have not a single after-tax real interest rate but an array of such rates, one for each tax bracket.

It has been suggested (Darby 1975, Feldstein 1976) that hypotheses such as ours should refer not to the simple real interest rate but to the after-tax real rate for some "representative" tax bracket or for the corporate tax rate paid by large corporations. There is a sort of intuitive plausibility to this suggestion. Consider two individuals in the same tax bracket who wish to make a three-month loan between them. No net taxes are paid by the two of them considered together since the borrower deducts interest paid equal to the amount declared as income by the lender. In effect, the government refunds τ times the interest rate from the lender to the borrower. In the face of inflation, if the individuals wish to keep the amount of real resources transferred in the terms of the loan the same as without inflation, they need only mark up their nominal rate by the inflation rate times $1/(1 - \tau)$.

If our tax system were neutral to inflation in other ways, and if all individuals paid the same marginal tax rate, then it would seem quite plausible that our hypotheses should refer to the after-tax real rate. The problem is that our tax system is not neutral in other ways to inflation. If the borrower in our example above wishes to use the funds to purchase physical assets for speculative purposes, then he will not be happy with an arrangement that keeps his real after-tax interest paid constant in the face of inflation, since he will be taxed on the inflation of the price of his investment. Indeed, with such short-term speculation for which gains are taxed as ordinary income, his profits after tax will remain constant in the face of inflation only if the simple (not after-tax) real rate is kept constant. The lender may then also be indifferent to either making the loan or investing in the physical asset himself. But if the borrower wishes to spend the money on a vacation (and the lender views the opportunity cost of the loan as a vacation foregone), then he may be happy with the constant after-tax real rate, precisely since he is not taxed on the "psychic" income from an investment in a vacation and hence inflation does not affect him in the same way. It is clear, then, that inflation affects taxes of individuals in different circumstances in different ways, and so it is not likely that hypotheses 1 through 3 above could be given a simple rationale in terms of any particular definition of the real interest rate.

One possible conclusion of our consideration of tax effects is that our empirical work should concentrate on the period before World War II, when income taxes were relatively negligible. Postwar monetary policy is not really "pure" monetary policy since it affects real taxes. If we are interested in the ability of "pure" monetary policy to affect real interest rates, then we had best confine our attention to the period when such policy was practiced. Our approach here is instead to consider both periods in terms of the simple real interest rate even though for the postwar period the hypotheses may be of less interest.

The Federal Reserve Policy Rule and Hypothesis Testing

We will suppose first that all relevant possible Federal Reserve policy rules can be summarized and indexed in terms of a parameter vector β in the form:

$$(1) \qquad f(r_t, M_t, \beta, \mathbf{I}_t, \phi_t) = 0,$$

where r_t is the interest rate, M_t is the log of high-powered money, $\mathbf{I}_t$ is a vector of state variables or information at time t which characterizes the economy before the Fed acts at time t and is known to the public as well as the Fed, and ϕ_t is an innovation in Fed policy that cannot be forecast by the public, that is, it is independent of the information vector $\mathbf{I}_t$. We have written the function in implicit form to allow for both interest rate rules and money stock rules or for combination rules.

The Fed confronts a public demand for high-powered money function, which we will write as:

$$(2) \qquad g(r_t, M_t, \mathbf{I}_t, \beta, \gamma, \delta_t) = 0,$$

where γ is a vector of parameters and δ_t is a vector of innovations in public behavior. Public behavior depends on β through their reaction to the Fed policy rule. Equation (2) is a reduced form equation for the rest of the macroeconomic model, taking either r_t or M_t as exogenous.

Equations (1) and (2) represent a two-equation model in two unknowns, r_t and M_t. The solution to the model, or reduced form is:

$$(3) \qquad r_t = h_1 (\beta, \mathbf{I}_t, \phi_t, \gamma, \delta_t)$$

$$(4) \qquad M_t = h_2 (\beta, \mathbf{I}_t, \phi_t, \gamma, \delta_t).$$

Another reduced form equation from the macroeconomic model gives the price level:

$$(5) \qquad P_t = h_3(\beta, \mathbf{I}_t, \phi_t, \gamma, \delta_t),$$

and from this equation we can derive the expected rate of inflation $E_t(P_{t+1} - P_t)$ and hence the rationally expected real interest rate:

$$(6) \qquad r_t - E_t(P_{t+1} - P_t) = h_4(\beta, \mathbf{I}_t, \phi_t, \gamma, \delta_t).$$

Hypotheses 2 and 3 concern the way this reduced form equation derived from the structural equations of our model depends on β.

One fundamental problem we face in explaining such models econometrically is finding identifying restrictions. One must find certain exogenous variables that we know shock equation (2) without shocking equation (1) and may be used as instruments to estimate (1) consistently and other exogenous variables that we know shock equation (1) without shocking equation (2) and may be used to estimate equation (2) consistently. The problem is that it is difficult to find *any* variable that we can be confident shocks one equation without shocking the other. When expectations are involved in the behavior that underlies (1) and (2), then *anything* that is publicly known might in principle affect both equations.

There is a literature on estimation of the demand for money and a smaller literature on the estimation of Fed reaction functions, which might be used to try to examine some of the hypotheses. We do not believe, however, that estimates are trustworthy for this purpose. One reason is that this literature generally does not handle the simultaneous equations estimation problem well. When instrumental variables are used there is generally no discussion, let alone a convincing one, to justify the assumption that the exclusion restrictions and exogeneity assumptions are justified. This defect is compounded by the fact that with slow-moving variables and short samples the small sample properties of the K-class estimators may differ widely from those predicted by the usual asymptotic sampling theory.

For the purpose of formulating policy, we need to know the model. For the purpose of evaluating the hypotheses noted in the introduction, however, it may not be necessary to estimate the model. It may instead be necessary to find some change in β.

The first hypothesis noted in the introduction asserts that the structure of the economy is such that $r_t - E_t(P_{t+1} - P_t)$ is independent of either the Federal Reserve parameter vector β or the random variable ϕ_t. If we can find ϕ_t or a change in β, then the real rate should be uncorrelated with it.

The second hypothesis implies that if $\phi_t = 0$ (i.e., the Fed is completely predictable), then $r_t - E_t(P_{t+1}) + E_t(P_t)$ is independent of β. Changes in the parameter β of the policy rule should not affect the random properties of the real rate. If ϕ_t is random, then this hypothesis has no unambiguous interpretation with a model of this generality. The division of Fed policy into "predictable" or "unpredictable" components might be achieved, for example, by positing a money stock rule of the form

(7) $$M_t = f_2(\mathbf{I}_t, \beta) + \phi_t,$$

and then we might interpret the hypothesis to mean that the behavior of real interest rates is independent of β.

The third hypothesis, like the second, cannot be defined unambiguously until we decide how to divide Fed behavior into components that were and others that were not predictable in advance by the policy effectiveness interval. If we write:

(7') $$M_t = f_3(\mathbf{I}_{t-k}, \beta) + g_3(\mathbf{I}_t, \phi_t),$$

so that $f_3(\mathbf{I}_{t-k}, \beta)$ is the component of Fed policy known in advance by the policy effectiveness interval k, then the hypotheses might be interpreted to imply that the interest rate is independent of β.

Unfortunately, although in casual discussions it is often assumed that the hypotheses are well defined, alternative interpretations are possible which would be represented by different versions of (7) or (7') and would in turn be subject to different approaches for testing them. For example, we might break down money into *multiplicative* predictable and unpredictable components, we might allow f_3 in (7') to be multiplied by a function of $\mathbf{I}_t$, or we might break down an *interest rate rule* into predictable and unpredictable components.

The only way we can discuss direct verification of the second or third hypothesis cited in the introduction to this paper is to identify periods during which the Fed policy rule had a stable, repetitive nature and also to identify the time when the transitions between these periods occurred (i.e., where β changed). Our guide in identifying changes in the policy rule will be to look only for changes that were announced by the Fed and well understood by the public. It is inherently a highly subjective business to try to identify periods in which the Fed policy rule might be described as repetitive and when it changed. To evaluate hypothesis 2 or 3 based on statistical analysis, however, we have no alternative but to try.

Measures of Real Interest Rates

As we have noted, it is impossible to measure the rationally expected real interest rate without a statement of faith in a model and, if there are unknown parameters in the model, an identification of a sample period of some length when the model held. If we take the model above, then, before looking at the data, we begin with prior distributions for the parameters β and γ and for the parameters of the distributions of ϕ and δ. We might then in principle update the priors with the data over a period when the policy rule was stable to get a joint posterior distribution of β and γ and other parameters. This distribution might then be used to produce a predictive distribution for the ex post real rate conditional on historical data: $f(r_t - \Delta P_{t+1} \mid \mathbf{I}_t)$, and we might define the rationally expected real rate as the expected value of $r_t - \Delta P_{t+1}$ from this predictive distribution.

This approach suffers from the problem of describing our uncertainty about the nature and structure of the model. A more parsimonious way to proceed is to seek a simple empirical forecasting relation by finding the optimal linear forecast of $r_t - \Delta P_{t+1}$ based on some small subset $\mathbf{I}_{0_t}$ of $\mathbf{I}_t$ which seems particularly likely to be important in determining the predictive distribution $f(r_t - \Delta P_{t+1} \mid \mathbf{I}_t)$. For example, we might regress $r_t - \Delta P_{t+1}$ on its own lagged value to produce an autoregressive forecasting relation. We will call the fitted values of such a regression based on the subset of information and regression coefficients the optimal linear forecast and denote it by $L(r_t - \Delta P_{t+1} \mid \mathbf{I}_{0_t})$. Now one property of such optimal linear forecasts is that $L(r_t - \Delta P_{t+1} \mid \mathbf{I}_{0_t}) = L(E(r_t - \Delta P_{t+1} \mid \mathbf{I}_t) \mid \mathbf{I}_{0_t})$; that is, the optimal linear forecast of the ex post real rate is the same as the optimal linear forecast of the true (unobserved) rationally expected real interest rate (see for example Shiller 1978).

It is a property of optimal linear forecasts that the variance of the forecast is less than or equal to the variance of the variable forecasted (i.e., $R^2 \leq 1$). If we know the optimal linear forecast variance, we can put bounds on the variance of the true rationally expected real interest rate, i.e., its variance must lie *between* the variance of the optimal linear forecast and the variance of the ex post real rate.

The essential point for our purposes is the following: if we can establish that the Fed can control the optimal linear forecast of the ex post real rate in the sense of one of our hypotheses (e.g., that it can, by changing β, and without relying on unforeseen shocks ϕ_t, affect the random properties of the optimal linear forecast), then it can affect the random properties of the true unobserved rationally expected real interest rate. Since the projection of the optimal linear forecast on $\mathbf{I}_{0_t}$ is the same as the projection of the true rationally expected real interest rate on $\mathbf{I}_{0_t}$, one cannot change the one without changing the other and hence one concludes that one *must* have changed at least the relationship of the rationally expected real interest rate with $\mathbf{I}_0$.

Empirical Verification Hypotheses

General Approach

Now we will explore interpretations and tests of the three hypotheses along the lines suggested above. We will consider whether the hypotheses are plausible in view of the observed behavior of nominal rates coupled with the fact that the precise timing and magnitude of Fed actions are probably exogenous and unforecastable. We will also consider the fact that the Fed apparently can (and *has*) pegged nominal rates, which means that there was a sharp reduction, to zero, in exogenous shocks to monetary policy at this time.

Next we will consider whether the history of the Federal Reserve system can be broken down into subperiods in which the policy rule showed a distinctly different stochastic behavior. The subperiods must be long enough so that it makes sense to try to identify the policy rule from the data. We will argue that there is some reason to divide the monetary history of the twentieth century into three long periods: the period 1900 to 1913, before the Fed was founded, the period 1914 to 1950 of early monetary policy (which was unfortunately disrupted by two world wars and a major depression), and the period 1951 to the present, when modern monetary policy was practiced.

Finally, we will consider Granger-Sims causality tests between real interest rates and money growth rates and Barro unanticipated money tests as ways of evaluating these hypotheses.

Behavior of Nominal Interest Rates

Members of the Federal Reserve Board—and of the Trading Desk at New York—have the distinct impression that they can, whenever they wish, influence nominal interest rates in a downward direction by increasing high-powered money and in an upward direction by decreasing high-powered money. This impression is very strong because they have seen it happen with great reliability. Moreover, since they were involved in the decision relating to the conduct of monetary policy, they have a clear idea whether their policy might be considered caused by economic circumstances and to what extent their policy might be viewed as a controlled experiment. Certainly the precise timing of their policy is determined by their own choices, and if interest rates immediately respond reliably when they do intervene, it is hard to question that they can control nominal interest rates in this manner.

If we accept, then, that when the Fed decides to intervene in the open market by increasing high-powered money the nominal interest rate declines, it would appear that the Fed must have some influence over real interest rates, and hypothesis 1 must be wrong. We usually think that increasing high-powered money is, if anything, a signal of higher inflation. It would seem implausible, then, that these lower interest rates are due to lower inflationary expectations. It is conceivable that exogenous increases in the money stock might be a sign of lower inflation over a certain time horizon if the parameters of our model were just right. But it seems inconceivable that such an explanation would reliably hold true for bonds of all maturities for the history of all monetary authorities for hundreds of years.

Even though the Fed knows it can drive the real interest rate at any moment in a desired direction, it does not follow that it can exert any *systematic* control over real interest rates; that is, hypothesis 2 or 3 may still be valid. To see how this might be the case, we may hypothesize a demand for high-powered money function of a form somewhat less general than expression (2) above:

$$(8) \qquad M_t = M_{t-1} + \mu(M^*_t - M_{t-1}) + \eta_t$$

$$0 < \mu \leq 1$$

where

$$(9) \qquad M^*_t = P_t + m_1 Y_t - m_2 r_t - m_3 (E_t(P_{t+1}$$

$$- P_t)) + m_4 Z_t$$

and all coefficients m_1, m_2, m_3, and m_4 are greater than zero. The term η_t is an unforecastable error. Here we have assumed a simple stock adjustment model although more general adjustment models would not affect the basic conclusions. The desired log money stock M^*_t is a function of the log price level P_t, a measure of aggregate economic activity Y_t, the nominal short interest rate r_t, the expected inflation rate, and other exogenous real variables Z_t. Substituting (9) into (8) and using $r_t = \rho_t + E_t(P_{t+1} - P_t)$, we get:

(10)
$$M_t = (1 - \mu)M_{t-1} + \mu P_t + \mu m_1 Y_t - \mu m_2 \rho_t$$
$$- \mu(m_2 + m_3)E_t(P_{t+1} - P_t) + \mu m_4 Z_t + \eta_t.$$

Taking expectations conditional on information at time t and solving for $E_t P_t$, we get:

(11)
$$E_t P_t = (1 - \lambda) E_t J_t + \lambda E_t P_{t+1}$$

where

$$J_t \equiv \Delta M_t / \mu + M_{t-1} - m_1 Y_t + m_2 \rho_t - m_4 Z_t - \eta_t / \mu$$
$$\lambda = (m_2 + m_3) / (1 + m_2 + m_3)$$
$$0 < \lambda < 1.$$

If we then solve this rational expectations equation and assume stable price behavior, that is, a price level that does not diverge to infinity unless the money stock is increased to infinity as suggested in the rational expectations literature, or in this specific context by Sargent and Wallace (1975), we find:

(12)
$$E_t P_t = (1 - \lambda) \sum_{i=0}^{\infty} \lambda^i E_t J_{t+i}$$

and

(13)
$$r_t = \rho_t + E_t(P_{t+1} - P_t) = \rho_t$$
$$+ (1 - \lambda) \sum_{i=0}^{\infty} \lambda^i E_t(\Delta J_{t+i+1}).$$

The model thus implies that the price level, as well as the nominal interest rate, embodies optimal forecasts of ΔJ_{t+1}, $i = 0, 1, \ldots$. We can thus see how it is that the Fed may have the *impression* that it influences the real rate and could do so systematically when in fact it cannot. Suppose we hypothesize a money stock rule of the form (7) above. Although the Fed may not be aware of it, the public has divided its behavior into two components: a predictable and an unpredictable component. The public has already formed anticipations of all future movements in the money stock based on information about Fed policy that has unfolded to that point in time. If the public anticipates a policy of greater increases in the money supply, then nominal interest rates will by (13) rise as soon as the public begins to collect information which enables it to anticipate this. If, on the one hand, the Fed *delays* expanding the money stock longer than the public expected, then interest rates may rise further still because of the effect on real interest rates of this "surprise" until the date when the Fed does intervene, when interest rates may drop back to the level given by (13).[6] If, on the other hand, the Fed increases the money growth rates *sooner* than the public expected, then interest rates may fall when they do this and may rise back to the level given by (13) when the Fed is on target again.

Whenever the Fed has the sense that its actions are volitional, that is, could not have been predicted by the market, it observes the customary negative relation between real rates and high-powered money. The Fed knows these shocks are exogenous and thus *knows* it has influence over real rates. But the Fed rarely observes the effect of its changes in its policy *rule* and, if it does not look deep into history, has no information on its *systematic* ability to control real interest rates.

This analysis does not necessarily suggest a scenario in which, as described, for example, by Friedman (1968), increases in high-powered money cause a decline in interest rates for a certain interval of time (the "liquidity effect" period) followed by a *rise* in interest rates above its former level due to engendered inflationary expectations. Friedman's scenario might come about if unforeseen shocks constituted evidence that further money growth rates would be higher, in which case inflationary expectations would be immediately adjusted upward, and if temporary effects on real interest rates were sufficient to offset the rise in inflationary expectations.

The crucial behavioral relation that gives the result that the Fed has no systematic influence over real interest rates is embodied in expression (12), coupled with hypothesis 2, which implies that the real variables in J_t are not subject to systematic Fed control. Expression (12) then says that the *price level* incorporates all information currently available about future money supplies. Without this relation, the Fed must be able to control real rates or the price level must be explosive, even with stable monetary policy. As an illustration, suppose the Fed announces that the money stock today will be decreased by 3% below what the public had expected, but that all future money growth rates will be unchanged. By (12), and hypothesis 2, and assuming for simplicity that $\mu = m_3 = m_4 = 0$, the price level must drop immediately, and by (13) the nominal rate will be unchanged. It seems unlikely that the price level would drop immediately by 3%, however. If the price level is sluggish, can we retain hypothesis 2? To retain it would mean that the real money stock falls and hence, by the money demand equation (9), that the nominal rates r_t must increase. If the real rate is constant, this must imply that expected inflation will increase. If this expected inflation is rational, then it must be the case that actual inflation increases, at least on average. Thus, the price level

---

6. If monetary shocks show persistence, i.e., serially uncorrelated movements in ϕ create serially correlated movements in the real rate, as represented, for example, in expression (14′) below, then the real rate will not return to "target" immediately.

tends to increase in the following period, rather than decrease, which throws the system further out of equilibrium. By the same reasoning the price level is expected to increase even faster during the following period, and, by induction, must explode to infinity even with a stable money supply.

If we assume only hypothesis 3, then (12) still must hold, but now we have lost the proposition that the future real rate and future real income terms in J_{t+i}, $i = 0, \ldots \infty$ are independent of the entire systematic component of monetary policy. Since our hypothesis then does not constrain these y and ρ terms in J, it says nothing about how the price level responds to current information about Fed policy, and so (12) has itself no content in this regard. Hypothesis 3 does imply that real variables are independent of information about monetary policy known earlier by the policy effectiveness interval. The price level, today, optimally incorporates all information about future monetary policy that was known then.

While this behavioral assumption in (12) may be plausible for prices of speculative commodities, this seems improbable for the *aggregate* price level judging from the way many prices are actually set. It is not just that prices are "sticky" or "sluggish," but that they are not set in anticipation of future monetary policy. It might not be too unreasonable to suppose that the prices of speculative commodities take into account a very simple, repetitive seasonal pattern in money growth rates. It is also conceivable that if the money stock has a simple predictable pattern over the business cycle, then the prices of certain speculative commodities might in effect incorporate this information. But will wages be set in this way? Will the price of haircuts? It seems likely that at least some modification of equation (12) is called for to allow for other factors that help determine the aggregate price level, and this will then invalidate hypotheses 2 and 3.

One reason that (12) and our hypotheses seem implausible is that the public is certainly not consciously aware of it. News reports routinely ascribe movements in the stock market indices to new information, but changes in aggregate price indices, while a subject of great public interest, seem *never* to be ascribed to new information about future monetary policy. Hypothesis 2 requires that if the Fed announces a change in its long-run target, the announcement itself (if credible, and not already discounted by the public) should have an immediate effect on the price level and on the nominal interest rate. Judging casually from the lack of public awareness of such an effect, we think that the effect is certainly not likely to be a very striking one.

Further evidence on the plausibility of (12) and (13) can be obtained by considering the effects of the Fed's announcing that interest rates will be pegged at a certain level. Before we consider this, we must point out that this has actually happened.

At the end of April 1942 the Federal Open Market Committee directed the twelve Federal Reserve Banks to purchase all treasury bills offered at a discount rate of ⅜ of 1% and in August directed the Federal Reserve Banks to give the seller an option to repurchase bills of the same maturity at the same rate. An ascending rate structure on government bonds was also pegged, peaking at 2.5% for the longest bonds. A demand for short-term bills persisted for a while with this structure, but, as confidence grew that the Fed would continue to peg long rates at this level, it evaporated. In July 1947, the Fed thus ended the peg on treasury bills. In December 1947 the Fed also lowered its buying price to near par on long-term bonds which, with the fixed rate structure, had come to sell above par, but felt obligated not to let bond prices fall below par, until after the Accord in March 1951. Some variation in long-term interest rates was allowed; in particular, the Fed allowed prices of long-term bonds to rise *above* the pegged price, which happened briefly in early 1946.

Price controls were also first imposed in April 1942, with the General Maximum Price Regulation and were finally lifted with the expiration of the Price Control Act on 1 July 1946. Price controls were not reimposed until the Korean conflict, when in January 1951 an official freeze on most prices and wages was announced. In the intervening period the only important efforts to control the aggregate price level were voluntary: the Economic Stabilization Agency efforts just before the price freeze with the Korean conflict, and the voluntary credit restraint program. We thus have a period of 4.5 years in which prices were free and long-term interest rates pegged and a one-year period in which prices were free and short-term interest rates were pegged. This time interval, moreover, came immediately after a four-year period which, although under price controls, was characterized by a development of "pent-up inflation" in the sense that the money supply increased dramatically under the pegged interest rate.

What does the model predict about the effects of an announcement by the Fed that interest rates are to be pegged at a certain level? Here we are confronted with a basic problem of the transition from one rational expectations equilibrium to another for which rational expectations models are no guide. Sargent and Wallace (1975) highlighted this problem when they pointed out that in their model, for which $\mu = 1$, the interest rate is related only to future *changes* in money; hence the money stock and price level are not determined by the fixing of the interest rate. Although in our model $\mu \neq 1$ so that a lagged money stock enters, it is unclear what relevance the money stock before the interest rate peg was announced has to the ultimate rational expectations equilibrium. The price level after a rational expectations equilibrium is reached is still not determined by the model.

If a rational expectations equilibrium is attained under hypothesis 2, then we do know that expression (13) must hold with r_t at the pegged rate, and this means that expected future changes in the money stock must move in such a way as to cause inflationary expectations to move opposite to the real rate. If, let us suppose, the real rate and exogenous factors are nearly constant, then the appropriate monetary policy is essentially to keep all changes in M at the appropriate level, equal to the pegged rate minus the real rate. The Fed, to keep interest rates low, essentially must merely keep money growth rates low. Fed policy must be to set an example with small money growth rates, rather than, as was actually the case, to conduct massive open market purchases when rates started to rise. The Fed does not try to offset movements in interest rates in the usual way; rather, it sets a monetary policy which implies deflation (and hence deflationary expectations) whenever the real rate is shocked upward, so that the public prevents the nominal rate from ever moving. Clearly, the Fed was not doing the right thing to cause the economy to converge on a rational expectations equilibrium with stable prices at the pegged rate, as they essentially said (though not in these words) in their arguments with the Treasury. We may say that the economy was not in a rational expectations equilibrium of the kind with stable prices, as described by (12) or (13). But it was not in an *un*stable rational expectations equilibrium either. When price controls were lifted in July 1946, we saw not a one-shot big increase in the price level but (after a relatively modest immediate jump in prices) a serially correlated smooth increase in prices (see fig. 4.5 below). This means that very negative real interest rates, apparently caused by monetary phenomena, could be *forecasted* during this transition period. This situation persisted for a while and then the economy settled in, not to a hyperinflation, but an ordinary recession.

Founding of the Federal Reserve System

In the original Federal Reserve Act of 1913 the first purpose of the Federal Reserve system defined in the opening paragraph is "to provide an elastic currency," and "to accommodate commerce and business" (section 14). From the discussion of the time there is at least one unambiguous implication of this purpose: namely, to provide a larger supply of currency toward the end of the year when the demand for currency was higher, in part because of the crop harvest and Christmas shopping.[7]

7. In its first annual report to Congress (1915), the Federal Reserve Board seems to say, in clear language, that it will mitigate seasonal fluctuations in interest rates: "It should not, however, be assumed that because a bank is a Reserve Bank its resources should be kept idle for use only in times of difficulty, or, if used at all

Under the national banking system, this higher demand for currency was not accommodated, and the result was pronounced seasonality of nominal interest rates. This seasonality in *nominal* interest rates apparently vanished after the establishment of the Federal Reserve system and was apparently replaced by a seasonality in currency in circulation as documented by Macaulay (1938). Carter Glass (1927) listed the elimination of this seasonality as one of the major achievements of his Federal Reserve Act.

The pronounced decline in seasonality in nominal interest rates after the founding of the Federal Reserve at the end of 1913 can be seen clearly in figure 4.1. An additive seasonal factor (plotted with the same scale as the nominal interest rate above) computed with the Census X-11 program is shown. This seasonal factor is computed as a 3×3 moving average of the difference of the corrected series from a 13-month average. This implies a triangular moving average extending over nearly 6 years. Thus, the fact that the seasonality does not disappear immediately in 1914 is mainly due to an artifact of the Census X-11 program. The seasonal pattern *does* show a marked decline about as soon as it could.

The question that apparently never occurred to anyone then was whether the Fed had, by adopting the announced policy of eliminating seasonal variations, eliminated a seasonal pattern in *real* interest rates. A stable seasonal pattern in ex post rates implies a seasonal pattern in ex ante rates since seasonal factors are forecastable. All our hypotheses may be taken to imply that the elimination of the seasonal factor in nominal rates should have changed the seasonal pattern in inflation rates so that the seasonal pattern in real interest rates should remain unchanged.

When we look at the seasonal pattern of the ex post real interest rates (fig. 4.2), we see an apparent disruption[8] in the seasonal pattern of real

---

in ordinary times, used reluctantly and sparingly. . . . Time and experience will show what the seasonal variation in the credit demands and facilities in each of the Reserve Banks of the several districts will be and when and to what extent a Reserve Bank may, without violating its special function as a guardian of banking reserves, engage in banking and credit operations. . . . There will be times when the great weight of their influence and resources should be exerted to secure a freer extension of credit and an easing of rates in order that the borrowing community shall be able to obtain accommodations at the lowest rates warranted by existing conditions and be adequately protected against exorbitant rates of interest. There will just as certainly, however, be times when prudence and a proper regard for the common good will require that an opposite course be pursued and accommodations curtailed." The Board said it gave "certain assurance that whatever funds might be necessary for the gradual and orderly marketing of the cotton crop would be available at moderate rates."

8. The disruption is not due to the spectacular deflation of 1920, since the Census X-11 program automatically excludes such outliers. The Census X-11 is still capable of producing spurious seasonal factors. Sargent (1971) demonstrated the existence

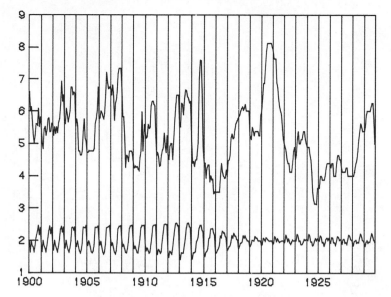

Fig. 4.1   Four-to-six-month prime commercial paper rate (above) and additive Census X-11 seasonal factors (below), monthly data. Vertical lines correspond to January of the year noted directly below. Source of prime rate series: 1900–1924, *Banking and Monetary Statistics, 1914–41*, Board of Governors of the Federal Reserve system 1943, table 120; 1925–29, Macro Data Library, Board of Governors of the Federal Reserve system.

interest rates after the founding of the Federal Reserve, but a reassertion of the seasonal pattern roughly as strong as before. One is tempted to interpret this disrupted period as a transitional period when the economy converged on a new rational expectations equilibrium in accordance with hypothesis 2. There is potentially an element of truth to this story; however, we note that the seasonal pattern in inflation rates had substantially greater amplitude than that in nominal interest rates, and so it is better to say that the seasonal pattern in inflation rates drowned rather than offset the declining seasonal pattern in nominal rates. All that we can conclude from this data is that we *can't* say with any confidence whether a policy of eliminating the seasonal pattern in nominal rates reduced the seasonal pattern in real rates. The seasonal pattern in inflation rates is so much bigger, and rather unstable itself, that we cannot find any

of a pre-1913 seasonal factor (as well as a post–World War II seasonal factor) in short-term interest rates with spectral analysis.

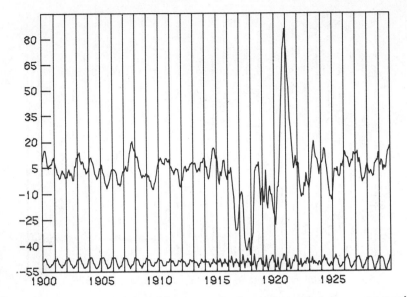

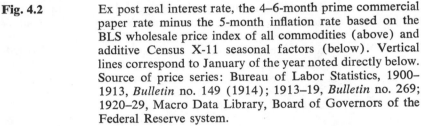

Fig. 4.2   Ex post real interest rate, the 4–6-month prime commercial paper rate minus the 5-month inflation rate based on the BLS wholesale price index of all commodities (above) and additive Census X-11 seasonal factors (below). Vertical lines correspond to January of the year noted directly below. Source of price series: Bureau of Labor Statistics, 1900–1913, *Bulletin* no. 149 (1914); 1913–19, *Bulletin* no. 269; 1920–29, Macro Data Library, Board of Governors of the Federal Reserve system.

evidence here contrary to the hypotheses. Carter Glass was too quick to congratulate himself on the real consequences of his Federal Reserve Act.[9]

A Policy Rule Change Marked by the Accord

It is commonly asserted that the Accord of March 1951 marked an abrupt change in Fed policy. This was the date that the Fed was freed

9. The seasonal pattern in real interest rates may be spurious. Since nominal rates showed less pronounced seasonality than inflation rates, there was an incentive in the fall, when agricultural prices were low, for farmers to hold their crops off the market and borrow at the nominal rate. Their efforts to do so were apparently hampered by credit rationing by the banks. It is possible that there was no seasonal factor in real rates actually available to farmers.

One effect of Fed policy not shown in the data may be the reduction of credit rationing in the fall. Hypothesis 2 would then suggest that the seasonal pattern in inflation should disappear, making for a spurious apparent reduction in real rate seasonality, which we do not observe. Instead, this interpretation suggests the Fed may have *introduced* a seasonal factor in real rates that did not exist before.

from the obligation to peg interest rates and a time of new-found concern with monetary aggregates and countercyclical monetary policy. One can see from figure 4.3 that the rate of growth of the money supply (M-1) before the Accord was less strongly seasonal and more distinctly marked by erratic longer-term movements. After the Accord (actually, after the war) the growth of the money stock was dominated much more by a very strong seasonal factor. The strong seasonal factor in the money stock, incidentally, first appeared around 1942, when interest rates were pegged and, of course, what seasonality in nominal interest rates still remained was then totally eliminated. It appears that the Fed revised its seasonal adjustment factors at this time and then, following the Accord, became concerned that the seasonally adjusted money stock should grow smoothly. In so doing, the Fed perpetuated the seasonal movements in the money stock that were appropriate to a short-term interest rate with no seasonal pattern for the period 1942–50. Subsequent estimates of

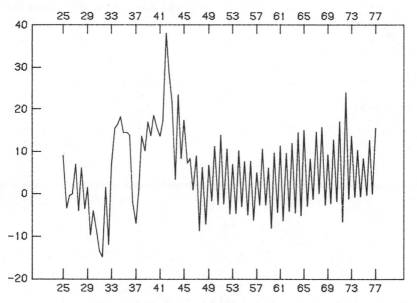

Fig. 4.3   Money growth rates before seasonal adjustment, 6-month percentage change in M-1 over succeeding 6-month period at annual rates, 1925–77, semiannually (June and December). Marks on horizontal axis correspond to June figure. Source: 1925–40, *Banking and Monetary Statistics, 1914–41*, Board of Governors of the Federal Reserve system, 1943, table 9; 1941–70, *Banking and Monetary Statistics, 1941–70*, Board of Governors of the Federal Reserve system, 1976, p. 5 and table 1.1; 1971–77, *Federal Reserve Bulletin*, passim.

seasonal factors would tend to remain unchanged as long as the Fed perpetuates this seasonal pattern. Apparently, the seasonal pattern in money demand became more pronounced after the war, and so a seasonal pattern in nominal rates has reappeared, as documented by Diller (1971) and Sargent (1971).

It appears, then, that there was a substantial change in the Fed policy rule after World War II. If we can assume that the stochastic structure of the rest of the economy did not show an equally substantial change following the war, then we can look at the behavior of the real interest rate and perhaps find some disconfirmation of our hypotheses if the behavior of real rates changes.

A plot of the ex post real short-term interest rate (the 4–6 month commercial paper rate minus the succeeding 5-month change in the wholesale price index) appears in figure 4.4 and the interest rates and inflation rates in figure 4.5. Indeed, there is a striking change at the time of the Accord. The last big movement downward in the real interest rate was due to the surge in inflation at the end of 1950 which provoked the Accord, as well as the price controls of the Korean conflict. After that, there was never again such a big movement in ex post real interest rates.

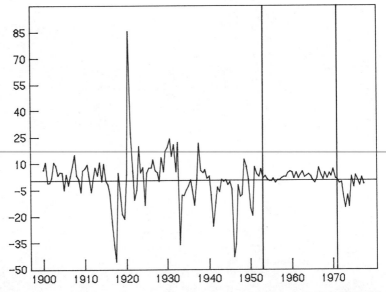

Fig. 4.4   Ex post real rate of interest, 1900:I to 1977:II, June and December, equal to the interest rate minus the inflation rate plotted in fig. 4.5. Marks on the horizontal axis correspond to the June figure. Fama's sample period is enclosed between vertical lines.

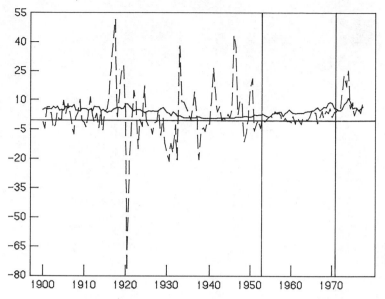

Fig. 4.5   Annualized percent change in the wholesale price index over succeeding 5 months (dotted line) and 4–6-month prime commercial paper rate (solid line), 1900:I to 1977:II, June and December. Marks on the horizontal axis correspond to the June figure. Fama's sample period is enclosed by vertical lines. Source of wholesale price index: Bureau of Labor Statistics, 1900–1913 *Bulletin* no. 149 (1914); 1913–19, *Bulletin* no. 269; 1920–77, Macro Data Library, Board of Governors of the Federal Reserve system. Source of prime commercial paper rate: 1900–1924, *Banking and Monetary Statistics, 1914–41*, Board of Governors of the Federal Reserve system, 1943; 1925–77, Macro Data Library, Board of Governors of the Federal Reserve System.

These ex post movements in the real interest rate before the Accord are not an indication of movements in rationally expected real interest rates unless they are forecastable. The apparent serial correlation in figure 4.4 suggests that they are, and this is confirmed by the simple autoregressions in table 4.1. The F tests indicate significant coefficients except for the period immediately after the founding of the Fed. The standard deviation of the fitted value (the lower figure in the last column) which is a measure of the standard deviation of the true rationally expected real interest rate is much higher before 1951 than after.

To the extent that we are willing to assume that the structure of the rest of the economy was the same before and after the Accord, these results clearly provide further disconfirmation of hypothesis 1. It is true

Table 4.1   Ex Post Real Rate Autoregressions

| Time Period | Coefficient of | | | | R^2 t_{next} | F Sig(F) | σ(RESID) σ(FITTED) |
	Const	Seasonal	Dep$_{-1}$	Dep$_{-2}$			
1901:II to 1913:I	1.73 (1.08)	4.79 (2.35)	.383 (2.02)	−.482 (−2.59)	.244 (−1.48)	3.47 3.54	4.56 2.59
1915:II to 1929:II	.620 (.107)	1.48 (.184)	.493 (2.49)	−.186 (−.942)	.104 (−.416)	2.08 12.87	21.6 7.36
1901:II to 1929:II	.236 (.081)	3.62 (.884)	.481 (3.55)	−.185 (−.137)	.151 (−.679)	4.31 .859	15.33 6.45
1915:II to 1950:II	−2.66 (−.926)	4.33 (1.07)	.493 (4.04)	−.116 (−.950)	.172 (−.327)	5.85 .131	16.9 7.71
1952:II to 1977:II	.100 (.135)	.375 (.369)	.324 (2.38)	.394 (2.91)	.360 (−1.01)	10.4 .002	3.59 2.69

NOTE

Dependent variable is the ex post real rate (i.e., the 4–6 month prime commercial paper rate minus the succeeding actual 5-month inflation rate computed from the wholesale price index) as shown in fig. 4.4. Data is semiannual, for June and December. Seasonal dummy is zero in June, 1 in December. Numbers in parentheses are t-statistics, t_{next} is t-statistic of dependent variable lagged one more time in a different regression (presented here instead of a Durbin-Watson statistic). The term σ(RESID) is standard error of regression; σ(FITTED) is estimated standard deviation of fitted values, equal to σ(RESID)$(R^2/(1-R^2))^{1/2}$.

that the period before 1951 was characterized by bigger wars than the period after. The depression also came before (although it is less clear that this represents a change in structure of the economy). Nonetheless, the change in the stochastic behavior of real rates with the Accord is so striking that one is tempted to conclude that the change in monetary policy had something to do with it.

Whether or not the change also disconfirms hypothesis 2 is not something we can say with any assurance. Indeed, given that the monetary policy is not deterministic, and cannot be described in terms of just a money stock rule or just an interest rate rule, then we have not given the hypothesis a precise enough definition to evaluate it formally.

One might attribute the greater movements in the real rate before the Accord merely to greater unforecastable monetary shocks before the Accord. By the same token the relatively low variance of real rates before the founding of the Fed might be ascribed to a more predictable monetary rule under the National Banking System. This argument would not apply to the pegged rate period, between 1942–51, when monetary policy was quite forecastable.

It is not obvious whether Fed policy was less predictable in the twenties, say, as compared with the sixties. One must remember that big movements in the money stock are no indication of unpredictability since presumably they were triggered primarily by economic conditions in a way that may well have been understood by businessmen at the time. Monetary policy actions need not be known in advance for there to be predictability in the sense of hypothesis 2 as long as these are revealed by public information before they take place.

We do know that a change in the policy rule occurred after the Accord. It would not be unreasonable to attribute the change in the behavior of real interest rates to the observed change in the systematic policy rule, and thus consider this change as evidence against hypothesis 2. Unfortunately, we cannot feel very comfortable in our assurance that this is so. We are left, then, with only a suggestion that hypothesis 2 might be misguided. Barring a controlled experiment contrasting alternative deterministic, announced policy rules, we are unlikely ever to find better information concerning the direct empirical implications of hypothesis 2.

Before we conclude, however, we note that recent literature on nominal interest rates for the period 1953–71 alone might seem to lead us to a different evaluation of the hypotheses. This literature, which was initiated by Fama (1975), has confined attention to this period because, it is claimed, it represents the only available time period in which the data on inflation rates are good and in which prices are uncontrolled. Fama said that to study real rates before 1953 is "meaningless" because the Bureau of Labor Statistics used poorer sampling techniques before 1953 in computing the consumer price index (which Fama used), in that it sampled more items on a three-month basis than it does today. If one looks at figure 4.4, one notes that this period (marked off between parallel lines) shows remarkable stability of the real rate of interest.[10] This was also a period when the Fed apparently *thought* it was conducting countercyclical monetary policy and is usually described as having caused at least one credit crunch. Fama's evidence appears then to be evidence which makes us less sure of our dismissal of hypothesis 1, that the Fed cannot influence real rates at all.

In his paper, Fama showed two remarkable results about short-term interest rates and prices for this sample period, both of which are consistent with his joint hypothesis that ex ante real rates of interest are constant and expectations are rational. First, while both short-term interest rates and inflation rates show significant autocorrelation, ex post real rates do not. This result can be seen again by looking at Fama's monthly data on one-month treasury bill rates and one-month inflation rates (fig. 4.6). The inflation rate appears approximately as white noise superimposed on the interest rate series, except for the period 1960–66, when the short rate shows a trend not matched by a trend in inflation rates. The serial correlation we observed in table 4.1 came about, apparently, from post-1971 data and perhaps also from our use of five-month inflation data, which is smoother than one-month data. Second, Fama showed that if inflation rates are regressed on interest rates the coefficient of the interest rate is nearly one (.97, $t = 10.0$, with his data) and then, when the lagged price level is added as a second explanatory variable, the coefficient of the interest rate remains near one (.87, $t = 7.2$) while the lagged inflation rate has a small coefficient (.11, $t = 1.6$) which is insig-

---

10. This figure shows the inflation as measured by the wholesale, rather than consumer price index, but the plots using the consumer price index, for the period for which it is available, look similar.

That Fama's hypothesis did not hold before is certainly well known. The famous "Gibson paradox," noted as early as 1884, was a positive correlation between interest rates and price *levels*, not rates of change of prices. While the correlation is most pronounced for long-term interest rates, it was also present with short-term rates for British data in the century before World War II, and over this period there was really no correlation between short rates and inflation rates (Shiller and Siegel 1977).

A plot of an ex post real British consol rate (subject to an arbitrary assumption about inflation rates past 1977 which makes the more recent real rates unreliable) from 1729 to the present appears in Shiller and Siegel 1977. This real long-term interest rate is very volatile and at times negative. It was found that nominal long-term rates over this period moved in such a way as to exacerbate, rather than mitigate, the effects of inflation on long-term real rates, i.e., nominal long rates were *negatively* correlated with the appropriately defined long-term inflation rate.

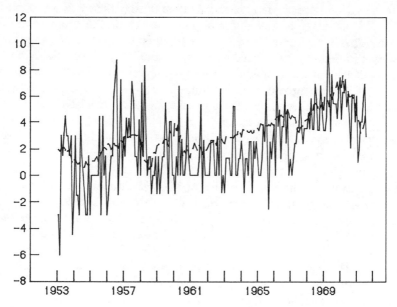

Fig. 4.6   Fama's data, February 1953 to July 1971. Solid line is inflation rate, equal to $-1200\,\Delta_t$ and dotted line is one-month treasury bill rate, equal to $1200\,R_t$ where Δ_t and R_t are defined in Fama 1975. Division marks on the horizontal axis correspond to the first month of the year numbered directly below. Data courtesy of E. Fama.

nificant.[11] It seems at first remarkable that the lagged inflation rate should be of so little benefit in forecasting inflation, but when one looks at the data one sees why this is the case. There is a great deal of month-to-month noise in the consumer price index, and so the lagged inflation rate is a poor indicator of current inflation. What is more remarkable is that the coefficient of the interest rate should come out so close to one, which is its theoretical value if the ex ante real interest rate is constant and inflation anticipations are true mathematical expectations.

It should be pointed out that under Fama's hypothesis residuals are serially uncorrelated, and if we wished to estimate the coefficient of the interest rate, then ordinary least squares is appropriate and the standard errors not compromised by possible serial correlation. If our theory is

11. Fama used the rate of change of the purchasing power of money as his dependent variable; i.e., his dependent variable is $\Delta_t = -(P_t - P_{t-1})/P_t$ rather than $(P_t - P_{t-1})/P_{t-1}$. When we used his data, we multiplied Δ_t by -1200 and called this the inflation rate. We have reserved the sign of his coefficient to accord with our definition.

that the after-tax real rate is constant, then this coefficient is an estimate of $1 - \tau$, where τ is the marginal tax bracket of the "representative investor." If we assume normal residuals, then ordinary least squares is clearly the appropriate procedure under Fama's hypothesis to estimate the coefficient in the regression.[12] Fama's regression of inflation on interest rates alone provided an estimate of $1 - \tau$ so close to one as to imply that the "representative tax bracket" is zero. Feldstein and Summers (1978a) concluded that the after-tax real interest rate relevant to the typical investment decision should be computed with, in effect, $(1 - \tau)$ roughly in the vicinity of .8 to 1.0, depending on depreciation and equity yields.[13] Fama's estimate of .87 with the inflation variable in the regression is dominated by the previous estimate, since by Fama's theory the inflation rate is an extraneous variable in the regression.

If, however, we are more interested in an alternative hypothesis that makes inflation rates unrelated to interest rates and serially correlated, then the ordinary t-test on the coefficient is not valid. The t-test is a likelihood ratio test in which the universe does not include the possibility of serially correlated residuals. Thus, we do not know from Fama's highly significant coefficient on the interest rate whether or not the observed relation between interest and inflation might easily have come about by a "trend" or "long cycle" or other low-frequency component in the interest rate which by sheer chance happened to be correlated with a similar component in the inflation series. Fama's good Durbin-Watson statistic is no assurance, as Granger and Newbold (1977) have pointed out, that this is not a problem. One can get some impression of the likelihood of such an alternative explanation of the correlation between interest and inflation by looking at figure 4.6. Clearly, the short-run movements in the price level are not explained by the interest rates. This impression is confirmed by running Fama's regression with the dependent variable lagged or led, to throw it out of alignment with his interest rate data. The fit of his equation is hardly changed. The R^2 rises from .29 in Fama's regression to .30 with a led inflation rate as the dependent variable and falls to .27 with a lagged inflation rate as the dependent variable.[14] In any event, the alignment is not really correct with Fama's regression either. Fama's interest rate data are based on midpoints of bid-asked

12. The residuals do, however, fail the David-Hartley-Pearson studentized range test of normality at the 5% level. The studentized range in the residuals regression of inflation on a constant and the interest rate for the full sample period is 6.42, and the Durbin-Watson statistic is 1.77.

13. Feldstein and Summers' arguments applied to long-term interest rates, which might be connected, via term structure phenomena, to short rates.

14. These statistics refer to a regression of the inflation rate on a constant and the interest rate over the longest possible sample with the data series shown in fig. 4.6.

spreads for the last day of the preceding month. The Bureau of Labor Statistics (1971) reports that it collects food prices on three consecutive days early in the month. Thus food prices, which in 1971 had a total weight of .224 in the consumer price index, are nearly 30 days out of alignment.[15] Rents and items for which prices are obtained by mail, in contrast, are reported as of the fifteenth of the month, and the pricing of other items priced monthly extends over the entire calendar month. Many items are still priced only every three months. We thus could not hope with such data to find a short-run (or high-frequency) relationship, and it is hardly appropriate to dismiss results based on earlier data for this reason.

The explanatory power in the interest rate series does not come about from a simple trend either. If one runs Fama's regression with a linear time trend term added, this variable does not come in as significant. The explanatory power instead comes primarily from a couple of humps in the interest and inflation series. The first hump begins at the bottom of the recession that occurred in 1954 and ends at the bottom of the recession that occurred in 1958. The other hump starts after the credit crunch of 1966 and ends in the recession of 1971. Some explanatory power also appears to reside in the downturn of interest rates in the recession of 1953–54, at the very beginning of the sample. In contrast, the period between 1958 and 1966 shows an upward trend in interest rates with no matching upward trend in inflation rates. Carlson (1977) showed that Fama's regression fits very poorly over this sample period, and the hypothesis that the coefficient is 1 can be rejected.

The remarkable thing about Fama's paper cannot be seen in the paper itself but in the fact that his critics did not find any regression results over the entire sample which strongly contradicted his. One would think that someone through data dredging could come up with another variable which dominated the interest rate as a predictor of inflation, but that appears not to be the case. Nelson and Schwert (1977) and Hess and Bicksler (1975) used the highly regarded Box-Jenkins forecasting techniques to produce a forecast of future inflation based on lagged inflation rates. When Nelson and Schwert added this forecast to Fama's regression of inflation on interest rates over the entire sample period (1953–71),

---

15. Fama's inflation rate is computed as $\Delta_t = (P_{t-1} - P_t)/P_t$, so the food price component of the change applies to the period from the beginning of the preceding month to the beginning of the current month. The interest rate series gives the treasury bill rate at the end of the preceding month, which matures over the current month.

The monthly change in the food price index is more volatile than other components and had a correlation of .71 with the monthly change in the consumer price index over Fama's sample period. Thus, the led inflation rate may be the more appropriate dependent variable.

the R^2 was increased only to .31 from .29. The coefficient of the interest rate fell from .97 in Fama's regression to .65, and the Box-Jenkins forecast had a coefficient of only .38. The coefficient of the Box-Jenkins forecast was significant (with a t-statistic of 2.4, in contrast to the t of 1.6 for the lagged inflation rate alone) and so Nelson and Schwert concluded that they had rejected Fama's hypothesis, but they were also forced to conclude that the interest rate carried additional information not in the Box-Jenkins forecast. Other critics were able to find other forecasting variables that pushed up the R^2 a little more. Carlson (1977) added the employment/population ratio to Fama's regression; this variable was highly significant and boosted the R^2 to .36. Still, the coefficient of the interest rate was .64. Joines (1977) added the three lagged values of the wholesale price index to Fama's regression, which were also highly significant, boosting the R^2 another increment up to .37, but still the coefficient of the interest rate remained at .77.

We thus concur with Fama that his results and the results of his critics do suggest that most of the variation in nominal short rates in his sample period can be attributed to inflationary expectations. Fama's results must give pause to those who believe that inflationary expectations are highly sluggish or follow a trend and that medium-run movements in short-term interest rates are movements in ex ante real rates.

It is possible to get an estimate of the variance of the ex ante real interest rate from Fama's regression of inflation on interest if one is willing to assume that the real rate of interest is uncorrelated with the predicted inflation rate. It is easy to see this as an application of the well-known theorem which states that, in a simple regression, if there is a measurement error in the independent variable, the probability limit of the estimated coefficient is biased downward by a factor which is the ratio of the variance of the true independent variable to the variance of the measured independent variable. Here, we take the variation in the real interest rate as the "measurement error." If we ascribe all of the deviation of the estimated coefficient of the interest rate from 1 to this source, then this implies that with an estimated coefficient of .98, the variance of the real rate is only about 2% of the variance of the observed interest rate, which implies that the standard deviation of the real rate is about 20 basis points. Nelson and Schwert used this kind of argument to arrive at an estimate of the variance of the real rate of interest, but they based their estimate on a different regression: of the change in the rate of inflation on the difference between the interest rate and the lagged inflation rate which produced a smaller coefficient (equal to .89). Under Fama's hypothesis, the coefficient should again be 1. If we take the real rate of interest again as the "measurement error" of a true independent variable which is the inflation forecast minus the lagged actual inflation rate and if we assume that the measurement error is uncorrelated with the true independent variable, then by the same reasoning we come up with an estimate of the variance of the real rate of interest which is $1 - .89 = .11$ times the variance of the interest rate minus the lagged inflation rate, which then implies a standard deviation for the real rate of 80 basis points.

These estimates of the variance are suggestive, although they must have substantial sampling error (not discussed by Nelson and Schwert). They do suggest smaller movements in real interest rates than many people expected to see.

Time Series Analysis of Real Rate and Money Stock Data

From the sound of the hypotheses, it would appear that a Granger or Sims test of causality (see Sims 1978) from money to real interest rates and a test of the effects of anticipated versus unanticipated money on real rates along lines suggested by Barro (1978), would be relevant to their evaluation.

Granger and Sims tests of causality from the change in the log of the money stock to ex post real interest rates as shown in figure 4.4 appear in table 4.2. Seasonality was handled in two ways. In some regressions, a seasonal dummy was added to the regression. For other regressions the data were first Fourier transformed, both real and imaginary parts were then set to zero in a band of width $\pi/12$ around the seasonal frequency and the series were then inverse Fourier transformed to produce a de-seasonalized series. Data for the Sims tests was also quasi-first differenced with filter $(1 - .75L)^2$.

The results of these causality tests are that, for the postwar period, money unambiguously causes real rates. Clearly the stochastic structure of the series has changed since the Accord, since no causality is found for the pre-Accord period.

Barro tests reported in table 4.3 use data series DM (change in the log money stock), DMR (Barro's estimate of the public's forecast error at time t for the change in the log money stock at time t), and G/y (real government expenditure over real GNP) from Barro (1978, tables 1 and 2). The dependent variable is the one-year (annual average) treasury bill rate or the rate on the treasury bill whose maturity is closest to one year minus the lead one-year inflation rate DP from Barro (1978, table 2). Neither the DM nor the DMR terms are significant in these regressions, which seems odd, since the Granger and Sims tests found, with different data, that money causes real rates. The F statistic is, however, nearly significant at the 10% level in the last regression. An interesting observation that arises here is that in the regression in which DM is excluded, all variables have the sign we would expect. All DMR terms have negative coefficients and G/y has a positive coefficient.

Table 4.2   **Granger-Sims Causality Tests**

Sample	Type	Seasonal Dummy	F Statistic	Degrees of Freedom
1928:II to 1977:II	Granger	No	3.09*	5, 87
1928:II to 1977:II	Granger	Yes	1.40	5, 86
1929:II to 1975:II	Sims	No	1.71	4, 80
1928:II to 1950:II	Granger	No	1.55	5, 33
1928:II to 1950:II	Granger	Yes	1.14	5, 32
1929:II to 1948:II	Sims	No	0.58	4, 26
1955:II to 1977:II	Granger	No	5.22**	5, 33
1955:II to 1977:II	Granger	Yes	3.05*	5, 32
1957:II to 1977:II	Sims	No	18.9**	4, 28

NOTES

Tests indicate whether the change in the log of the money supply (from time series illustrated in fig. 4.3) causes real rates (from series shown in fig. 4.4). Data is seasonally adjusted unless seasonal dummy appears. For Sims tests, data is quasi first differenced with filter $(1 - .75L)^2$. Ex post real rate based on nominal rate in a given quarter is considered contemporaneous with the change in the log of the money stock from the preceding quarter to the given quarter. Granger tests involve regressing real rate on five lagged values of the real rate and money variable, a constant, a linear time trend and, if noted, a seasonal dummy. F statistic is test of hypothesis that all lagged money coefficients are zero. Sims tests involve regressing the money variable on 4 lead, a contemporaneous and 6 lagged real rate variables, as well as a constant and linear time trend. F statistic is test of the hypothesis that all lead real rate coefficients are zero.

*Significant at 5% level.
**Significant at 1% level.

What do these results mean? One interpretation along lines suggested by the literature on rational expectations and the natural rate of unemployment hypotheses follows from the assumption of a structural relation implying that real interest rates respond *linearly* to the change in the log money stock and expectations of future changes in log money stocks:

$$(14) \qquad \rho_t = \zeta_t + \sum_{i=0}^{n_1} \phi_i \Delta m_{t-1} + \sum_{i=0}^{n_2} \sum_{j=0}^{n_3} \psi_{ij} E_{t-i}(\Delta m_{t-i+j}),$$

Table 4.3 **Barro Type Regressions**

	Coefficient of														
Const	DMR	DMR_{-1}	DMR_{-2}	DMR_{-3}	DM	DM_{-1}	DM_{-2}	DM_{-3}	Time	G/y	R^2	D.W.	S.E.	F	F_b
.372	−23.8	−7.15	−17.0	−29.3	—	—	—	—	.023	—	.218	1.46	1.28	1.06	—
(.627)	(−1.22)	(−.371)	(−.900)	(−1.55)	—	—	—	—	(.582)	—					
−7.64	−27.0	−9.45	−31.7	−38.2	—	—	—	—	.191	46.9	.366	1.82	1.18	1.73	—
(−1.93)	(−1.48)	(−.52)	(−1.68)	(−2.13*)	—	—	—	—	(2.12*)	(2.04)					
2.93	11.4	87.7	−30.2	68.5	−39.8	−75.4	36.9	−96.0	.251	—	.550	1.82	1.10	2.03	2.75
(2.53*)	(.192)	(1.40)	(−0.50)	(1.87)	(−.74)	(−1.20)	(.572)	(−2.30*)	(2.87*)	—					
−2.95	17.6	85.0	−42.2	55.2	−52.4	−74.9	46.2	−79.1	.353	34.4	.594	2.04	1.08	2.04	1.96
(−0.60)	(.300)	(1.38)	(−.694)	(1.46)	(−.971)	(−1.22)	(.723)	(−1.83)	(2.96*)	(1.23)					

NOTES

Dependent variable is the annual average monthly one-year treasury bill rate series (or 9–12-month rate series when 12-month rate is unavailable) from *Banking and Monetary Statistics 1941–70*, Board of Governors of the Federal Reserve System, 1976, and *Federal Reserve Bulletin*) minus 100 times Barro's 1978 inflation variable (DP) for the following year. All other data are from Barro 1978. DM is the change in the log of the money stock, DMR is the residual in Barro's DM forecasting equation, G/y is real government expenditure over real GNP. Time is 1 in 1952 and 25 in 1976. Sample period is 1952–76. F_b is F statistic to test hypothesis that coefficients of all DM terms are zero. The t statistics are in parentheses.

*Significant at 5% level.

where ρ_t is the rationally expected real interest rate, m_t is the log money stock, ζ_t is a stochastic process representing the real forces that cause movements in the real rate even when the money stock is predictably growing along a constant growth path, ϕ_i and ψ_{ij} are coefficients, and E_{t-i} denotes expectation conditional on information available at time $t-i$.

The ex post real rate $r_t - p_{t+1} + p_t$ equals the rationally expected real interest rate plus an error term: $r_t - p_{t+1} + p_t = \rho_t + \eta_{t+1}$, where the error term is uncorrelated with all data known at time t and hence is itself serially uncorrelated but may be correlated with information acquired between t and $t+1$.

In terms of this formulation, hypothesis 1 may be interpreted to mean that ϕ_i and ψ_{ij} are all zero, so that $\rho_t = \zeta_t$ and $r_t - p_{t+1} + p_t = \zeta_t + \eta_t$. We shall assume for the moment that ζ_t is constant. Then, Fama's tests are appropriate and Barro's tests should find all DM and DMR terms insignificant (as we in fact found) although a DMR_{t+1} term may be significant insofar as it affects η_{t+1}. Granger or Sims tests should show that money does not cause real rates, since, as Fama noted, ex post real rates will be unforecastable white noise.

Hypothesis 2 may be interpreted as a restriction on the coefficients of (14), namely:

$$(14')\qquad \rho_t = \zeta_t + \sum_{i=0}^{n} a_i(\Delta m_{t-i} - E_{t-i}(\Delta m_{t-i})),$$

so that only surprises in monetary policy $\Delta m_t - E_t \Delta m_t$ affect real rates. The lagged terms are included to allow for persistence in the effects of these surprises. Now, Fama's tests are no longer appropriate even if ζ_t is constant. The Barro type tests should show all DM terms insignificant, but the DMR terms, which are supposed to represent $\Delta m_t - E_t(\Delta m_t)$, might now be significant. Since ρ_t is a simple moving average process whose innovation $m_t - E_t m_t$ is uncorrelated with past data, a Sims or Granger test using the true ρ_t would show that money does not cause ρ_t, that is, $\rho_{t-1}, \rho_{t-2}, \ldots$ contain all information available for forecasting ρ_t and hence further information in terms of lagged m is of no value.

Hypothesis 3 might be interpreted as a less stringent restriction on (14):

$$(14'')\qquad \rho_t = \zeta_t + \sum_{i=0}^{n} a_{0,i}(\Delta m_{t-i} - E_{t-i}(\Delta m_{t-i}))$$

$$+ \sum_{i=0}^{n} a_{1,i}(\Delta m_{t-i} - E_{t-i-1}(\Delta m_{t-i}))$$

$$+ \ldots + \sum_{i=0}^{n} a_{s,i}(\Delta m_{t-i} - E_{t-i-s}(\Delta m_{t-i}))$$

where s is the policy effectiveness interval. The restriction imposed by this hypothesis is that long-term forecast errors (i.e., for a forecast horizon greater than s) have in themselves no effect on ρ. This hypothesis now implies nothing for any of the tests we have examined. One might have thought that it would perhaps imply that, with a Granger causality test, money terms lagged more than s periods would have no effect, but this is not the case. The only test that seems immediately suggested by it would be an extension of the Barro test found by estimating a battery of 0-period, 1-period, 2-period, and so on, forecasting equations, and then taking their residuals as estimates of the terms $\Delta m_t - E_t(\Delta m_t)$, $\Delta m_t - E_{t-1}(\Delta m_t)$, and so on. One could then estimate (14″) using for ρ the ex post real interest rate. Hypothesis 3 would then imply that coefficients of $\Delta m_t - E_{t-j}(\Delta m_t)$, $j > s$ should be zero, which is in principle testable.

While the above analysis seems to suggest that Granger, Sims, or Barro tests, or extensions thereof, might well be used to examine the hypotheses, it is useful to bear in mind the stringent assumptions that must be made. These assumptions have for the most part already been pointed out in different contexts by, for example, Sargent (1976) and Sims (1977), so we will cite them only briefly here.

We have assumed first that ζ_t is constant. In fact, it is plausible that real factors have had an impact on real interest rates and that the forecast of ζ_t may be related to lagged money. For example, wartime increases in government expenditure may themselves influence ζ_t and are also correlated with the wartime increases in money. On the one hand, this may mean that Barro, Granger, or Sims tests would find that money has an effect on real rates even if hypothesis 1 or 2 is true. Barro's contemporaneous G/y term may well fail to correct for such effects. On the other hand, even if all the hypotheses are false, it is possible, as Sims (1977) has pointed out in a more general context, that if the Fed has been trying to stabilize real interest rates, that is, offset ζ_t, causality tests might lead one to conclude that money has no effect on real interest rates. These problems seriously limit the usefulness of the above tests for the purpose of examining our hypotheses.

Another problem with the Granger or Sims tests in this context is that our hypotheses relate to unobservable rationally expected real rates and we use in the tests the ex post real rates. With either the Granger or Sims tests the real rate must appear on the right-hand side of the equation, so we have an errors in variables problem (which is not completely solved by using some other estimate of the rationally expected real rates). Then, even if hypothesis 2 is true, m may appear to cause real rates, since lagged Δm may provide information about $\Delta m_{t-i} - E_{t-i}\Delta m_{t-i}$ not obtainable from the lagged real rate.

This problem would not arise if we were willing to assume in hypothesis 2 that there is no persistence in the effects of monetary surprises on real interest rates, that is, $a_i = 0$, $i \geq 1$. Then (so long as problems of time variation in ζ_t do not arise) we could test the hypothesis by checking whether ex post real rates can be forecasted. In effect, we could eliminate the lagged real rate terms from the Granger test by theoretical considerations. Similarly, if the summations in (14″) are known to contain only the first term (i.e., $a_{ji} = 0$, $i \geq 1$, all j) then hypothesis 3 could be tested merely by regressing ex post real rates on information known s periods earlier, which should not contribute to a forecast of real rates. However, those who have suggested our hypotheses have made it clear that they are not willing to rule out persistence, so these tests cannot be used.

Another problem with the Barro tests is that it is perhaps not possible to identify the contemporaneous forecast errors, since these rely necessarily on an arbitrary characterization of the forecasting relation and information set of the public. His forecasting equation depends on one contemporaneous variable (a government expenditure term) which appears no more likely to be known at any point of time than is the money stock itself. This term is essential to the model, since without it his forecasting relation would be autoregressive, in which case the DM terms would be linear combinations of lagged DMR terms and hence not distinguishable in the regression.

Finally, whatever we learn about (14) under one policy rule, we do not necessarily know that (14) is a structural relation which is invariant under alternative policy rules, as Sargent (1976) has emphasized.

Conclusion

We will conclude here by listing the salient facts that seem relevant to each of the three hypotheses. Since the hypotheses are nested, evidence against any hypothesis also serves as evidence against the hypotheses preceding it.

Hypothesis 1. The Federal Open Market Committee knows it can influence nominal rates because it has conducted what Friedman and Schwartz (1963) called "quasi-controlled experiments"; that is, it has moved the money stock in ways and at times that could not be ascribed to reverse causality from economic variables to the money stock. It seems highly improbable that the outcome could be explained in terms of the reaction of inflationary expectations to the shock. We thus feel we can safely say that hypothesis one is wrong.

Fama's evidence serves principally to cast substantial doubt on the conventional argument that medium-run movements in nominal rates must be due primarily to movements in ex ante real rates since inflationary expectations are very sluggish. The correspondence of movements in post-Accord nominal rates and the optimally forecasted inflation rates is fairly impressive. One must bear in mind that really short-run movements in nominal rates did not occur enough in the sample period for us to say anything about these movements in nominal interest rates. Fama probably exaggerates the problems with earlier data and our results with these incline us to the conclusion that the relative constancy of real rates in his sample is due to Fed behavior, not the inability of the Fed to shock them. An interesting unanswered question is: Why did the Fed behave so as to keep the pretax real rate constant? Was this behavior due to their concern with some other variable which responds reliably to this rate?

Hypothesis 2. Direct evidence against this weaker hypothesis can be found only if we can find policy rule changes which affect the predictable component of monetary policy. Barro claims to have decomposed changes in the money stock into predicted versus unpredicted components for the postwar period, but his claim is not terribly convincing and in any event he assumed a constant policy rule. Granger or Sims causality tests are suitable as tests of this hypothesis only under some artificial assumptions.

One policy change that appears to relate to the way the Fed reacts to public information is marked by the Accord in 1951. This change was a once-and-for-all change ascribable largely to factors whose origin lay in politics and theoretical economics, and in this sense it too was exogenous. There is a dramatic change in the behavior of real interest rates that seems, looking at the data, to coincide with the Accord. Unfortunately, we do not know for sure that this change is due to a change in the systematic policy rule or just a change in the magnitude of the random components. It is also possible, moreover, that other changing variables were responsible for the change in the real rate's behavior. We also saw, for example, a dramatic rise in income tax rates dating from World War II, and although this change does not coincide with the change in real rate behavior, one could not rule out that the two are related. Paradoxically, pretax real interest rates were more stable *after* the tax rates were increased, when the theoretical case for constant pretax real rates was apparently weakened.

Hypothesis 3. Direct evidence against this yet weaker hypothesis can be found only if we can discover changes in the monetary policy rule which relate to information known in advance for a length of time exceeding the policy effectiveness internal. We considered one such shock to policy which relates to information forecastable into the indefinite future; that is, the seasonal factor. At the time it was founded, the Fed announced a policy of reducing the seasonal shock in nominal rates. The Fed succeeded in reducing it, but there is no evidence that it affected the seasonal factor in real rates.

The most important potential source of evidence against this hypothesis, as well as hypothesis 2, comes not from the macroeconomic data but from other considerations. If we combine hypothesis 3 with a demand for money equation and a stability condition, then we are led to the conclusion that the price level bears a certain relationship to information about monetary policy known in advance by more than the policy effectiveness interval. While it is plausible that in some alternative steady states characterized by, say, different money growth rates, this might work out to be true, it does not seem likely that new information about discrete Fed policy actions would become optimally incorporated in the price level over any policy effectiveness interval. Most prices do not seem to be set that way.

We conclude that none of the hypotheses is likely to be so strictly correct as to rule out completely a predictable effect of systematic monetary policy on expected real interest rates. This does not by itself establish that there is a role for monetary policy in improving economic welfare. This conclusion, moreover, rests on our impression of how prices are set and not on any formal statistical evidence, which cannot be effectively brought to bear either for or against our conclusion. We hope, however, to have clarified why the complete noncontrollability of expected real interest rates should not be, as many seem to have concluded recently, a cornerstone for macroeconomic modelling.

Comment   Phillip Cagan

Economists have long assigned to monetary changes an effect on the real rate of interest. In a famous passage Ricardo stated that changes in the money stock would not affect interest rates in the long run, because price increases would take the economy to the same equilibrium in real terms that it started from.[16] I interpret the word "permanently" in Ricardo's statement to mean that monetary increases temporarily depress interest rates (both real and nominal—though such a distinction was not typically

16. "The interest for money is not regulated by the rate at which the [central] Bank will lend, whether it be 5, 4, or 3 per cent; but by the rate of profits, which can be made by the employment of capital, and which is totally independent of the quantity, or of the value of money. Whether a bank lent one million, ten millions, or a hundred millions, they would not *permanently* alter the market rate of interest; they would alter only the value of the money which they thus issued" (Ricardo 1817, Everyman's Edition, p. 246; italics added).

made in the classical literature). Mill alludes to an effect which was apparently widely accepted at the time and was later elaborated and made famous by Wicksell (1898, 1906) as an effect of "cumulative inflation."[17] Wicksell considered a continual increase in the money stock through bank expansion (either by a falling reserve ratio or growth of the monetary base). Since the new money enters the economy through credit markets and is assumed initially to augment the supply of loanable funds, the real rate of interest is reduced. Although the inflation that ensues reduces the purchasing power of all money, the inflow of new money continues to command resources and can be viewed as a continual addition to bank loans in real terms. Unlike Ricardo's proposition, the Wicksell effect does not pass away but holds the real rate of interest lower so long as the money supply increases. The Wicksell effect involves a redistribution of spending in the economy; most recent models of the economy and Shiller's review of them put aside distributional effects of money creation and so neglect this effect.

Recent contributions to monetary theory clarify the assumptions underlying these earlier propositions. If we assume, contrary to the classical economists, that prices are perfectly flexible and expectations are rational, Ricardo's long-run equilibrium is achieved very rapidly and, in so far as changes in the money stock are anticipated, immediately. Hence, in some recent models, as Shiller explains, changes in prices nullify the potential real effects of monetary changes, and the short-run changes implied by Ricardo's statement cited above never occur.

Price flexibility and rational expectations do not dispose of the Wicksell effect, however, since its redistributional effect is not eliminated in real terms by price increases. In an earlier work I analyzed the Wicksell effect as a situation in which *all* the revenue from money creation was used by the issuers to increase their saving to acquire more assets (Cagan 1972). Such a lopsided disposition of the income from money creation is questionable and not the most plausible assumption. If bank owners treat such income as they do all other income, I showed that the Wicksell effect disappears. It can sneak back in, however, if bank owners save a high proportion of income from money creation because it is unanticipated or uncertain or if the Federal Reserve deliberately uses its revenue from money creation to retire the national debt. We can still cut off this last effect if, as suggested by Ricardo (1817) and Barro (1974), we treat the public as knowledgeable stockholders of the government and

17. "The paper currency in common use, being a currency provided by bankers, is all issued in the way of loans, except the part employed in the purchase of gold and silver. The same operation, therefore, which adds to the currency also adds to the loans: the whole increase of currency in the first instance swells the loan market. Considered as an addition to loans it tends to lower interest" (Mill 1865, p. 646).

assume that individuals privately offset whatever saving the Federal Reserve does on their behalf.

To the question, Can the Fed control real interest rates? a broadly accepted answer in the profession even today would be that, for the short-run impact, yes; but that over time the effect diminishes to zero (ignoring second-order effects on the capital stock); and the more monetary actions are anticipated and adjusted to, the smaller the effect, while in some cases perhaps these adjustments make it zero in the short run. (This says nothing about the desirability of having the Fed use this capability.)

Shiller appears to share this general view. But he asks an auxiliary question, What solid evidence do we really have that the Fed affects real rates? Given the difficulties of testing rational expectations and whether policy actions are anticipated, the evidence must be examined with considerable sophistication. This Shiller does, and his paper is very good from this point of view. The counterpart to being sophisticated is that straightforward statistical evidence is slim, and in that respect his paper makes only a limited case for the affirmative view that the Fed affects real rates. Yet Shiller analyzes some qualitative empirical evidence that is of special interest in answering the question even if it does not resolve all the issues raised. He looks at some extreme cases most likely to provide evidence for the affirmative. These are pegging of interest rates during World War II and after, the decline in seasonal variation of nominal interest rates after the founding of the Federal Reserve system, and the decline in the variance of monetary growth and real interest rates since World War II. (As Shiller notes, the fact that nominal rates adjust to expected inflation does not mean that monetary changes have not produced changes in real rates.)

To use these facts to derive an affirmative answer to the question of his paper, it is necessary to conclude that the changes in behavior of nominal rates also produced changes in real rates and that the changes reflected a change in Federal Reserve behavior. Shiller has done a better job of persuading me (who needed little) than himself. But he is right to be careful, because rigorous statistical evidence on the real rate to support the affirmative position is not easy to establish. I am persuaded more by what I know of those events from historical research on monetary developments.

Consider the pegging episode, in which the Federal Reserve held nominal interest rates at a low level. If expected real rates were not also reduced by that action, the expected rate of change of prices had to be negative, which meant that expected monetary growth had to be reduced appreciably. It is difficult to interpret the pegging period as conforming to that scenario. As a matter of fact, the period appears to conform to the

Wicksell scenario, in which the rate of monetary growth is increased by the pegging, prices rise, and the real rate of interest is reduced. Surely most of these changes were widely expected. Indeed, it is difficult to see how the economy, given the pegging policy, could have avoided this outcome.

A similar interpretation can be applied to the reduction of seasonal variations in nominal interest rates, which the Federal Reserve engineered and claimed credit for (one of the limited number of cases in which its claim to have contributed to the stability of something appears valid, though whether the policy was desirable or not is debatable). Although Shiller finds that the effect on seasonal variations in real rates of interest is unclear, it seems to me that they, too, were probably reduced and were expected to be. The Federal Reserve operated by increasing monetary growth in the autumn and Christmas season, supplying seasonal increases in currency and credit in order to hold down the traditional second-half rise in nominal rates. This certainly facilitated the corresponding variation in trade; whether prices also increased seasonally is unclear, but it is likely that they did. If so, nominal rates rose less in the second half and prices more, or at least not less; hence real rates rose less or fell as a result of the Fed's policy.

As possible counter evidence to the affirmative view, Shiller notes that the quarter century since World War II displays an increasing correspondence between nominal interest rates and the rate of change of prices; that is, real rates have risen and fluctuated much less than have nominal rates. To be sure, based on the reduced variations in monetary growth over the same period, this suggests that monetary policy influenced real rates. But it can also be viewed as evidence that real rates are often independent of monetary developments. There is disagreement in the literature on whether real rates can be viewed as constant over this period and what it would mean if they have been constant. In any event, I would not take this as evidence against the affirmative view. The statistical relationship between nominal interest rates and the rate of inflation pertains mainly to the long-run movement; none of it shows that real rates did not fluctuate over the business cycle or that all the fluctuations were unrelated to monetary developments. The financial stringencies of 1966 and 1969 were "real" enough, and the evidence that they were engineered by monetary restraint is very persuasive to me.

I grant that these stringencies may have been largely unanticipated, and that our world is changing. As Friedman and Schwartz (1976) note, financial markets are *learning* to conform to the "Fisher effect" (with due regard for taxes, of course).

The duration of monetary effects on real rates of interest is therefore a crucial consideration. While the long-run effect never existed or is now disappearing, the short-run effect appears strong and, for the present at least, long enough to make monetary policy and how it is conducted a very serious matter.

Comment   Charles R. Nelson

Robert Shiller has undertaken a particularly difficult but correspondingly important task in trying to shed some light on the question of whether the Federal Reserve can control real interest rates. Shiller begins by providing three specific hypotheses to be considered. Briefly, they are: (1) the Fed cannot affect expected real rates at all; (2) the Fed can affect real rates only through surprise moves in policy; and (3) Fed policies known far enough in advance will have no effect on expected real rates. To this list I would add another hypothesis, which turns out to be surprisingly difficult to reject, namely, that there is no variation whatever in expected real interest rates. Shiller's paper is primarily concerned with reviewing the evidence in favor of or contrary to these hypotheses including some which are relevant to the last hypothesis.

The essence of the problem is, of course, that the ex ante real rate is not generally observed. An exception would be the case of index bonds, which are not traded in the U.S. Shiller argues that if index bonds did exist, then the Fed could control their price and therefore their (real) yield simply by standing ready to buy or sell at a target level. In a world of rational expectations, however, it is not at all clear that the Fed would not face a perfectly elastic supply of such bonds since the implications of its actions for the rate of inflation would be immediately and completely understood. Thus, an attempt to depress the yield on index bonds would raise both the expected rate of inflation and *nominal* discount rates by the same amount, making market participants unwilling to hold *any* index bonds at anything less than the initial equilibrium real yield.

Shiller also discusses the possibility of controlling the real rate measured with respect to the consensus of published inflation forecasts and argues that the Fed "can choose a real interest rate, add to that the latest consensus inflation forecast, and then 'peg' the nominal rate at their sum." If I understand this sequence of events correctly, namely, that this real rate is measured relative to a *given* prior forecast, the ability to control it would appear to be of as little interest as the ability to control ex post realized real rates.

The important question, of course, is whether the Fed can affect or control real rates measured relative to rationally expected inflation. After reviewing the difficulties of addressing this question in the context of an explicit model, Shiller turns to the possibilities for deriving implied behavior in observable magnitudes, in particular the behavior of the ex post realized real rate. For example, Shiller shows that the variance over time in the linear forecast of realized rates based on past realized rates places a lower bound on the variance of the true rationally expected ex ante real rate. Similarly, Fama (1975) has argued that autocorrelation in realized rates would constitute evidence of variation in ex ante real rates since the pure forecast error on inflation must be serially random if expectations are rational. In principle, then, the impact of changes in the regime of monetary policy on the behavior of ex ante real rates may have observable implications. Unfortunately, as Nelson and Schwert (1977) have demonstrated, the very large variance of inflation forecast errors makes it difficult to reject any plausible hypothesis about the behavior of ex ante real rates on the basis of realized rates of return. For example, Fama was unable to reject the hypothesis that ex ante real rates are constant. Although Nelson and Schwert were able to reject this extreme null hypothesis using more refined tests, the basic problem of inferring the behavior of a signal buried in substantial noise remains. This also answers the question posed by Shiller about why Fama's critics did not find some variable that would dominate in an R^2 sense the nominal interest rate as a predictor of inflation. Similar limitations crop up in Shiller's intriguing examination of whether the Fed altered the seasonal pattern in real rates when it moved soon after its establishment to eliminate the seasonal in nominal interest rates. When Shiller applies tests for autocorrelation analogous to Fama's for the period before the Accord, clear evidence of autocorrelation in realized rates and therefore variation in ex ante real rates seems to be indicated. But the inflation measure used is the wholesale price index and the well-known shortcomings of that index in reflecting list rather than transaction prices make the presence of autocorrelation in realized returns less convincing evidence of movements in ex ante rates. Interestingly enough, the empirical evidence would not seem to be nearly so ambiguous in the case of real returns on common stocks. Nelson (1976) and others have presented strong evidence that both ex post and ex ante returns on common stocks are negatively related to inflation.

Shiller also discusses the available "experimental evidence" on the ability of the Fed to influence real rates. Evidently, the Trading Desk can in fact drive down nominal short-term rates on any given day by buying bills. Since such an increase in high-powered money could hardly be construed as diminishing expected inflation, the clear implication is that the Fed can, at will, drive down the real rate at least temporarily. Shiller makes it clear that in a rational expectations context the Fed may well be able to engineer such movements in real rates by surprising the market, but that *systematic* control is by no means implied by this evidence. Empirical tests to distinguish the impact of expected as opposed to unexpected open market actions by the Fed on short-term rates designed along the lines of analogous work by Robert Barro (1977) relating to unemployment and monetary policy have been made by Shiller, but of course are subject to the same statistical problems that have been raised by discussants of Barro's paper at this conference.

Comment   James L. Pierce

Bob Shiller is to be congratulated for having written yet another highly informative and interesting paper. The paper uses the recent literature on rational expectations as a basis for examining the question of whether or not the Federal Reserve can control rationally expected real interest rates. Shiller points out that it is difficult to convert much of the discussion about real interest rates into testable hypotheses. His development of the various hypotheses and his discussion of the difficulty in testing them is, in itself, a valuable contribution.

After developing a simple model to determine the nominal interest rate and rationally expected inflation in which policy, and the public's response to it, are endogenous, Shiller spends most of his efforts in searching for data that will provide identifying restrictions for the model. He has to find exogenous shocks that affect the Fed while leaving the public unaffected. The trick is to find shifts in regimes in which the stochastic processes driving the system are altered, that is to say, when the system moves from one rational expectations equilibrium to another. Ordinary time-series analysis is not useful for the task. Shiller shows considerable skill and tenacity in looking for appropriate episodes. For example, he looks for changes in the seasonality of interest rates following the founding of the Federal Reserve system and for changes in the stochastic behavior of "real" interest rates following the Accord of 1951, when the Fed abandoned its peg on government security prices.

Despite his many efforts, Shiller is unable to provide unambiguous evidence on the question of whether the Fed can control real interest rates because the very shifts in regimes that could allow identification of parameters might have affected other parameters in the system. But he does find some evidence to support the proposition that the Fed can affect real interest rates.

It is possible that more evidence could be brought to bear on the issues if additional structure were introduced. The real interest rates that Shiller considers are real in Fisher's sense, that is, the real interest rate is taken to be the nominal interest rate less the expected rate of inflation. The Fisher approach is then applied to financial assets. But there is also a real return on real assets. There is no guarantee that these two interest rates are always equal, but one would expect agents to exploit arbitrage opportunities between them. These opportunities drive the kind of model developed by Wicksell.

There is substantial evidence that some combination of Fed policy and inflationary shocks can drive a wedge between the real return on financial assets and that on real assets. For example, the real return on short-term financial assets has been negative for much of the period from 1974 to the present, yet many real assets such as commodity inventories and houses have enjoyed a substantial real return. Apparently, asset markets are more specialized and segmented than many observers have thought. It is difficult to remove by arbitrage differences in real return between treasury bills and houses. When wide margins do exist between the return on financial assets and that on real assets, such episodes can provide additional identifying restrictions for tests of relevant hypotheses concerning the Fed's ability to influence real interest rates. It is conceivable that this ability is considerably greater for financial than for real assets.

Comment   Martin Feldstein

The basic economic decisions to save and invest do not depend on the real interest rate as such but on the *net-of-tax* real interest rate. The relevant question about the neutrality of monetary policy should therefore be restated as, "Can the Fed Control the Real *Net* Interest Rate?" I think that there can be little doubt that this is so.

It is important to note first that if the real interest rate remains unchanged, the real *net* rate will be significantly altered. This occurs because the tax rate applies to the nominal interest rate, making the effective tax rate a function of the rate of inflation. Consider, for example, an individual with a 50% marginal tax rate. If the interest rate is 4% and there is no inflation, the real rate is obviously 4% and the real net rate is 2%. If a 6% inflation rate keeps the real rate unchanged, the nominal rate becomes 10%; the net-of-tax nominal rate is 5% and the net real rate is −1%. So even if monetary policy is neutral in the sense that the 4% real interest rate is unchanged, the 6% rate of inflation can turn a 2% real net yield into a real net yield of −1%. Of course, for a borrower with a 50% marginal tax rate, the 6% inflation also causes a corresponding reduction in the real net cost of borrowing.

The assumption of a fixed real pretax interest rate also represents an extreme and unlikely case. In several papers, I have examined the theoretical and empirical aspects of the effect of inflation on the interest rate that business investors would be willing to pay if the real marginal product of capital remained constant (Feldstein 1976, Feldstein, Green, and Sheshinski 1978, Feldstein and Summers 1978*a*). This analysis suggests that, with current tax rates and depreciation rules, each 1% of inflation raises the interest rate that firms would be willing to pay by somewhat more than 1%. The net effect of inflation depends also on the way in which tax rules affect the supply of funds and the demand for funds in other markets. Because of differences in tax rules, it is clear that inflation will not affect investment in housing in the same way it affects investment in industrial plant and equipment.

These results have important implications about the interpretation of the existing evidence on the "neutrality" of monetary policy. Evidence that each 1% of expected inflation raises the interest rate by 1% has incorrectly been viewed as implying such neutrality. Just the opposite is true. A demonstration that the real interest rate remains unchanged should be interpreted as evidence of nonneutrality because it implies a change in the real *net* rate of interest.

A sustained increase in the rate of growth of money thus alters the real net interest rates that govern individual decisions. The complexity and distortions introduced in this way should be regarded as a major reason for opposing such inflation.

General Discussion

Shiller was asked whether under the hypotheses he was testing, the nominal interest rate should not have fallen by 500 basis points in 1971 when Phase I of wage-price controls reduced the inflation rate by 5%. He replied that only the first hypothesis carries this implication; he did not doubt that hypothesis 1 could be rejected. In connection with Nelson's proposed hypothesis that the real rate is constant, he noted that the Fama results could be rejected for periods other than 1951–73; he had to reject the hypothesis with a sample extended to 1977 for instance.

In response to a criticism that the paper was overly skeptical Shiller argued that he had clearly rejected hypothesis 1. While prima facie evidence against hypotheses 2 and 3 could not be found, it seemed unlikely that either was strictly true. He found it implausible that the aggregate price level should optimally incorporate information about future monetary policy, as these hypotheses imply. Shiller said that he had concentrated on short rather than long rates in this study, but that his work with Siegel on British consol yields over 250 years found that long-term real yields showed large movements. Movements in nominal long-term yields worked in the direction of *increasing* the amplitude of the movement in real long-term yields.

Robert Hall suggested that the paper was missing an analysis of the economic forces that might stabilize the real interest rate. Arbitrage is the potential link between the behavior of nominal interest rates and prices. The consumer price index is not representative of the goods subject to arbitrage over time, since it includes perishables.

It was suggested that arbitrage could not account for the behavior of interest rates during 1975 and 1976, since ex ante real treasury bill rates then were clearly negative. Paul Samuelson replied that arbitrage possibilities of the type discussed by Hall did not necessarily rule out nonnegativity of real interest rates. If there were commodities storable at zero cost, then the real rate, at least as measured in terms of those goods, could not become negative. In the absence of such commodities, the real rate could indeed be negative.

Herschel Grossman argued that the fact that money supply data are revised several times tends to support the view that confusion about the level of the money stock contributes to the business cycle. He was not confident that existing theories based on incomplete information were enough to explain business cycles, but also doubted that existing theories based on nonclearing of markets could provide the full explanation.

References

Barro, R. J. 1974. "Are Government Bonds Net Wealth?" *Journal of Political Economy* 82:1095–117.

―――. 1977. "Unanticipated Money Growth and Unemployment in the United States." *American Economic Review* 67:101–15.

―――. 1978. "Unanticipated Money, Output, and the Price Level in the United States." *Journal of Political Economy* 86:549–80.

Bureau of Labor Statistics. 1971. *Handbook of Methods*. Washington, D.C.: U.S. Government Printing Office.

Cagan, P. 1972. *The Channels of Monetary Effects on Interest Rates.* New York: Columbia University Press and National Bureau of Economic Research.

Carlson, J. A. 1977. "Short-Term Interest Rates as Predictors of Inflation: Comment." *American Economic Review* 67:469–75.

Darby, M. R. 1975. "The Financial and Tax Effects of Monetary Policy on Interest Rates." *Economic Inquiry* 13:266–76.

Diller, S. 1971. "The Seasonal Variation in Interest Rates." In *Essays on Interest Rates*, edited by J. Guttentag, 2:35–133. New York: Columbia University Press and National Bureau of Economic Research.

Fama, E. F. 1975. "Short-Term Interest Rates as Predictors of Inflation." *American Economic Review* 65:269–82.

———. 1977. "Interest Rates and Inflation: The Message in the Entrails." *American Economic Review* 67:487–96.

Federal Reserve Board. 1915. *First Annual Report of the Federal Reserve Board.* Washington, D.C.: U.S. Government Printing Office.

Feldstein, M. 1976. "Inflation, Income Taxes, and the Rate of Interest: A Theoretical Analysis." *American Economic Review* 66:809–20.

Feldstein, M.; Green, J.; and Sheshinski, E. 1978. "Inflation and Taxes in a Growing Economy with Debt and Equity Finance." *Journal of Political Economy* 86, pt. 2, pp. S53–S70.

Feldstein, M., and Summers, L. 1978*a*. "Inflation, Tax Rules, and the Long-Term Interest Rate." *Brookings Papers on Economic Activity* 1:61–109.

———. 1978*b*. "Inflation and Taxation of Capital Income in the Corporate Sector." National Bureau of Economic Research Working Paper no. 312. *National Tax Journal*, forthcoming.

Fischer, S. 1977. "Long-Term Contracts, Rational Expectations, and the Optimal Money Supply Rule." *Journal of Political Economy* 85:191–205.

Friedman, M. 1968. "Factors Affecting the Level of Interest Rates." In *Savings and Residential Financing.* 1968 Conference Proceedings. Chicago: United States Savings and Loan League.

Friedman, M., and Schwartz, A. J. 1963. *A Monetary History of the United States.* Princeton, N.J.: Princeton University Press.

———. 1976. "From Gibson to Fisher." *Explorations in Economic Research* 3:288–91.

Glass, C. 1927. *An Adventure in Constructive Finance.* New York: Doubleday.

Granger, C. W. J., and Newbold, P. 1977. "The Time Series Approach to Econometric Model Building." In *New Methods in Business Cycle Research*, pp. 7–21. Minneapolis: Federal Reserve Bank of Minneapolis.

Hess, P. J., and Bicksler, J. L. 1975. "Capital Asset Prices versus Time Series Models as Predictors of Inflation: The Expected Real Rate of Interest and Market Efficiency." *Journal of Financial Economics* 2:341–60.

Joines, D. 1977. "Short-Term Interest Rates as Predictors of Inflation: Comment." *American Economic Review* 67:476–77.

Lucas, R. E. 1973. "Some International Evidence on Output-Inflation Tradeoffs." *American Economic Review* 63:103–24.

Macaulay, F. R. 1938. *The Movements of Interest Rates, Bond Yields, and Stock Prices in the United States since 1856.* New York: National Bureau of Economic Research.

Mill, J. S. 1865. *Principles of Political Economy.* New York: Kelley, reprinted 1961.

Nelson, C. R. 1976. "Inflation and Rates of Return on Common Stock." *Journal of Finance* 31:471–83.

Nelson, C. R., and Schwert, G. W. 1977. "Short Term Interest Rates as Predictors of Inflation: On Testing the Hypothesis That the Real Rate of Interest Is Constant." *American Economic Review* 67:478–86.

Phelps, E. S., and Taylor, J. B. 1977. "Stabilizing Powers of Monetary Policy under Rational Expectations." *Journal of Political Economy* 85:163–89.

Poole, W. 1976. "Rational Expectations in the Macro Model." *Brookings Papers on Economic Activity* 2:463–505.

Ricardo, D. 1817. *The Principles of Political Economy and Taxation.* Everyman's Edition. London: J. M. Dent & Sons, 1911.

Roll, R. 1972. "Interest Rates on Monetary Assets and Commodity Price Changes." *Journal of Finance* 27:251–77.

Rutledge, J. 1974. *A Monetarist Model of Inflationary Expectations.* Lexington, Mass.: D. C. Heath.

Sargent, T. J. 1971. "Expectations at the Short End of the Yield Curve: An Application of Macaulay's Test." In *Essays on Interest Rates,* edited by J. Guttentag, 2:391–412. New York: Columbia University Press and National Bureau of Economic Research.

———. 1976. "The Observational Equivalence of Natural and Unnatural Rate Theories of Macroeconomics." *Journal of Political Economy* 84:631–40.

Sargent, T. J., and Wallace, N. 1975. "Rational Expectations, the Optimal Monetary Instrument, and the Optimal Money Supply Rule." *Journal of Political Economy* 83:241–54.

Shiller, R. J. 1978. "Rational Expectations and the Dynamic Structure of Macroeconomic Models." *Journal of Monetary Economics* 4:1–44.

Shiller, R. J., and Siegel, J. J. 1977. "The Gibson Paradox and Historical Movements in Real Interest Rates." *Journal of Political Economy* 85:891–907.

Sims, C. A. 1977. "Exogeneity and Causal Ordering in Macroeconomic Models." In *New Methods in Business Cycle Research,* pp. 23–43. Minneapolis: Federal Reserve Bank of Minneapolis.

Wicksell, K. 1898. *Interest and Prices.* London: Macmillan, reprinted 1936.

———. 1906. *Lectures on Political Economy.* Vol. 2. London: Macmillan, reprinted 1935.

5　A Competitive Theory of Fluctuations and the Feasibility and Desirability of Stabilization Policy

Finn Kydland and Edward C. Prescott

Introduction

Can fiscal policy be used to stabilize the economy? In this essay we first develop an equilibrium theory of fluctuations consistent with the observed persistence of unemployment and then address this question within the framework of that theory. We conclude that fiscal policy rules, which alter relative prices facing firms and households, can and have had important effects upon the stability of the economy. Some rules increase fluctuations and others smooth out the business cycle. In choosing among rules the criterion used is the cost-benefit measure of neoclassical public finance, which has been applied to numerous problems involving important effects of government policies upon resource allocation.[1] Our conclusion is that tax rates should remain constant or nearly constant over the cycle with the budget being balanced on average. This does not minimize fluctuations but does minimize the deadweight burden of financing government expenditures.

Need for Rules

At this point we emphasize that the choice is from a set of fiscal policy *rules*. Only if businesses and households have a basis for forming expectations of future policies do they have well-defined decision problems, a prerequisite for the application of modern public finance theory. Only

We would like to thank the discussants, the editor, V. V. Chari, and Walter Dolde for comments. Research was partially supported by the National Science Foundation.

1. See for example Feldstein 1974 for his analysis of the effects of the Social Security System upon capital accumulation.

then is the behavior of the economic agents econometrically predictable. This is just the point made by Lucas (1976) in his critique of current econometric policy evaluation and will not be dwelt upon here. We emphasize that the fixed-rule procedure we advocate does not necessarily imply constant values or constant growth rates of the policy instruments. Feedback rules with the tax parameters varying systematically with economic conditions are considered. A policy rule, however, is needed before one can predict what equilibrium process will govern the economy.

The policy problem considered is that of choosing from a set of fiscal policy rules for setting tax rates and levels of government spending. Rather than characterizing the rule that is best in the cost-benefit sense of modern public finance, principles are sought for the design of policy rules that do well in terms of this criterion. This is done for three reasons. First, the policy that is best, relative to the specified objective, may be very complicated and not explainable to the public. This negates its usefulness, for the democratic policy selection process is not well suited to making subtle second- and third-best distinctions. Second, the determination of optimal policy requires precise estimation of the parameters of preferences and technology, and these estimates are not available and probably not obtainable. Third, the optimal policy will almost surely be time inconsistent, as we have previously shown (Kydland and Prescott 1977). Even for deterministic dynamic optimal taxation problems, if one again solves the optimization problem subsequent to the initial period, taking as given decisions already made, the resulting optimal plan for the remainder of the planning horizon is inconsistent with the initially optimal plan. Besides invalidating the principle of selecting the action which is best given the current situation, a principle needed to justify discretionary policy, the computation of the optimal taxation programming problem when there is uncertainty is beyond our current capabilities. This time inconsistency does not arise because of a conflict between social and private objectives except insofar as people value consumption of public goods and prefer not to pay taxes. The problem is present even if the social objective is the welfare of the representative individual.[2]

2. Calvo (1977), in a very interesting paper, has demonstrated the time inconsistency of an optimal monetary policy. Since inflation can be viewed as a tax on liquidity, his is an optimal taxation analysis. The authors (1978a) have explored further the problems of computing optimal policy. Bellman's principle of optimality was shown to hold if policy is constrained to rationalize *past* decisions of private agents. In that paper the standard optimal taxation problem is extended to dynamic environments.

Need for a Theory Consistent with Facts

A prerequisite for the application of neoclassical public finance is an equilibrium theory, that is, a specification of preferences and technology which rationalizes choices of the economic actors. The puzzle of the business cycle is why output does not vary smoothly over time but rather fluctuates about trend. In the postwar period some of these deviations of measured output from trend have exceeded 5% of trend output. The rate of capital accumulation, in particular the production of producer and consumer durables, is highly correlated with output (all variables are measured as percentage deviation from trend); however, the percentage fluctuations are of much greater amplitude. Fluctuations in labor supplied are also positively and strongly correlated with output and have amplitudes comparable with those of real output. An equilibrium theory must explain these well-known facts about the comovements of these aggregate economic time series.

A second set of observations that confronts a theory of business fluctuations is the persistence of deviations of output from trend. Indeed, these persistent deviations have been taken by many as an argument against the use of equilibrium models with rational expectations to explain business cycle phenomena. Modigliani (1977, p. 6), in his presidential address, states: "But the most glaring flaw of MREH (Macro rational expectations hypothesis) is its inconsistency with the evidence: if it were valid, deviations of unemployment from the natural rate would be small and transitory—in which case *The General Theory* would not have been written and neither would this paper."

An indication of this persistence can be obtained by regressing the detrended log of real output on itself lagged one period and on the lagged rate of change. The estimated equation from quarterly data for the 1947–77 period is

$$y_t = .909y_{t-1} + .477(y_{t-1} - y_{t-2}).$$

$$(.026) \qquad (.082)$$

$$S.E. = .00011 \quad R^2 = .908$$

This second-order difference equation is stable with largest eigen-value .75. Given this fact and that there are 120 observations, large sample theory should provide nearly valid inference.

For this difference equation the expected deviation from trend this period is a function not only of last period's deviation but also of the rate of change in the deviation. This latter dependency, which we label momentum, results in the response to an innovation not being greatest in the initial period but rather increasing to a peak in a period subsequent to the innovation before subsiding (see fig. 5.1).

Additional evidence for persistence and momentum is the research of Barro (1977, 1978). He finds that the effects of unanticipated monetary shocks upon output initially increased before dampening. Sims's (1979) estimates of response functions of real output to innovations in the vector autoregressive process display a similar pattern.

The Monetary Shock Theory

Lucas (1972) developed an equilibrium business cycle theory with monetary shocks to explain the negative correlation of output and the consumption of leisure or non-market-produced goods and services. Monetary shocks confound relative price shifts resulting in correlated supply errors in a decentralized economy. Crucial to this theory is the intertemporal substitutability of leisure, which implies that temporary changes in expected real wages have important effects upon labor supply even though permanent changes have little or even slightly negative effects. We find the theory that monetary shocks have important effects on real aggregates appealing and the evidence supportive. But we think shocks to technology and fiscal policy shocks, which affect relative prices, are also important in triggering economic fluctuations. The following analysis of the deterministic equilibrium growth model suggests that variations in factors affecting the equilibrium rate of capital accumulation could give rise to fluctuations in investment of the magnitude observed in the postwar period. We emphasize that this analysis is not a substitute for a rational expectations theory with shocks, which is de-

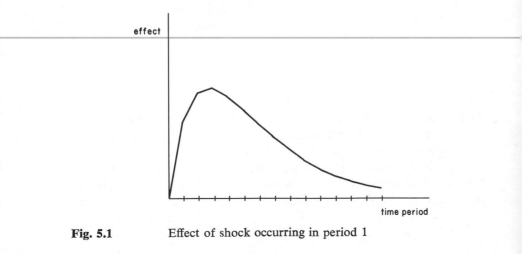

Fig. 5.1   Effect of shock occurring in period 1

veloped subsequently. Rather, it is a simple exercise to bring to bear prior knowledge about preferences and technology to determine whether such factors should be ruled out as a *quantitatively* important source of fluctuations.

Quantitative Importance of Real and Policy Shocks

Policies that affect the relative price of capital goods, leisure, and consumption have important effects upon the stationary capital stock. Abstracting from growth, as our concern is with deviations from trend, the stationary capital stock k^s satisfies

$$(1 - \theta) \, f_k(k^s, n^s) = q(\delta + \rho),$$

where θ is the corporate tax rate, f_k the marginal product of capital, n^s the stationary labor supply, q the effective price of new capital, δ the exponential depreciation rate of capital, and ρ the subjective time discount rate.

The effective price of capital is related to fiscal policy parameters and the inflation rate as follows:

$$q = 1 - \tau - \frac{\theta \, \psi}{\psi + \pi + \rho},$$

where τ is the investment tax credit rate, ψ the capital consumption allowance rate allowed for tax purposes, and π the inflation rate.

This is the standard rental price analysis of Jorgenson except for the last term, which is the present value of reductions in future tax liabilities and is obtained by summing the present value of capital consumption allowances t periods hence,

$$\frac{\psi(1 - \psi)^t}{(1 + \rho + \pi)^{t+1}},$$

from t equal zero to infinity and multiplying by the corporate tax rate θ.

For purposes of obtaining order of magnitude estimates of effects of policy parameters upon stationary capital stock, we assume a Cobb-Douglas production function with capital's exponent being .25. If the time period is a year, the initially assumed values for the other parameters are $\rho = .05$, $\psi = .10$, $\delta = .10$, $\pi = 0$, and $\tau = 0$. We also assume that changes in the policy parameters have a negligible effect upon the stationary labor supply. This is not an unreasonable approximation given the small change in per person labor supply that has occurred over the last forty years, a period in which there was a large increase in the real wage.

With these assumptions the effect of a 10% investment tax credit is to increase the stationary capital stock by 20%. Because a 10% investment tax credit was introduced in the early sixties and the depreciation schedule accelerated (ψ increased), the rapid rate of capital accumulation over much of that decade is no surprise. More surprising, at least to us, is the large effect that changes in the anticipated future inflation rates have upon the capital stock. A change in the average inflation rate from zero to 7% more than offsets the effect of a 10% investment tax credit, at least for the assumed parameter values. The increase in the average inflation rate that occurred in the seventies may be the principal cause of the low rates of capital accumulation in recent years.

This structure considers only plant and equipment in the corporate sector. This stock is only a fraction of the physical capital stock and is approximately three-quarters of annual GNP for the American economy. Other components of the capital stock comparable in size are inventories, housing stock, stock of consumer durables, and the public capital stock. Considering all of these components, the reproducible capital–annual output ratio is about 3 for the American economy.[3] A shock to technology, such as the increase in the price of imported oil that occurred in the early seventies, might reduce our production possibilities set by 2.5% and therefore stationary capital stock by 10% of annual GNP.[4]

This stationary point analysis indicates that policy and technology shocks have effects upon the stationary capital stocks of the order of 10% of annual GNP. Depending upon the rate of adjustment along the equilibrium path, these shocks might or might not have effects comparable in magnitude to observed fluctuations. To address this issue of speed of adjustment, additional assumptions about preferences are necessary. We assume that the utility function of the representative household can be approximated in the neighborhood of the stationary point by

$$\sum_{t=0}^{\infty} (1+\rho)^{-t} \{\ln c_t + 2 \ln (1 - n_t)\}.$$

We also assume that the production relationships are

$$f(k_t, n_t) = k_t^{1/4} n_t^{3/4}$$

and

$$c_t + k_{t+1} \leq f(k_t, n_t) + (1 - \delta)k_t.$$

The rest point values for this growth model are $k^s = .6132$, $n^s = .3103$, $c^s = .3066$, and stationary GNP $= .3679$.

3. These numbers were taken from *The Statistical Abstract of the United States* (1976), table 695, p. 428.

4. We are assuming stationary capital–output ratio of three, a Cobb-Douglas production function with coefficient of capital equal ¼, and a 2.5% reduction in the multiplicative factor of the production function.

We substitute $f(k_t, n_t) + (1 - \delta)k_t - k_{t+1}$ for c_t in the utility function and make the quadratic approximation about the stationary values. We find that for this approximate problem the equilibrium law governing the capital stock is

$$k_{t+1} - k^s = .7544(k_t - k^s).$$

This solution to the approximate problem is the first-order Taylor series approximation at k^s to the equilibrium rule for the growth problem being considered.

The stationary capital–annual output ratio for the growth problem is 1.7, and the rate of adjustment of capital to the stationary value is almost 25% per year. That is, in three years more than half the gap between current and stationary capital stock is closed along an equilibrium growth path. If capital is 10% below its stationary value, labor supply is about 2.1% above its stationary value, output 1% below its stationary value, gross investment 2.4% of stationary output above its value, and consumption 4.1% below its value. These numbers are not consistent with the observed correlations: other features must be introduced before we have an explanation of fluctuations. These numbers do indicate that capital-theoretic elements cannot be ruled out as a quantitatively important source of economic fluctuations.

A Theory of Economic Fluctuations

Ours is a competitive theory which combines the Lucas (1972) monetary shock model with the model of capital accumulation in an environment with shocks to technology.[5] We choose the infinitely lived family rather than the overlapping generation abstraction because it facilitates bringing to bear prior knowledge and is easier to analyze. Such structures with a single capital good do give rise to the observed comovements of economic aggregates and persistence of deviations of output from trend when plausible parameters are assumed. For the examples considered, however, momentum for the equilibrium process governing real output was not obtained. Possibly introducing information diffusion, a feature of Lucas's (1975) extension of his business cycle theory, is the way to obtain momentum. We think a more plausible explanation is that more than a single period is required to build a new capital good. The work by Jorgenson (1963, 1971) and recent estimates by Hall (1977) suggest that there are long lags from the time when changes in its determinants call for an increase in the capital stock until the time when the new capital starts yielding services.

5. See Brock 1978 for the theory laid out in detail or Prescott and Mehra 1978, where recursive methods are used. Black (1978) has argued that real factors can explain aggregate fluctuations.

Supposing that the process of designing, ordering, and installing capital can be described by a fixed distribution of lags, Hall (1977) found the *average* lag to be about two years. Evidence of a different kind is reported by Mayer (1960). On the basis of a survey he found that the average lag (weighted by the size of the project) between the decision to undertake an investment project and the completion of it was twenty-one months. To this must be added any lag that occurs between the arrival of information and the decision to carry out the investment. If anything, this estimate is likely to be an underestimate of the actual lag during a period of general expansion. If most firms decide to expand almost simultaneously, delivery lags are likely to be substantially longer than would be the case if investments were evenly spread out over time. It should also be noted that lags are generally longer for larger projects.

Once a project is begun, the cost will be distributed over the period of time it takes for it to become productive. According to Mayer, the construction period for a typical plant is fifteen months. During the time period of half a year or so before start of construction, plans are drawn, financing is arranged, and the first significant orders are placed before construction can begin. There was, of course, a lot of variation in lead times. For example, in his sample of completed plants, 20% required ten months or more from start of drawing of plans to start of construction. These findings, which are probably low estimates for periods of generally high capital accumulation, suggest that only a small fraction of additions to capital stock that are decided on in a given year show up as investment expenditures in the same year. Most of the expenditures will be incurred during the next year, with a not insignificant fraction being left over for the subsequent year.

To our knowledge, the first analysis incorporating this feature within a dynamic equilibrium framework was done by the authors (1977). The typical firm in a competitive industry was assumed to make investment plans in period t on the basis of the state of the economy at that time, the investment tax credit, and expectations about future prices. Part of the expenditures were incurred in the same period and the rest in period $t + 1$. The new capital stock was assumed to become productive in period $t + 2$. Expectations were rational in the sense that, when aggregated across firms, the investment behavior did indeed lead to the distribution of future prices on which individual decisions were based. In that model the propagation of random demand shocks or changes in the tax rate was fairly slow.

In this paper we present an abstraction in which durables play the role of capital, although they were assumed, directly or indirectly, to enter the consumer's utility function. Thus, durables as a proportion of total output are thought of as being roughly equivalent in magnitude to the sum of consumer and producer durables. In general, suppose additions to the stock of durables planned in period $t - L$ do not produce services before period $t + 1$, as expressed by the equation

$$(1) \qquad d_{i,t+1} = (1 - \delta_d) d_{it} + s_{iLt},$$

where d_{it} is the stock of durables held by individual i at the beginning of period t, s_{iLt} is the plan made in period $t - L$ for an addition to the stock of durables, and $0 < \delta_d < 1$ is a depreciation rate. The expenditures, however, are distributed with a fraction ϕ_0 in the planning period $t - L$, a fraction ϕ_1 in period $t - L + 1$, and so on. Total investment expenditures in period t are then

$$(2) \qquad z_{it} = \sum_{j=0}^{L} \phi_j s_{ijt},$$

where $\sum_{j=0}^{L} \phi_j = 1$. On the basis of empirical evidence, it seems reasonable that L would be at least two years, that ϕ_0 would be relatively small, and that ϕ_1 would be at least 0.5.

Lucas and Rapping (1969) and Ghez and Becker (1975) found ample evidence that leisure time in one period is a good substitute for leisure time in another period. This suggests that intertemporal substitution is an important feature of people's preferences. Greater intertemporal substitutability can be modeled by introducing a quasi-capital element in the utility function which measures how much workers have worked in the past, with relatively more weight on the more recent past, say given by

$$(3) \qquad a_{i,t+1} = (1 - \delta_a) a_{it} + n_{it},$$

where n_t is hours worked in period t, and δ_a is a depreciation rate. Both a_t and n_t enter the current-period utility function. The higher the value of a_t in a given period, the more utility is derived from leisure in that period. This model is consistent with the observation that labor supply is elastic with respect to transitory changes in the real wage rate, but inelastic with respect to permanent changes.

In this economy we have a large number of people who have identical preferences. Each maximizes expected discounted utility

$$\sum_t \beta^t u(c_{it}, d_{it}, n_{it}, a_{it}), \quad 0 < \beta < 1,$$

where c_{it} is consumption of nondurables. This is not a time-separable utility function because a_{it} is a function of previously supplied labor. But it is determined recursively, a property which is needed to insure that resulting equilibrium decision rules are stationary.

We assume that the function u is such that after using the budget constraint to eliminate c_{it}, the resulting function can be approximated by a quadratic function over the range of fluctuations. Resulting equilibrium decision rules are then linear, as required for most econometric time series analyses, and the equilibrium is computable.

For the examples presented here we do not permit loans among individuals. The consumer has a store of value, namely capital, so our somewhat arbitrary exclusion of this market should not significantly affect our conclusions. Some preliminary results (see Kydland and Prescott 1978b) support this conjecture and we would be very surprised if the inclusion of a consumer bond market would alter any conclusions. With these apologetic statements the consumer is faced with the sequence of budget constraints:

$$(4) \qquad c_{it} = \lambda_{it} n_{it} - z_{it}$$

indexed by t where λ_{it} is his real wage. Another set of constraints he faces is:

$$(5) \qquad s_{i,k,t+1} = s_{i,k-1,t} \text{ for } k = 1, \ldots, L.$$

The number of new projects initiated k periods prior to next period will be the number of projects initiated $k - 1$ periods prior to the current period.

We do not assume a standard production function with capital, labor and a technology shock parameter because of the computation problems that would result. Rather we assume that the sum of consumption and gross investment is constrained by the sum of individuals' outputs, $\lambda_{it} n_{it}$. The curvature of our (indirect) utility function, we think, captures the substitutability of capital for labor in the production process.

The exogenous stochastic elements giving rise to fluctuations are shocks to productivity. We assume the individual λ's are distributed about an economy wide mean Λ_t, which is subject to change over time. More explicitly, we assume Λ_t is subject to a first-order autoregressive process:

$$\Lambda_{t+1} = \rho \Lambda_t + \mu + \xi_{t+1}$$

$$\lambda_{it} = \Lambda_t + \epsilon_{it} \text{ for all } i.$$

The ϵ_{it} are distributed independently over individuals and for simplicity over time as well. By the law of large numbers, the average ϵ_{it} over the continuum of individuals is zero with probability 1. In addition, the disturbances ξ and ϵ are normally distributed with means of zero and variances σ^2_ξ and σ^2_ϵ.

In order to simplify subsequent analysis we represent the relationships as

$$(6) \qquad \lambda_{ti} = \Lambda^e_t + \xi_t + \epsilon_{it},$$

where

(7) $$\Lambda^e_{t+1} = \rho\Lambda^e_t + \rho\xi_t + \mu.$$

The Λ^e_t is the expected real wage at time t conditional upon observations with index less than t.

Using the convention of letting capital letters denote the aggregate or per capita quantities of the corresponding individual variables, we can write

(8) $$A_{t+1} = (1 - \delta_a)A_t + N_t,$$

(9) $$D_{t+1} = (1 - \delta_a)D_t + S_{Lt}, \text{ and}$$

$$Z_t = \sum_{j=0}^{L} \phi_j S_{jt}.$$

Some might question whether the real wage does move procyclically as the theory requires if there is to be persistence and momentum. First, if the elasticity of labor supply with respect to cyclical variations in the real wage is high, only small fluctuations in the real wage, say a percent or two, are needed to explain the observed fluctuations in employment. Measurement errors could very well introduce a *cyclical* bias in the measurement of the real wage of this magnitude. In boom periods a given worker may be assigned to a job which is higher on the internal job ladder and has higher pay, and being less experienced, he will cost the firm more per unit of effective labor service in the boom period.[6] Another potential source of cyclical measurement bias is that, with the implicit employment contract, payments are not perfectly associated over time with labor services supplied. Thus, we do not consider it damaging to our theory that there is little evidence of procyclical movement of the real wage.

The theory presented assumes a single capital good. Generalization to multiple capital goods with different time periods required for construction (i.e., different L's) and different distributed resource allocations (i.e., different sets of ϕ_j's) is straightforward. Such generalizations were not attempted because, besides significantly increasing the costs of computing the fixed-point problem that must be solved to determine the competitive equilibrium, they were not needed to explain persistence of shocks nor did we see any reason why policy conclusions would be at all sensitive to the simplification.

In our model so far we have measured the wage rate in terms of the price of output (durables or nondurables). An important extension is to allow for monetary shocks. The individual observes only his own nominal wage rate (or the wage rate on his "island") before making the decision

---

6. See Reder 1962 for a further discussion.

on how much to work in period t. From the observed nominal wage rate, say w_{it}, and knowledge of variances of shocks, he can infer only with error his own real wage rate, λ_{it}, and the economywide real wage, Λ_t.

To be specific, assume that

(10) $$w_{it} = \lambda_{it} + \eta_t,$$

where η_t is due to monetary shocks and is assumed to be normally distributed with mean zero and variance σ^2_η. The worker will want to supply more labor when his real wage is high relative to what he can expect to earn in the future, of which the economywide real wage rate is an indication. He will therefore try to infer λ_{it} and Λ_t from the observation of w_{it}. Given the assumptions above, the conditional expectations are

$$E(\Lambda_t \mid w_{it}) = (1 - \psi_1) \Lambda^e_t + \psi_1 w_{it},$$

where $\psi_1 = \sigma^2_\xi / (\sigma^2_\xi + \sigma^2_\epsilon + \sigma^2_\eta)$, and

$$E(\lambda_{it} \mid w_{it}) = (1 - \psi_2) \Lambda^e_t + \psi_2 w_{it},$$

where $\psi_2 = (\sigma^2_\xi + \sigma^2_\epsilon) / (\sigma^2_\xi + \sigma^2_\epsilon + \sigma^2_\eta)$. It is instructive to write these conditional expectations in a different form:

(11) $$E(\Lambda_t \mid w_{it}) = \Lambda^e_t + \psi_1(\epsilon_{it} + \eta_t + \xi_t)$$

(12) $$E(\lambda_{it} \mid w_{it}) = \lambda_{it} - (1 - \psi_2) (\xi_t + \epsilon_{it}) + \psi_2 \eta_t.$$

Of course, some of the variables on the right-hand sides of the last two equations are not observable.

In this setup, if the agent observes a change in w_{it}, he does not know how much of it is due to the monetary shock (η_t), to the economywide productivity shock (ξ_t), or to the difference between his own and the average productivity (ϵ_{it}). His knowledge of relative variances for the three shocks, however, allows him to form conditional expectations. Having decided how much labor to supply, he subsequently observes his real income. If it is, say, higher than anticipated, optimal behavior is to allocate a larger proportion of his income to durables, yielding services in future periods, than he would have otherwise.

Definition of Equilibrium

An individual at a point in time is characterized by his state variable vector $y_t \equiv (d_t, a_t, s_{1t}, \ldots, s_{Lt})$ and wage w_t. The subscripts i are omitted because individuals with the same (y_t, w_t)-pair are indistinguishable and consequently choose the same decision vector, (c_t, s_{0t}, n_t), in that period. The vector y_t was selected to summarize all relevant aspects of past decisions upon current and future decisions.

The state of the economy is the distribution of the y_t over the implicitly assumed continuum of individuals plus Λ^e_t. For our structure only the first moment of this distribution matters in the sense that equilibrium values of aggregate economic variables and prices are a function of the population averages only. The convention of using the corresponding capital letter to denote a variable's population average is adopted in the subsequent discussion. The economywide state is the pair (Y,Λ^e). A second important feature of our structure—that it is recursive—results in time invariant, or stationary, equilibrium laws of motion for the economy, as is required for the application of standard econometric time series analysis. Equilibrium prices and aggregate variables are a function of the economy state variable while optimal individual decisions are functions of both individual and economy state variables. Equilibrium requires that the individual decision rules imply the aggregate relationships, that expectations are rational, and that markets clear. We now make this more explicit.

Let value function $v(y,w,Y,\Lambda^e)$ be the (equilibrium) expected discounted utility for an individual with initial state (y,w) if the initial economy state is (Y,Λ^e). Primes denote the value of a variable in the subsequent period. By Bellman's principle of optimality, this value function must satisfy the following functional equation:

$$v(y,w,Y,\Lambda^e) = \max_n E \{\max_{c,s_0} [u(c,d,a,n)$$

$$+ \beta E \, v(y',w',Y',\Lambda^{e'})] \mid w,\Lambda^e\}$$

subject to constraints (1)–(5). In the above, the first expectation is conditional on his observed nominal wage w. The maximization with respect to n is outside the expectation because the labor supply decision is on the basis of the nominal wage prior to deducing the value of the nominal shock. At the time of the consumption-savings decision, realized real wage, nominal shock, and therefore economywide average real wage as well are known.

The one variable whose distribution is not yet well defined is Y'. A (linear) law of motion $Y' = F(Y,\Lambda^e,\xi,\eta)$, where ξ and η are the economywide real and nominal shocks, is assumed. Given function F, the decision problem of the household is well defined, and there are resulting (linear) optimal decision rules for individuals:

$$n = n^e(y,w,Y,\Lambda^e)$$

$$c = c(y,n,Y,\Lambda^e,\epsilon,\eta,\xi).$$

$$s_0 = s_0(y,n,Y,\Lambda^e,\epsilon,\eta,\xi).$$

Equations (6) and (10) are used to obtain labor supply as a function of individual and economywide states and the three shocks or

$$n = n(y, Y, \Lambda^e, \epsilon, \eta, \xi).$$

Averaging variables (note that average ϵ is 0 because ϵ is independent across individuals), one obtains (N, C, S_0) as a linear function of $(Y, \Lambda^e, \eta, \xi)$, which along with (8) and (9) can be used to obtain Y' as a function of $(Y, \Lambda^e, \eta, \xi)$. For equilibrium, this implied law of motion must equal the assumed law of motion F.

Our method of determining an equilibrium is to use backward induction to solve for the first-period equilibrium decision rules and law of motion for finite-period problems. As the horizon increased, in all cases, these equilibrium first-period decision rules converged. This limiting rule is a solution to the infinite-horizon equilibrium problem and is computable.

Except for the monetary shocks, our abstraction is very much a Robinson Crusoe economy. This we consider a virtue, for, other things being equal, we prefer a simple easily understood explanation to a complicated one. For public finance applications, the introduction of a government debt state variable and a market for government bonds is necessary. This extension is conceptually straightforward but within our computability requirement a nontrivial extension. This is the subject of current research, and we are optimistic that the technical problems can be solved.

Some Results

The theory is not complete until the parameters of preferences and technology and the variances of the shocks are specified. One approach would be to estimate the parameters using, say, maximum likelihood techniques. But since this is impractical given current computational methods and existing computers, an alternative approach was adopted. We simply specified what we think are reasonable values for the parameters and then varied some of the parameters to see if the results were sensitive to the specified value.

The parameters of technology, that is the coefficients of the distribution of investment expenditures, are $\phi_0 = \phi_1 = 0.3$ and $\phi_2 = 0.4$. We think the evidence previously cited provided strong prior support for a pattern not too unlike this one, and we do not think results should be very sensitive to the values assumed for the ϕ_i, provided a significant fraction of the expenditures occurred in each of the periods. We did find that momentum was not obtained when investment projects initiated during this period became part of the productive capital stock during the subsequent period. It would have been of some interest to vary these parameters, but, given the sizable cost of each example, resources were best allocated to varying the shock variances, about which our prior knowledge is weak. The parameters of the preference were selected so that stationary values of the variables would be consistent with the data and "long-run" labor supply inelastic. We did some sensitivity analysis with respect to these parameters and found the results varied little.[7]

Our first example assumes no monetary shocks ($\sigma^2_\eta = 0$) and highly persistent real shocks ($\rho = .9999$).

Figure 5.2 shows that the effect of a shock on labor supply and production of durables peaks two periods subsequent to the shock and then approaches a limit with some fluctuation. In the case of employment, the new limit is essentially zero. We have taken after-shock productivity to be one, so that aggregate output and employment are comparable in magnitude. We see that, although purchases of durables represent roughly one-third of total output, their degree of fluctuation is comparable with that of total output. The shape of the curve for employment looks very much like the one derived in figure 5.1 from the estimated relation. In this example we have not assumed any cost of adjustment of changing employment from one period to another, as is emphasized in some of Sargent's work. Such an assumption can easily be incorporated in our framework as well and would have made the curve for employment (and output) even more similar to the estimated one.

This example illustrates the effects of permanent real shocks to the economy without any monetary shocks or imperfect information. The results were not sensitive at all to the choice of parameters of preferences. The most important feature of our model in producing this kind of persistence and momentum is the distributed lag. As we have argued earlier, there is strong a priori information on this lag, and this evidence

7. The values of the parameters can be obtained from the authors. For technical details see Kydland and Prescott 1978*b*.

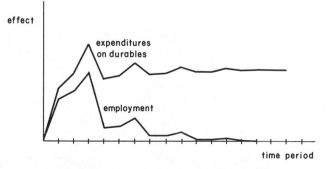

has been incorporated in our model. In conclusion, this example shows substantial persistence and momentum as a result of a permanent innovation to technology.

We next determined the equilibrium process when there were monetary shocks ($\sigma^2_\eta \neq 0$) but no real shocks ($\sigma^2_\xi = 0$). The results obtained correspond to those of Lucas (1975) in his equilibrium model of the business cycle with capital accumulation. There was no momentum, and the effect of the shock was offset in subsequent periods. A similar result was obtained when there were transitory real shocks only ($\sigma^2_\eta = 0$ and $\rho = 0$). The only important difference was that with positive real shocks agents rationally supplied more labor services and accumulated more capital in and for a period subsequent to the period of the shock, whereas with positive monetary shocks agents were tricked into supplying more labor services and initiating more investment projects than were optimal.

When there are simultaneously both transitory real and monetary shocks, however, greater persistence and some momentum result. This point is illustrated in figure 5.3, which depicts the response to an innovation in the productivity process. The effect on employment is larger in the third period than in the first. There is then a negative effect reflecting partly a reduction in purchases of durables (since the steady state has not changed) and partly the increased value of leisure resulting from the increased labor supplied in the previous period. This response is consistent with the argument that monetary shocks can be used to delay a recession but not to avoid it. Offsetting real shocks with monetary shocks results in a more severe recession at a later time.

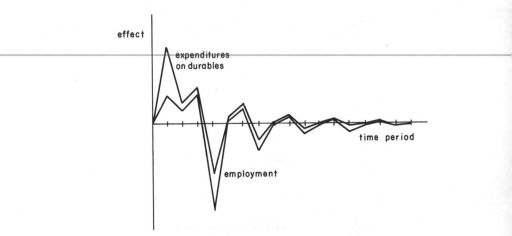

Fig. 5.3   Effect of transitory real shock occurring in period 1

Policy Implications

Most would agree that some fluctuations in output and employment are not a social problem and may even be socially desirable. For example, seasonal fluctuations, which are of the same order of magnitude as postwar business cycle fluctuations, generally are not considered to be a matter of great social concern. Indeed, the most widely reported and watched time series are all seasonally adjusted. Most would also agree that the 6% average difference in seasonally unadjusted output between the fourth and first quarters could be eliminated by providing a modest wage subsidy in the first quarter and wage tax in the fourth to induce an intertemporal substitution of labor supplied, but that this should not be done.

What differentiates fluctuations resulting from seasonal factors from those arising as the result of shocks to the technology of production and exchange? The answer sometimes given is that the seasonal components are predictable, whereas shocks, by definition, are not. The implication of competitive theory under uncertainty, and therefore the implication of our theory, is that this argument is flawed. It is true that with anticipated events adjustment can occur prior as well as subsequent to the event although for a shock there can be no prior adjustment. This does not invalidate the first theorem of welfare economics, that, in the absence of externalities, competitive equilibria, including those of the dynamic stochastic variety, are Pareto optimal.[8] Consequently, in the absence of a public sector, the policy implication of our theory of fluctuations is that the cost of stabilizing the economy exceeds the benefits in the cost-benefit sense advocated by Phelps (1972). It also follows that the monetary authorities should behave as predictably as possible. This would not eliminate monetary shocks but would reduce them and result in the improved performance of the economy.

Once a public sector is introduced into a competitive model, one can no longer rely upon the first theorem of welfare economics to answer the desirability of stabilization policy question. Rather one must apply modern public finance and the theory of efficient taxation.[9] Assuming that sufficiently precise estimates of the parameters are available, our theory predicts that greater stability could be achieved by an appropriate cyclical manipulation of tax rates than if a noncyclical tax rate policy

8. A few other weak conditions are needed for this result. For example, if there is nonsatiation, convex preferences, and the individuals' consumption possibility sets are convex, the result follows (Debreu 1954, theorem 1).

9. We found Sandmo's 1976 survey a good introduction to the optimal taxation literature. Diamond and McFadden 1974, Diamond and Mirrlees 1971, and Harberger 1964 were also useful.

were pursued. To achieve the greater stability, the tax rates must be adjusted in response to shocks so that more labor is supplied in states in which employment would otherwise be below average and less in states in which it would be above. For example, temporary investment tax credits reduce the cost of future consumption in terms of current leisure inducing an increase in current labor supplied. Similarly a temporary wage tax affects the relative costs of current and future leisure resulting in intertemporal substitutions.

The issue then is whether the gains from manipulating tax rates cyclically to achieve greater stability exceed the costs. The answer to this question is no and follows from the well-known principle of public finance (Ramsey 1927), that the loss in consumer surplus per dollar collected from taxing a commodity is greater the more elastic is its demand. Capital goods produced in different periods that are close in time are close substitutes as are both market-produced and non-market-produced goods in adjacent periods. The elasticity of demand for a product with close substitutes is high. Thus varying tax rates over time to induce a particular state-contingent intertemporal reallocation of labor supplied is inconsistent with efficient taxation, at least to a first approximation. Cyclical variations in tax rates add to the burden of financing society's demands for public goods and income redistributions.

Summary

The principle for fiscal policy that emerges from this exercise in neoclassical public finance is that tax rates should not respond, at least not much, to aggregate economic fluctuations. These are just the principles laid down by Friedman (1948) thirty years ago. His conclusions, however, were based in large part upon ignorance of the timing and magnitude of the effects of various policy actions. With our analysis, these conclusions follow even if the structure of the economy is well understood and the consequences of alternative stabilization policy rules are econometrically predictable. We did not determine the rule with the best operating characteristics for a particular estimated structure, as Taylor (1979a) did. This was unnecessary because the conclusion follows from well-known principles of modern public finance.

The issue was addressed within a competitive equilibrium framework which requires maximizing behavior and market clearing. Part of the maximizing assumption is the efficient use of information or, equivalently, rational expectations. Equilibrium also requires that the set of markets assumed be sufficiently rich that it is not in the mutual interest of economic agents to organize additional markets. We argued that the persistence of deviations of output from trend can be explained within the equilibrium framework by requiring multiple periods to build new capital goods. Considerable persistence of the effects of monetary, fiscal, and technological shocks and momentum characterize the equilibrium behavior of our models, which incorporate this factor as part of the technology.

The implication of this equilibrium analysis is that the economy, like a single-commodity market, can be stabilized but like the commodity market, the costs of stabilization exceed the benefits. Cyclical variations in tax rates, whether they increase or decrease fluctuations, increase the burden of taxation.

Comment   Martin Feldstein

There are many things that I like about the Kydland and Prescott paper, particularly the authors' attempt to link modern public finance analysis with current macroeconomic theory. But I remain unconvinced by their discussion of the equilibrium business cycle and I do not think that they have presented a new case for restricting fluctuations in tax rates for either stabilization or revenue reasons.

Let me begin with the part I like best: the authors' use of a more general description of the role of fiscal effects than is typical in macroeconomic analyses. Instead of limiting their analysis of fiscal policy to variations in lump sum taxes or government spending, Kydland and Prescott recognize the importance of tax rules that change relative prices. In particular, I agree very strongly with their emphasis that the effect of inflation on real depreciation has been one of the most significant fiscal effects on the economy in the 1970s. Larry Summers and I recently estimated that the use of "original cost depreciation" for tax purposes without any adjustment for inflation caused taxable profits of U.S. corporations in 1977 to be overstated by $40 billion or 39% (Feldstein and Summers, 1978b). Because of the rise in the inflation rate during the past decade, the effective tax rate on real corporate profits rose from 54% in 1967 to 66% in 1977 despite a series of statutory changes designed to reduce the tax rate. Although I have analyzed some of the long-run implications of the depreciation effect in papers with Summers (Feldstein and Summers 1978a) and with Green and Sheshinski (1978), the Kydland and Prescott paper is the first that I know that emphasizes the way in which changes in the rate of inflation can cause cyclical instability.

I have only one small quarrel with their analysis of this issue. There is no doubt that the introduction of the investment tax credit in the 1960s and the effect of inflation on real depreciation in the 1970s would have major effects on the desired capital stock if the relevant discount rate remained unchanged, that is, if these changes in the effective tax rate on capital income were fully shifted. But this *conditional* statement is very different from asserting that these tax changes would actually increase the capital stock. If the supply of private saving is inelastic, the induced increases in the demand for industrial capital can be satisfied only at the expense of residential construction and government demand. The net effect of this substitution on employment is surely not unambiguous.

But this is a question about their analysis and not about the historical facts. Let us accept, as historically accurate, the following sequence of events described by the authors: (1) Accelerated depreciation in the 1960s and then the adverse effects of the original cost depreciation in the inflationary 1970s caused changes in the desired capital stock. (2) These changes in desired capital caused the actual capital stock to adjust with a distributed lag of investment. (3) This pattern of capital stock adjustment caused fluctuations in output and employment.

The key question is: *How should the change in employment be interpreted?* There are three quite different possibilities and each has different implications about the rest of the analysis.

Kydland and Prescott regard any change in employment as an equilibrium intertemporal substitution of leisure in the manner of the original Lucas and Rapping paper. An alternative interpretation is the Friedman-Phelps view, namely, that increases in nominal wages fooled workers into accepting jobs with a lower real wage than they otherwise would have accepted. Finally, there is the traditional Keynesian view that in the early 1960s there was a temporary disequilibrium—that is, short-run involuntary unemployment—and that the increase in aggregate demand permitted the unemployed to find jobs; according to this Keynesian view, the reverse process of creating disequilibrium unemployment occurred in the mid-1970s.

Although Kydland and Prescott present a consistent model interpreting the facts in the first framework, they provide no evidence or logic to make this first interpretation more plausible than either of the other two or than some combination of all three. While I believe in the intertemporal substitution of leisure in some circumstances (e.g., that social security induces earlier retirement and might cause more work during preretirement years), I doubt the relevance of intertemporal substitution to unemployment fluctuations. I certainly do not think it is the sole explanation. I remain to be convinced that there is any persuasive evidence, let alone the "ample evidence" to which Kydland and Prescott refer.

The authors' characterization of unemployment is important in another context. In the paper they raise a general methodological issue by asserting the applicability of public finance efficiency arguments to the analysis of stabilization policy. That position is correct only if all cyclical insta-bility in employment represents *equilibrium* intertemporal substitution of leisure. More generally, if there is a temporary disequilibrium (i.e., short-run involuntary unemployment) or if workers are temporarily "fooled" by changes in nominal magnitudes, the conditions required for the application of traditional welfare analysis are not satisfied. With dis-equilibrium unemployment, the observed prices are not market-clearing ones and certainly do not measure the marginal evaluations of the private agents. If workers are being "fooled," the observed prices may clear the market, but the workers' actual marginal rates of substitution between goods and leisure equal what they (falsely) believe to be the real wage rates rather than the observed real wage rates.

In practice, the authors do not try to apply the traditional welfare argument to stabilization policy. Instead, they use it to analyze the ap-propriate mix of fluctuations in debt and in taxes in response to exog-enously determined changes in government spending. The use of tra-ditional welfare economics in this context is quite appropriate since un-employment as such is irrelevant. But I find their argument for fluctua-tions in borrowing rather than in tax rates far from compelling. It rests on the assertion that current labor supply is very sensitive to small dif-ferences between the current real wage rate and the future real wage rate. It requires that individuals can distinguish permanent tax rate changes from temporary ones and can adjust their labor supply accord-ingly. Moreover, the analysis in the paper appears to assume a fixed capi-tal stock so that variation in debt only affects consumptions and not changes in capital or production. Let me emphasize that I do not disagree with the authors' conclusion about the appropriate fluctuations in debt and taxes. But I think a more complete analysis is required to make a convincing case.

Let me return now to the authors' key conclusion that "tax and in-vestment credit rates should not be varied in an effort to stabilize the economy." This conclusion follows directly from their view that all employment fluctuations represent equilibrium intertemporal substitution of leisure. If there are costs of adjustment, asymmetries of information, or other reasons why observed fluctuations in unemployment represent temporary disequilibrium, there is a potential role for good macroeco-nomic policy. The choice among fiscal and monetary instruments de-pends on issues of timing and of the mix of demands to be affected. The government's limited ability to forecast the future course of the economy and the effects of different stabilization policies is to me still the main reason for limiting policy activism.

Comment   Robert E. Hall

Given its very strong premises, the paper by Kydland and Prescott reaches a sharp conclusion—minimization of the deadweight loss of fiscal programs requires equalization of tax rates over the present and the future. When new information arrives, tax rates should move in tandem. Temporary fiscal moves are never planned, though they may happen unexpectedly. The paper is the application of a very general proposition about optimal planning when the present and future instruments enter the objective function symmetrically. Other applications can be made to consumption, where the rational consumer never plans a temporary adjustment of consumption, and to the dividend policy of the firm.

The provocative issue raised by this paper is the relevance of the general principle—that is, whether it is true that the deadweight loss of present and future fiscal moves are symmetrical on the margin. The case made for the application of the principle in the paper rests on the equilibrium interpretation of aggregate fluctuations—cyclical changes in employment represent movements along an aggregate supply function for labor. The premise of the paper is that the cyclical labor supply schedule reflects the true valuation of workers' time. That valuation is not very sensitive to the amount of work done, on the margin, because people have valuable alternative activities. A recession is just a spell when the financial reward for work is low and other activities become attractive. This contrasts strikingly with the Keynesian view that there is a strong externality operating in a recession: the marginal value of labor's time drops far below the marginal product of labor, and genuine involuntary unemployment results. Under the Keynesian view, the premise of the paper is quite wrong and something like a temporary investment subsidy to offset a recession makes good economic sense.

In its most carefully stated form, for example, in this paper, the equilibrium theory of business cycles interprets the observed combination of interest rates, current and expected future wages, and level of employment as a point on an intertemporal labor supply function. Employment will be low when the current reward to labor is low relative to its discounted future value. Kydland and Prescott continue the tradition of emphasizing fluctuations of the real wage as the most important ingredient in this calculation, though it has been pointed out by several authors that movements in interest rates could be the principal source of changes in the optimal intertemporal labor supply plan of the worker.

Testing of the equilibrium–labor supply hypothesis has been no better than rudimentary. Its proponents have cited some fragmentary evidence on the intertemporal substitutability of alternative uses of time. Its many critics have generally asserted that the hypothesis is too foolish to be taken seriously (for example, Robert Solow in his paper for this conference) or that it was refuted by simple evidence. It has often been said that the equilibrium theory predicts that quits should rise in a recession, so the theory must be wrong because quits actually fall.

My own view is that the equilibrium theory deserves a serious examination and that it is not self-evident that it is completely wrong or completely right. With respect to the long-standing and basic criticism that the theory makes all cyclical movements in labor supply "voluntary," one of the branches of modern theory of labor contracts suggest a possible answer—under labor contracts, workers cede to employers the right to determine the level of employment subject to prescribed rules about compensation. If the rules respect the value of the worker's time, then it could both be true that employers make unilateral employment decisions and that the observed movements are along the true labor supply function.

This line of argument only weakens one of the elements of the case against the equilibrium theory. The real task of the proponents of the theory is to show that the intertemporal substitutability is high enough to explain observed cycles. The evidence on this point is mixed. What we seem to have learned from the various negative income tax experiments, for example, is fairly weak substitution toward nonwork activities under temporary reductions of wages in the order of 50%. But contract theory may help explain the weakness of that response, since contracts have not been written to take account of the appropriate adjustment of employment in response to an experimental temporary tax. All I can say at this stage is that much more thought and work is needed.

Comment   John B. Taylor*

In their paper Kydland and Prescott present a novel technique for answering an old macroeconomic question: Can fiscal policy be used to stabilize the economy? The technique combines "equilibrium business cycle modelling" with modern tools of public finance and contrasts sharply with the conventional techniques—such as econometric model simulation—now commonly used to answer such questions. Although the technique confronts some difficult modelling and computational problems, it offers a promising alternative to the more traditional methods of quantitative policy evaluation.

The first stage of the Kydland-Prescott policy evaluation method is the development of an equilibrium business cycle model which displays the major empirical regularities of macroeconomic fluctuations. For example,

*A grant from the National Science Foundation is gratefully acknowledged.

they model *contemporaneous* correlations between the major aggregates by assuming limited information about aggregate disturbances in local markets. More difficult however, is modelling *serial* correlations which characterize business cycles. Kydland and Prescott summarize these intemporal correlations in terms of an estimated second-order stochastic difference equation in the linearly detrended log of real GNP (y_t):

(1) $$y_t = 1.4y_{t-1} - .5y_{t-2} + \epsilon_t.$$

This can be written equivalently as a distributed lag in the shock ϵ_t. That is,

(2) $$y_t = \sum_{i=0}^{\infty} \psi_i \epsilon_{t-i}$$

where $\psi_0 = 1$ and the ψ_i weights first increase before starting to decline toward the neighborhood of zero.[10] The primary explanation given by Kydland and Prescott for this "humped" pattern is the delay between actual expenditures and planned expenditures for many components of GNP. For example, investment expenditures are a distributed lag of investment plans, and empirically this lag is "humped"; hence output should also have a humped lag distribution similar to the observed ψ_i values in equation (2).

Although this type of investment behavior will indeed produce the desired correlation pattern, I feel it has two basic difficulties as a central mechanism for generating output persistence in this model. First, in order for such a mechanism to qualify as an essential propagator of business cycle fluctuations, the impulse variables (in this case investment plans) should be serially uncorrelated. If the impulse variables themselves are serially correlated, then another propagation mechanism is necessary to explain this persistence. In fact, investment plans do appear to be highly correlated serially. For example, capital appropriations and construction permits, which are rough proxies of expenditure plans, have high serial correlation properties. Moreover, this correlation is very similar to that of investment expenditures.[11] Since the expenditure–planning lag hypothesis does not explain these fluctuations, it is insufficient as a mechanism to generate business cycle movements without other sources of persistence.

A second difficulty is related to the "parameter variation" problem emphasized by Robert Lucas. As stated by Kydland and Prescott, avoid-

10. Many such empirical regularities are presented in Hodrick and Prescott 1978, where alternative detrending methods are also examined.

11. Many variables which are representative of expenditure plans, such as permit authorizations, are thought to be leading indicators of actual expenditures. As leading indicators, they tend to have serial correlation properties which are similar to expenditures, but are slightly out of phase.

ing policy-induced shifts in parameters is a major motivation for developing models like the one they propose here as an alternative to conventional econometric models. Yet, the expenditure–planning lag emphasized by Kydland and Prescott is not derived explicitly from a maximizing model and, hence, in principle is subject to such policy-induced shifts. Moreover, one might expect such shifts in the expenditure–planning lag mechanism to be important in practice. For example, construction of previously planned projects might be accelerated in anticipation of higher costs—perhaps induced by a policy change. If the effect of policy on this acceleration is not accounted for, then a wrong— and possibly destabilizing—policy might be used. While all existing econometric models are subject to this same problem, I emphasize it here because one of the main reasons for using these techniques is to avoid such problems.

A number of other explanations of the pattern of serial correlation summarized in (2) have been proposed by business cycle researchers. The flexible accelerator mechanism will generate such correlation for suitable parameter values, and attempts have been made to develop this mechanism in a simple rational expectations model (see Pashigian 1969). Another explanation comes from some of my own research on staggered contracts with rational expectations (see Taylor 1979a). Serial persistence patterns similar to (2) may be due to short-lived wage and price rigidities which cause purely random shocks to accumulate for a number of periods before their effect diminishes toward zero. A review of U.S. data suggests that contracts about one year in duration may be sufficient to generate business cycle persistence similar to what has been observed during the postwar period. One advantage of this alternative type of rational expectations model is that it also generates a persistence of inflation. In fact a good argument can be made that the persistence of inflation is at least as big a theoretical challenge to rational expectations theorists as the persistence of output or employment fluctuations: if policymakers form expectations rationally and the world behaves according to the market-clearing rational expectations model described by Kydland and Prescott, then there is no explanation for the inflation-supporting aggregate demand policies which we have observed during much of the postwar period. The inflation-output trade-offs evident in contract models provide at least a partial explanation.

With the exceptions noted above, Kydland and Prescott build their equilibrium business cycle model upon the assumption of utility maximization. That is, they posit a representative household utility function which depends on consumption, leisure, and government expenditures, and they assume that households maximize this utility function subject to budget constraints. An important and welcome feature of their policy analysis is the use of this same utility function to evaluate fiscal stabilization policy. No additional policy criterion function—such as a quadratic loss in output and inflation fluctuations—is needed for the analysis. Since the maximized value of the household utility functions depends on the parameters of government decision rules, the welfare effects of policy can be evaluated directly by examining the improvement or deterioration of individual utilities as policy changes.

In principle, such an approach is preferable to the more standard procedure of postulating a simple aggregate policy criterion which is only indirectly related to individual welfare. But the indirect approach has practical advantages. There are many reasons why macroeconomic policy should aim to reduce the size of output and price fluctuations—simply maintaining a stable and relatively certain environment for private decision making is one reason. Such reasons have not, however, been formally linked to a basic household utility function analysis. Apparently a fairly complex and complete model must be developed to formalize such a link. Until this development, a simple aggregate criterion may serve well as a first approximation.[12]

Using this model and this procedure for evaluating policy, Kydland and Prescott conclude their analysis by examining whether taxes or borrowing should be used to finance temporary government expenditures. They find the model indicates that it is better to finance temporary expenditures (such as wars) by bond finance, leaving more lasting expenditures to tax finance. Intuitively, this result is due to the assumption that labor supply and the demand for durables are very elastic in the short run, but not in the long run. If so, then the Ramsey inverse elasticity rule—lower taxes on high elasticity items—suggests the resulting debt finance mix. It is reassuring that the formal techniques give answers which correspond to this intuitive finding.

This result, which is the main conclusion of the policy analysis, certainly has important implications for fiscal stabilization policy. For example, it gives a rationale for stability of tax rates and hence for including the major tax instruments of fiscal policy in aggregate criterion functions—policy variables are usually included for pure computational reasons and to prevent the embarrassment of instrument instability. It is not clear, however, why this result is particularly relevant to the central question of the paper. An analysis of other fiscal policy issues, such as the usefulness of the automatic stabilizers, might have been more helpful. Nevertheless, developing and applying an equilibrium business cycle model to a central problem of public finance represents an important and unique contribution to the problem of policy evaluation in a rational expectations setting.

12. An example of the potential empirical advantages of such a criterion is given in a rational expectations setting by Taylor (1979).

General Discussion

In response to the comment by Taylor that the lag weights in his equation (2) would themselves change with policy rules, Prescott suggested that the weights were dependent on technology and would thus be policy invariant. He also remarked that procyclical movement of the real wage was needed for persistence effects, even though real wage movements need not be large.

On the persistence issue raised by Taylor, Robert Barro commented that it was difficult to reconcile the behavior of prices with that of real output and unemployment. Disequilibrium or contracting models imply a pattern of price persistence that matches the pattern of output and unemployment persistence.

Edmund Phelps suggested that the terms "equilibrium" and "disequilibrium" were being used in confusing ways. Markets might well clear even with disequilibrium; he defined equilibrium as an evolution of events in which expectations were borne out—and this did not require or imply that demand equaled supply in every market.

Robert Hall preferred a definition of equilibrium as a situation where people think they have no further opportunity to make themselves better off, and where the basic efficiency conditions are met.

Phelps also voiced concern about the time inconsistency of optimal policy. Time inconsistency implies that if generation "zero" conducts policy based on a utilitarian or other social welfare function, then subsequent generations would find it desirable to deviate from the policy that had previously been optimal. He did not see why the use of rules would solve this problem—since the later generations would still be better off if they broke the rules.

Charles Nelson noted that stability required the sum of the coefficients in the Kydland-Prescott autoregressive equation for output to be less than unity. If the stochastic process for output were unstable, parameter estimates might still tend to indicate stationarity even though it did not obtain; he was thus worried about how close the Kydland-Prescott equation was to instability. William Poole did not see any persuasive reason for technological change and relative price shifts to occur over time in such a way that per capita income should return to trend.

Alan Blinder commented on Hall's remarks on testing the degree of intertemporal substitution of leisure that it might be useful to examine the evidence from temporary tax cuts, such as that of 1968. Robert Solow pointed out that the intertemporal substitution of leisure mechanism implied that the demand for leisure complements, such as ski equipment, color TV sets, should be countercyclical. This could easily be tested.

Robert Weintraub picked up on the argument that high real interest rates would induce an increase in the labor supply in the current period and suggested that people should answer unemployment surveys by saying "I'm waiting for real interest rates to rise." He was similarly bemused by the fact that Barro's paper explained the behavior of prices using the nominal interest rate: now he could agree with those who blamed inflation on high interest rates.

Frank Morris commented that the policy prescription of Kydland and Prescott had been followed by Lyndon Johnson, who refused to change tax rates during the Vietnam intervention: it was good to know that policy had then been optimal.

References

Barro, R. J. 1977. "Unanticipated Money Growth and Unemployment in the United States." *American Economic Review* 67:101–15.

―――. 1978. "Unanticipated Money, Output, and the Price Level in the United States." *Journal of Political Economy* 86:549–80.

Black, F. 1978. "General Equilibrium and Business Cycles." Sloan School of Management, MIT.

Brock, W. A. 1978. "Asset Prices in a Production Economy." Report of the Center for Mathematical Studies in Business and Economics, University of Chicago.

Calvo, A. G. 1978. "On the Time Consistency of Optimal Policy in a Monetary Economy." *Econometrica* 46:1411–28.

Debreu, G. 1954. "Valuation Equilibrium and Pareto Optimality." *Proceedings of the National Academy of Science* 40:588–92.

Diamond, P. A., and McFadden, D. L. 1974. "Some Uses of the Expenditure Function in Public Finance." *Journal of Public Economics* 3:3–21.

Diamond, P. A., and Mirrlees, J. A. 1971. "Optimal Taxation and Public Production I, II." *American Economic Review* 61:8–27, 261–78.

Feldstein, M. 1974. "Social Security, Induced Retirement, and Aggregate Capital Accumulation." *Journal of Political Economy* 82:1325–39.

Feldstein, M.; Green, J.; and Sheshinski, E. 1978. "Inflation and Taxes in a Growing Economy with Debt and Equity Finance." *Journal of Political Economy* 86, pt. 2, pp. S53–S70.

Feldstein, M., and Summers, L. 1978a. "Inflation, Tax Rules, and the Long-Term Interest Rate." *Brookings Papers on Economic Activity* 1:61–109.

―――. 1978b. "Inflation and the Taxation of Capital Income in the Corporate Sector." National Bureau of Economic Research Working Paper no. 312. *National Tax Journal*, forthcoming.

Friedman, M. 1948. "A Monetary and Fiscal Framework for Economic Stability." *American Economic Review* 38:245–64.

Ghez, G. R., and Becker, G. S. 1975. *The Allocation of Time and Goods over the Life Cycle.* New York: National Bureau of Economic Research.

Hall, R. E. 1977. "Investment, Interest Rates, and the Effects of Stabilization Policies." *Brookings Papers on Economic Activity* 0:61–101.

Harberger, A. 1964. "Measurement of Waste." *American Economic Review* 54:58–76.

Hodrick, R. J., and Prescott, E. C. 1978. "Post-War U.S. Business Cycles: A Descriptive Empirical Investigation." Paper presented at the Econometric Society Meetings, Chicago.

Jorgenson, D. W. 1963. "Capital Theory and Investment Behavior." *American Economic Review* 53:247–59.

————. 1971. "Econometric Studies of Investment Behavior: A Survey." *Journal of Economic Literature* 9:1111–47.

Kydland, F., and Prescott, E. C. 1977. "Rules rather than Discretion: The Inconsistency of Optimal Plans." *Journal of Political Economy* 85:473–92.

————. 1978a. "Rational Expectations, Dynamic Optimal Taxation, and the Inapplicability of Optimal Control." Carnegie-Mellon University Working Paper.

————. 1978b. "Persistence of Unemployment in Equilibrium." Carnegie-Mellon University Working Paper.

Lucas, R. E. 1972. "Expectations and the Neutrality of Money." *Journal of Economic Theory* 4:103–24.

————. 1975. "An Equilibrium Model of the Business Cycle." *Journal of Political Economy* 83:1113–44.

————. 1976. "Econometric Policy Evaluation: A Critique." In *The Phillips Curve and Labor Markets,* edited by K. Brunner and A. H. Meltzer, pp. 19–46. Carnegie-Rochester Conference Series no. 1. New York: North-Holland.

Lucas, R. E., and Rapping, L. A. 1969. "Real Wages, Employment, and Inflation." *Journal of Political Economy* 77:721–54.

Mayer, T. 1960. "Plant and Equipment Lead Times." *Journal of Business* 33:127–32.

Modigliani, F. 1977. "The Monetarist Controversy, or Should We Forsake Stabilization Policies?" *American Economic Review* 67:1–19.

Pashigian, P. 1969. "Growth and Oscillations of Income When Expectations Are Consistent." Unpublished.

Phelps, E. S. 1972. *Policy and Unemployment Theory: The Cost-Benefit Approach to Monetary Planning.* London: Macmillan & Co.

Prescott, E. C., and Mehra, R. 1978. "Recursive Competitive Equilibrium: The Case of Homogeneous Households." Columbia Graduate School of Business Working Paper.

Ramsey, F. P. 1927. "A Contribution to the Theory of Taxation." *Economic Journal* 37:47–61.

Reder, M. 1962. "Wage Differentials: Theory and Measurement." In *Aspects of Labor Economics*. Princeton, N.J.: Princeton University Press and National Bureau of Economic Research.

Sandmo, A. 1976. "Optimal Taxation: An Introduction to the Literature." *Journal of Public Economics* 6:37–54.

Sargent, T. J. 1977. "Aspects of the New Classical Macroeconomics." Working Paper. Minneapolis: Federal Reserve Bank of Minneapolis.

Sims, C. A. 1979. "Macroeconomics and Reality." *Econometrica*, forthcoming.

Taylor, J. B. 1979a. "Aggregate Dynamics and Staggered Contracts." *American Economic Review* 69:108–13.

———. 1979b. "Estimation and Control of a Macroeconomic Model with Rational Expectations." *Econometrica* 47:1267–86.

United States Department of Commerce, Bureau of Census. 1976. *Statistical Abstract of the United States*. Washington, D.C.: U.S. Government Printing Office.

6   Rules, Discretion, and the Role of the Economic Advisor

Robert E. Lucas, Jr.

Introduction

I take the purpose of this session to be to elicit views on economic policy from economists of different points of view.[1] The particular title of the session, "Macroeconomic Policy, 1974/75: What Should Have Been Done?" does not seem to me useful for this purpose, as I will explain below, so I will adopt a somewhat different approach. I will begin by stating a variation on the policy proposals advanced by Milton Friedman in "A Monetary and Fiscal Framework for Economic Stability" (1948) and *A Program for Monetary Stability* (1959). After some speculations on why the Friedman program has had so limited an impact,[2] I will identify and discuss some recent developments suggesting that its acceptance and influence may be greater in the near future. The paper concludes with an assessment of the case for the Friedman program as it stands today, a brief discussion of problems of transition, and some concluding remarks.

In centering the discussion around a proposal Friedman formulated, in its essentials, thirty years ago, I run an admitted risk of locking myself and others into positions we may have taken up years ago and not rethought seriously since. The alternative strategy of repackaging this proposal in more current language is one I find distasteful, and, in any case, it

The revision has benefitted from the suggestions of Stanley Fischer, Milton Friedman, and Robert Weintraub.

1. EDITOR'S NOTE: Comments and discussion for chaps. 6 and 7 appear in chap. 7.

2. Of course, Friedman's work in general has had an enormous impact on many dimensions. I am here referring only to his recommendation that monetary and fiscal policy be conducted according to fixed rules.

would quickly be found out. I will begin, then, on familiar ground and, for the most part, remain there.

A set of aggregative policies which would I believe, lead, and have led, to satisfactory general economic performance are, compactly described:

1. A 4% annual rate of growth of M1, maintained as closely as possible on a quarter-to-quarter basis
2. A pattern of real government expenditures and transfer payments, varying secularly but not in response to cyclical changes in economic activity
3. A pattern of tax rates, also varying secularly but not in response to cyclical changes in economic activity, set to balance the federal budget *on average*
4. A clearly announced policy that wage and price agreements privately arrived at will not trigger governmental reactions of any kind (aside from standard antitrust policies and the general policy of government preference for low over high bids)

The first three of these policy rules are taken directly from Friedman's writings.[3] The fourth is simply a recognition of the fact that, since the time Friedman's proposals were originally formulated, intervention in the details of private price and wage negotiations has ceased to be viewed as an emergency measure so that a position on the generally accepted aspects of aggregative policy cannot omit mention of this fact.

In restating these recommendations, I have tried to follow Friedman in being concrete and operational concerning exactly which policies are being advocated. Under the principle that *natura non facit saltum*, these particular policies must have neighbors that would have nearly the same consequences, and one would certainly like to have an analytical framework within which one could assess the consequences of variations on them. The provision of such a framework is far beyond the scope of the present paper. I will proceed, instead, in an entirely different direction: first by recalling some of the main features of the intellectual environment, both within and without our profession, into which Friedman's framework was introduced and then by tracing some of the changes since in this environment.

The Employment Act of 1946

The dominant events influencing the minds of the intended readers of Friedman's "Framework" were the Great Depression of the 1930s and

---

3. Rules 2 and 3 are paraphrases of those in Friedman 1948 (1953, pp. 136–37). Rule 1 is from Friedman 1959, pp. 87–92, there presented as a desirable but second-best alternative to the requirement of 100% reserve banking advocated in Friedman 1948.

the "prosperity" (as measured by unemployment rates) of the Second World War. It is difficult to imagine a sequence of events that could more forcefully illustrate both the costs of high unemployment and the ability of government policy to affect unemployment. In all capitalist countries, this "lesson" had profound influences on policy. In the United States, it was embodied in the Employment Act of 1946.

To some contemporaries, the Employment Act was "a weak and meaningless wraith" (Bailey 1950, p. 253), and in some respects it is easy to see why. The act granted the executive no powers which had not been fully assumed during the New Deal period preceding, nor did it specify either the economic targets to be achieved or the policy tools to be utilized. The act did, however, require the executive in very explicit terms to forecast the state of the economy in the coming year and to prescribe policies designed to alter this state in a desirable direction. Moreover, it was clear in specifying exactly where the expertise required to carry out this task could be found: The Council of Economic Advisors was established by the act as the channel by which this expertise could be brought to bear on practical policy.

It would be a difficult and subtle task to trace the effects of the Employment Act on the policy performance of the U.S. government in the postwar years. There is nothing subtle, however, in the effects of the act (or of the events immediately preceding it) on the practice of monetary economics in the postwar period. Renamed *macroeconomics*, this subdiscipline *defined* itself to be that body of expertise the existence of which was presupposed in the Employment Act, and its practitioners devoted themselves to the development and refinement of forecasting and policy evaluation methods which promised to be of use in the annual diagnosis-prescription exercise called for by the act.

In many respects, the assumption of this rather specific, applied role had a very healthy effect on monetary economics. The set of common, agreed-upon substantive objectives helped to unify the field and lent it a quantitative, operational character in sharp contrast with the literary, doctrinal emphasis of so much prewar monetary and business cycle theory. A great number of talented scientists found this new character congenial.

The highly productive, collective effort to make the Employment Act "work" was just getting underway when Friedman's "Framework" was published in 1948. This was a proposal "concerned . . . with structural reform [which] should not be urged on the public unless and until it has withstood the test of professional criticism" (Friedman 1948 [1953, p. 156]). Perhaps this description may be taken as a comment on the haste with which Keynesian theory, at that time regarded as difficult and controversial, understood by only a handful of American economists, had been embodied in federal legislation. In any case, it is an accurate description of the proposals which are, implicitly, a prediction that the diagnosis and prescription process called for in the Employment Act *cannot* be made to work, given the level of scientific understanding of monetary dynamics at the time. The proposals are offered rather as a *compromise*, promising economic performance superior to that which had been observed historically, yet promising less than the performance goals which are implicit, if vague, in the Employment Act. They constituted, Friedman hoped, "a minimum program for which economists of the less extreme shades of opinion can make common cause" (Friedman 1948 [1953, p. 135]).

In retrospect, it is clear that Friedman underestimated by far the extent to which his colleagues were united in the belief that the Employment Act, together with the Federal Reserve Act as supplemented by changes in the 1930s, provided a workable policymaking apparatus. Post–World War II macroeconomics has shown little interest in reforms of the institutional framework within which economic policy is conducted, and virtually no concern with formulating legislative guidelines or limits on monetary, fiscal, and now, "incomes," policy. The professional forum for debating alternative monetary institutions to which Friedman addressed his proposals did not analyze them, consider them, reject them in favor of others. It simply passed out of existence. Instead, within the existing institutional framework, the role of the economic expert as day-to-day manager expanded rapidly, and the role of the academic macroeconomist became that of equipping these experts with ideas, principles, formulas which gave, or appeared to give, operational guidance on the tasks with which these economic managers happened to be faced.

From the perspective of this new role for aggregative economics, the difficulty with the Friedman proposals was not so much that they were demonstrably dominated by others, but that they were irrelevant. They speak to the question: Under what rules of the game, remaining predictably in force over long periods, can we expect satisfactory economic performance? The economic manager responsible for advising on, say, the size of the coming fiscal year deficit is simply uninterested in this question: it seems to him merely an academic exercise, unrelated to the tasks he has taken it upon himself to perform.

On one level, this reaction to the Friedman proposals is understandable. General economic performance in the twenty years following the passage of the Employment Act was, by any historical standard, highly successful. It is not surprising, then, that there was little general discussion of institutional change during this period and that this lack of interest was reflected in economists' choice of research problems. Yet the history of monetary and fiscal institutions, in the United States and elsewhere, is one of repeated failure, and failure at very high social cost. One is not surprised that a large fraction of the profession found it worthwhile to attempt to provide the expertise presupposed by the existing institutions. Similarly, it should surprise no one that others continued to question the viability of these institutions and focused their work on the design of alternative frameworks which might ultimately replace them.

Some Signs of Change

Events of the current decade have brought about important changes in both public and professional confidence that economic expertise can deliver satisfactory performance within the framework provided by the Employment and Federal Reserve acts. They also provide examples of mechanisms, quite outside those established by this legislation, by which public opinion may be brought to bear on economic policy. In this section, I will briefly review a few of these, beginning with what is surely the most important: the experience of stagflation.

In a first course in econometrics, students discover upward-sloping demand curves and production functions which impute negative productivity to capital. Students find these shocking experiences for which nothing in their theory courses has prepared them. This is a standard developmental crisis, like discovering that one's parents are not perfect, and experience shows that if it occurs in a reasonably protected and supportive environment, it can be survived and resolved with no lasting harm done.

There is a tendency on the part of many economists involved with Keynesian macroeconometric models to view the inflation and unemployment rate forecast errors of the 1970s in much the same terms. That is, the error itself is not denied (this is hardly a possibility) but is interpreted as indicating nothing deeper than a neglect in controlling for some other factors which, when properly taken into account, reveal the original basic structure to be sound. Thus we show our econometrics students that by controlling for income and other variables and by reducing contamination from supply side effects, the law of demand is revealed as clearly in the data as it is in the theory chapters of their textbooks.

I have argued elsewhere, most recently and comprehensively in collaboration with Thomas Sargent (Lucas 1975, Lucas and Sargent 1978), that these two cases are not at all analogous scientifically and that the misforecast of the stagflation period is in fact a symptom of much deeper problems. But a second, even clearer, difference in these two cases involves the context in which the error occurred. The stagflation error did not occur in the privacy of the seminar room, a puzzle of interest to professionals only. It occurred *after* the idea of a stable inflation-unemployment trade-off had become accepted by the public generally as *the* central construct in discussing macroeconomic policy, and *after* wide public acceptance of the idea that movements along the Phillips curve were technically within the control of economic managers. Even if it were true (and I believe it is not) that the sources of this error are easily correctible and unlikely to be repeated, an enormous and far-reaching change has already taken place in the political climate in which economic issues are discussed.

Two early symptoms of this change are Arthur Laffer's influential "Laffer curve" and Arthur Okun's proposal for controlling inflation by a complex system of taxes and subsidies on individual producers. Though both can be supported by theory of sorts, provided one uses the term "theory" with sufficient looseness, neither follows in any way from any widely accepted theoretical framework, neither has received serious analysis by either proponents or critics, neither was even *mentioned* in the academic literature prior to the last year or so.

This is the legacy of stagflation: a general loss of confidence, whether scientifically warranted or not, in the formerly accepted framework guiding discretionary economic management. Since the demand for discretionary policies remains strong, we are seeing the proliferation of new "solutions" to "short-run" policy problems, defended by the promise of particular results but without basis in either theory or historical experience. Given the entry costs into economic advising of this sort, is there any real doubt what the future holds if economists continue to view themselves in a day-to-day management role?

The experience of stagflation has, then, brought about important changes in the nature of the postwar dialogue by means of which policy-oriented economists attempt to advance their ideas and to satisfy the immediate needs of economic managers. Recently, there have been a number of important developments occurring outside the now-traditional dialogue among experts and economic managers, the most striking of which has been the passage of California's Proposition 13, limiting property taxes. Similar measures are under consideration in other states and there are analogous attempts underway to influence the federal budget at the constitutional level.

The main impetus for this "tax revolt" is surely dissatisfaction over the general level of taxes and government spending, and not over the nature of stabilization policy. Yet there is a clear and instructive connection at the political level. In policies of either type, it is evidently impossible for large numbers of people to form opinions and exercise influence at anything like the level of detail at which legislators and economic managers and their advisors carry on their discussion. In contrast, it is clearly possible for people to impose limits on these technical discussions, to *bound* levels and rates of change of economic aggregates. Public opinion generally can do little to *guide* the exercise of discretionary economic authority, but it has enormous potential to limit its scope.

To this point I have stressed developments external to the economics profession, as opposed to internal, scientific developments, as influences on the way economists and noneconomists view the possibilities open to us for influencing economic policy. This choice of emphasis reflects the opinion that public opinion generally (or what used to be called "political feasibility") was far more important than were scientific considerations in influencing professional reaction to Friedman's "Framework," and that this situation is not at all unusual. (This observation is not intended as a lament: there is little to be said for isolating economics from general contemporary social thought, and the consequences of trying to do so tend to lead to reliance on sterile aesthetic criteria in guiding theoretical work.)

Nevertheless, research based on the idea of *rational expectations* has played a role in buttressing the case for thinking about policy, as Friedman argued we should, as a problem in selecting stable, predictable policy *rules*. The main argument turns out to be a positive (as opposed to normative) one: our ability as economists to predict the responses of agents rests, in situations where expectations about the future matter, on our understanding of the stochastic environment agents believe themselves to be operating in. In practice, this limits the class of policies the consequences of which we can hope to assess in advance to policies generated by fixed, well understood, relatively permanent rules (or functions relating policy actions taken to the state of the economy).

I have developed the reasoning underlying this point elsewhere (Lucas 1975). (Indeed, it follows from modern control-theoretic views of policy evaluation almost independently of one's views on expectations formation.) I have been impressed both with how noncontroversial it seems to be at a general level and with how widely ignored it continues to be at what some view as a "practical" level. One could ask for no better illustration of this than the question motivating this session: "Macroeconomic Policy, 1974/75: What Should Have Been Done?" The question presupposes one of two possible situations. The first is that households and firms in 1974/75 were describable by a fixed set of decision rules, so that given any hypothetical selection of 1974/75 policies, one could simply read private-sector responses off these fixed curves to determine the response of the economy as a whole. The second situation under which this question is meaningful imagines firms and households attempting to solve maximum problems involving not only current policy actions but expected, future actions as well. The economist evaluating 1974/75 policy is in this case required to understand what these expectations about the future were, and how they would have been influenced by policy actions taken in 1974/75.

Does anyone seriously argue that either of these two situations prevails in fact? If so, on what scientific ground? If not, then why are we discussing this spuriously practical question at all?

This seems to me by far the most fundamental sense in which recent work on expectations reinforces the viewpoint toward policy which Friedman espoused in his 1948 paper. It emphasizes the fact that analysis of policy which utilizes economics in a scientific way *necessarily* involves choice among alternative stable, predictable policy rules, infrequently changed and then only after extensive professional and general discussion, minimizing (though of course never entirely eliminating) the role of discretionary economic management.

Though an agreement to focus on alternative policy *rules* would, in my view, be the major step toward restoring some degree of rationality to aggregative policy discussions, it does not necessarily follow that the particular set of rules advocated by Friedman would dominate others. On the one hand, several researchers have developed particular examples in which a 4% monetary growth rule is not dominated by monetary policies which react to the state of the economy (Sargent and Wallace 1975, Barro 1976, Lucas 1972). Moreover, Sargent (1976) has shown that one can find models of this class which account very well for the behavior of postwar, U.S. time series. On the other hand, John Taylor (1979) has developed an empirically implemented example in which monetary policies which react to the state of the system dominate (in a particular sense) a fixed monetary growth rule, though the latter is also shown, in this context, to dominate actual postwar policies. It seems clear at this point that the choice among alternative sets of policy rules will necessarily depend on the answer to difficult substantive questions involving the sources of business cycles and the nature of business cycle dynamics. Though there seems good reason to expect that the principle of rational expectations will prove to be a powerful tool in attacking these questions, it is clearly not sufficient in itself to dictate the nature of desirable countercyclical policies.

The Case for the Friedman Program

I began this paper with a brief summary of a variant of Milton Friedman's well-known program for stabilization policy, and then advanced some conjectures of a sociological nature about why professional discussion of this program has been so unsatisfactory in the past and some reasons for believing that the terms of the discussion may now be shifting toward those which Friedman presupposed in his 1948 paper. Yet beyond an unelaborated endorsement of this program, I have devoted no space to its defense or to an assessment of its likely consequences, if adopted.

To an extent which, until a recent rereading, I had forgotten, this absence of a clear defense and assessment also characterizes Friedman's "Framework." There, in outlining his strategy, Friedman says that "I deliberately gave primary consideration to long term objectives. That is, I tried to design a framework that would be appropriate for a world in which cyclical movements other than those introduced by 'bad' monetary and fiscal arrangements, were of no consequence. I then examined the resulting proposal to see how it would behave in respect to cyclical fluctuations. It behaves *surprisingly* well . . ." (Friedman 1948 [1953, p. 133]; italics mine). How well is this? "The proposal may not succeed in reducing cyclical fluctuations to tolerable proportions. . . . I do not see how it is possible to know now whether this is the case" (Friedman 1948 [1953, p. 156]).

The strategy, then, was to design a workable stabilization policy not dependent in any way on detailed knowledge of business cycle dynamics. The program would (I think on this there is no serious professional disagreement) *fully* protect the economy against sustained inflation. It would *fully* insure against the kind of monetary collapse which was so important a factor in the early stages of the Great Depression of the 1930s. It would entirely eliminate erratic monetary and fiscal shocks as independent sources of instability. Surely these are modest claims when compared with what can be accomplished via the application of optimal control to purely hypothetical economies which provide a *complete* description of business cycle dynamics. Yet as compared with actual performance in both the distant and recent past, their appeal is evident.

In my view, recent research has added little to strengthen Friedman's case, except in what might be called a negative way. Friedman's case was built largely on the presumption of *ignorance* of the nature of business cycles. Many of us confused the methodological advances in economic dynamics that took place in the 1950s and 1960s with the substantive narrowing of this ignorance and consequently with the increasing feasibility of sophisticated, reactive countercyclical policy. We have learned, I believe, that the list of economic propositions sufficiently well grounded in theory and evidence to be useful in formulating aggregate policy is no longer now than it was in 1948. This situation is discouraging and also, I think, improvable, but in the meantime we should be grateful that, in the face of our ignorance, we can still do "surprisingly well."

The Problem of Transition

From the point of view of those involved in economic management, the position that policy should be dictated by a set of fixed rules seems at best a partial response to the question: What should be done, now? To one with some responsibility for monetary policy in 1974, say, it is not very helpful to observe that monetary growth "should have" proceeded at a constant 4% rate for the 25 years preceding. Moreover, even if a move toward a policy of fixed rules were desired, it could be done in innumerable ways, presumably with different consequences, and a criterion based on long-run average performance offers no help in choosing among them. What advice, then, do advocates of rules have to offer with respect to the policy decisions before us *right now*?

This question does have a practical, men-of-affairs ring to it, but to my ears, this ring is entirely false. It is a king-for-a-day question which has no real-world counterpart in the decision problems actually faced by economic advisors. In the current system of discretionary economic management, no one or no small group has the job of deciding what to do right now and into the middle distance with respect to the main aggregative decision variables. None of these managers is in a position to influence the economy in any significant way toward a regime of fixed, nonreactive policy rules. They are simply reacting, sometimes well, sometimes badly, to current difficulties, with no more capability of affecting policy five years hence than of affecting what happened five years before.

Economists who pose this "What is to be done, today?" question as though it were somehow the acid test of economic competence are culture-bound (or institution-bound) to an extent they are probably not aware of. They are accepting as *given* the entirely unproved hypothesis that the fine-tuning exercise called for by the Employment Act is a desirable and feasible one. In criticizing Friedman's 1948 proposal from this point of view, they are simply missing its main point. It is not a recipe for making the Employment Act "work" but rather a prediction that it *cannot* be made to work, and an outline of an alternative set of policy arrangements.

If one does try to think in a politically serious way about possible scenarios leading to a fixed-rule regime, one is led to assign the primary roles to actors *outside* the executive–central bank system of economic management. An encouraging example is provided by the House Concurrent Resolution 133, requiring that the Federal Reserve Board announce monetary growth targets in advance and account for deviations afterward.[4] One can imagine this resolution hardening into legally binding

---

4. The substance of this resolution became an amendment to the Federal Reserve Act in 1977. See Weintraub 1978.

limits on monetary growth rates. A second example is politically less advanced: movements for constitutional limits on the federal budget deficit.[5]

In cases such as these, existing economic managers will not program a transition in any formal way, though they could certainly help to minimize disruption. But the inherent gradualism of the legislative and constitutional processes will mean that any actual move toward fixed rules will necessarily occur with ample advance warning and a great deal of prior adjustment on the part of both government and the private sector. Analytical elegance will clearly not be one of the virtues of such a transition, but I see no reason to expect large economic disruption, at least by the sorry standards of the past decade, to be an inevitable or even a likely consequence.

Concluding Remarks

As an advice-giving profession we are in way over our heads. The Employment Act of 1946 placed heavy demands on the ability of economists to guide executive authority granted very broad powers. In the early postwar years, and even through the sixties, it appeared that the framework provided by the Keynesian theory of income determination was, intelligently applied, capable of meeting these demands. As confidence has ebbed in our ability to use general monetary and fiscal policy to carry out the aims of the Employment Act, professionals and nonprofessionals alike have turned to a wide variety of complex, selective interventions in individual markets. Even to begin to assess the likely consequences of these policies in anything like a scientific way is clearly well beyond the current limits of our discipline.

One response to this situation is to attempt to deal with this ever broadening range of management questions, working and hoping for advances sufficiently dramatic to enable us to regain the intellectual control we thought we had in the sixties. If, as I believe to be the case, this will require scientific improvements of a fundamental or basic nature, then this response is not likely to succeed. Basic research, to be successful, requires some degree of control over the questions to be asked and the results that can be delivered. Though stimulated by practical demands, it is rarely carried out by those in an active managerial role, even at one remove.

An alternative response is to attempt to make clear to our fellow citizens the questions that currently available expertise can hope to answer

---

5. For a proposed amendment to this effect, together with an economic and political analysis, see Buchanan and Wagner 1977.

successfully, to base policy recommendations on the well-understood and empirically substantiated propositions of monetary economics, discouragingly modest as these may be, and to make it as clear as possible that the main task of monetary and fiscal policy is to provide a stable, predictable environment for the private sector of the economy.

References

Bailey, S. K. 1950. *Congress Makes a Law*. New York: Columbia University Press.

Barro, R. J. 1976. "Rational Expectations and the Role of Monetary Policy." *Journal of Monetary Economics* 2:1–32.

Buchanan, J. M., and Wagner, R. E. 1977. *Democracy in Deficit*. New York: Academic Press.

Friedman, M. 1948. "A Monetary and Fiscal Framework for Economic Stability." *American Economic Review* 38:245–64. Reprinted in *Essays in Positive Economics*. Chicago: University of Chicago Press, 1953.

———. 1959. *A Program for Monetary Stability*. New York: Fordham University Press.

Lucas, R. E., Jr. 1972. "Expectations and the Neutrality of Money." *Journal of Economic Theory* 4:103–24.

———. 1975. "Econometric Policy Evaluation: A Critique." In *The Phillips Curve and Labor Markets*, edited by K. Brunner and A. H. Meltzer, pp. 19–46. Carnegie-Rochester Conference Series no. 1. New York: North-Holland.

Lucas, R. E., Jr., and Sargent, T. J. 1978. "After Keynesian Macroeconomics." In *After the Phillips Curve: Persistence of High Inflation and High Unemployment*, pp. 49–72. Conference Series no. 19. Boston: Federal Reserve Bank of Boston.

Sargent, T. J. 1976. "A Classical Macroeconomic Model for the United States." *Journal of Political Economy* 84:207–54.

Sargent, T. J., and Wallace, N. 1975. " 'Rational' Expectations, the Optimal Monetary Instrument, and the Optimal Money Supply Rule." *Journal of Political Economy* 83:241–54.

Taylor, J. B. 1979. "Estimation and Control of a Macroeconomic Model with Rational Expectations." Econometrica, forthcoming.

Weintraub, R. E. 1978. "Congressional Supervision of Monetary Policy." *Journal of Monetary Economics* 4:341–62.

7 On Activist Monetary Policy with Rational Expectations

Stanley Fischer

This paper discusses the potential effectiveness and desirability of activist monetary policy[1] and also rules versus discretion. Recent academic discussions of the role of monetary policy have been heavily influenced by the rational expectations approach to macroeconomics: it has been argued that, from the viewpoint of the behavior of output, any monetary policy rule strictly adhered to is as good as any other (e.g., Sargent and Wallace 1975, Barro 1976). This theoretical viewpoint receives support from empirical work by, among others, Sargent (1976a) and Barro (1977a, 1978), which appears to show that only unanticipated changes in the money stock affect output.

This paper accepts both rational expectations, as a theory of expectations, and the view that "unanticipated" changes in the money stock have a greater impact on real output than anticipated changes in the money stock. It argues nonetheless that systematic countercyclical monetary policy can affect the behavior of output and that activist monetary policy should be used for that purpose.

The argument starts by asking why economic agents have not made contingent arrangements—for example, wage rates indexed to the money stock or very short contracts—that would insulate them from the effects of unanticipated changes in the money stock. The answer is that such contingent arrangements are costly; the private sector is therefore willing

I am grateful to David Modest for research assistance and to Olivier Blanchard, Rudiger Dornbusch, Jacob Frenkel, Robert Gordon, Robert Hall, Michael Rothschild, Frank Schiff, and members of the M.I.T. Money Workshop for comments. Research support was provided by the National Science Foundation.

1. While I concentrate on the same issue as Franco Modigliani in his 1977 AEA Presidential Address, the approach will be seen to differ from his.

to bear the costs imposed on it by the output deviations resulting from unanticipated money changes.

The potential role for monetary policy is created by those same costs of insulating the private sector from disturbances. The case for active monetary policy is that it is more efficient for the Fed to offset aggregate disturbances than it is for the private sector to do so. The efficient division of labor between the private and public sectors leaves it to macroeconomic management to deal with aggregate disturbances.

The perspective of this paper is one that views the private and public sectors as potentially cooperating in responding to economic disturbances; it contrasts with the view associated with rational expectations theorists that tends to regard monetary policy as working mainly through deception. Once the cooperative view of policy is adopted, the relevant questions about the desirability of activist monetary policy become those familiar from Milton Friedman's (1960) argument for a constant growth rate rule: they concern the possibility that attempts to control the economy could be destabilizing (long and variable lags) and the alleged propensity of the Fed to misbehave.

Although I do not accept the policy perspective of much of the rational expectations literature, this is not an attack on the rational expectations hypothesis. The rational expectations theory of expectations —that individuals form expectations optimally on the basis of the information available to them and the costs of using that information—has become and will remain the leading theory of expectations.[2] But there is nothing inherent in the hypothesis that implies that activist policy is either impossible or undesirable.

Since the paper ranges widely, it is useful to outline the argument. Given recent claims about the ineffectiveness of systematic monetary policy, and the evidence apparently supporting such claims, I have first to establish that there is something to talk about. Sections 1 and 2 therefore lay the groundwork for the claim that, rational expectations-oriented work notwithstanding, systematic monetary policy matters for the be-

2. It is worth distinguishing between the "strong form" of rational expectations, which assumes that individuals' subjective probability distributions are the same as those implied by the models in which they are presumed to be agents, and the "weak form," which is defined in the text. ("Semi-strong" forms of rational expectations may be defined to require that the first n moments of subjective probability distributions coincide with those of the model.) I believe that rational expectations in the weak form, will be the leading theory of expectations in the same sense that utility theory (or its equivalents) is the leading theory of consumer behavior. We frequently use models in which behavioral functions are not explicitly derived from maximization, but are uneasy in doing so, and are reassured if it can be shown that the behavioral functions are consistent with maximization. Similarly, economists will continue to use adaptive and other prespecified models of expectations, but will feel constrained to apologize for, and attempt to justify, doing so.

havior of output. Assuming that claim is established, the issue of whether activist policy *should* be used remains. Section 3 discusses the desirability in principle of activist policy; section 4 discusses activist policy in practice; and, finally, section 5 considers rules versus discretion.

In more detail, it is shown in section 1 that there is a variety of mechanisms through which even fully anticipated monetary policy can affect the behavior of output. These mechanisms, however, are not central to the case for countercyclical monetary policy, which hinges on short-run considerations.

Section 2 therefore reviews some of the evidence that only unanticipated changes in the money stock affect the behavior of output. If it could be established that any systematic monetary policy had no real effect on output, then there would be little to discuss about countercyclical policy except to the extent that price level behavior matters. Recent empirical work by Barro (1978) does indeed appear to establish that only unanticipated money matters for the behavior of output, but in fact Barro's results are quite consistent with the view that systematic monetary policy can be used to affect output: the crucial issue for the potential effectiveness of policy is whether output is affected by expectations that were formed before the monetary authority had to commit itself to a particular level of the money stock. Results presented in the appendix show that if Barro's mechanism of expectations formation is accepted, then the data do not reject the hypothesis that two-year-ahead forecast errors of the money stock affect the behavior of output. Since the Fed can clearly react to events with less than a two-year lag, Barro's results do not force an end to further discussion of countercyclical monetary policy.

Section 2 argues that systematic monetary policy *can* be used to affect the behavior of output. The case in principle for using activist policy is made in section 3, where it is argued that the same factors that make the economy vulnerable to "unanticipated" money suggest that monetary policy should be used to offset aggregate disturbances—if the use of active policy is not itself destabilizing. The discussion in section 4 accordingly centers on older arguments about monetary policy relating to the long and variable lags with which policy works and the lessons of history.

On the issue of rules versus discretion, I conclude with a presumption in favor of a monetary policy that leaves the Fed an important measure of discretion.

1   Equilibrium Considerations: Nonneutralities of Anticipated Money

Since any systematic monetary policy would eventually come to be anticipated, it seems that such a policy can continue to affect output only if anticipated changes in the money stock can affect output;[3] accordingly, the natural place to start in considering the case for activist monetary policy appears to be with the nonneutralities of anticipated money. In this section, I will discuss the nonneutralities of fully anticipated money, by which I mean changes in the money stock that are anticipated at the time decisions relevant to the determination of output are made.

The neutrality of money has always been a central concern of monetary theory, precisely because it has long been obvious that money is not neutral. The implications of this fact for monetary policy depend on the source of the nonneutralities. Traditional discussions of neutrality distinguished between the transitional effects of a once-and-for-all change in the money stock, which were generally thought to affect real variables, and the long-run or equilibrium effects of the change, which analysis suggested were insubstantial.[4] Modern analysis has added two important distinctions to the discussion: (1) that between the neutrality and superneutrality of money, corresponding respectively to the effects of changes in the stock of money and growth rate of money, the latter producing changes in the inflation rate; and (2) that between anticipated and unanticipated changes in the money stock.[5]

Anticipated Inflation

In this section we concentrate on nonneutralities of money that arise from anticipated changes in the money stock and consequent changes in the expected rate of inflation. Informational considerations are deferred to section 2. As long as money pays no interest, changes in the expected rate of inflation change the expected real return from the holding of money, affecting the demand for real balances, and creating the possibility that anticipated changes in the growth of money affect real variables.[6]

---

3. I shall argue below that this statement is in important respects misleading. A systematic *policy*, i.e., a rule that specifies money supply responses to disturbances, will itself eventually be anticipated, but actual changes in the money stock under such a policy may not have been anticipated as of an earlier date when decisions relevant to the determination of output were made.

4. See, for instance, Irving Fisher 1922.

5. Both distinctions were at least implicit in the older discussions. First, there was typically mention of the elasticity of expectations, suggesting awareness of the importance of changes in the expected rate of inflation. Further, the typical money stock change had people waking in the morning to discover the good news of a doubling of their holdings, reflecting awareness also of the distinction between anticipated and unanticipated events.

6. Two assumptions are maintained until further notice. First, there are no interest payments on money. Second, the government does nothing other than distribute money to the economy through transfer payments, which, however, are not related to individual holdings of money by the transfer recipients. The second as-

Consider first the standard two-period lifetime consumption loans model in its simplest form: there is no production and each individual has an endowment of a nonstorable consumption good in the first period of his life; money is the only vehicle for saving. Changes in the growth rate of money affect the intergenerational allocation of resources in such a model if, say, the lump sum transfers are made to the old. If endowments varied stochastically over time, and there was a somehow agreed-upon social welfare function for weighting generational expected utilities, the government might optimally want to vary the growth rate of money. But since output is exogenously determined, monetary policy obviously does not affect the level of output.

The monetary authority's ability to affect the allocation of resources depends in this case on its ability to affect the real interest rate and thus saving. Higher rates of monetary expansion reduce the real interest rate by raising the expected rate of inflation. If we now allow for the inclusion of an endogenous labor supply (but do not yet add productive capital to the model), it will still be true that the monetary authority affects the real interest rate by varying the growth rate of money. Labor supply, and thus output, will respond to variations in the real rate of interest. A case for activist monetary policy in a context in which there were variations in the productivity of labor could once again be made, given a social welfare function.

Expansion of the menu of assets makes it necessary to provide a rationale for portfolio diversification, particularly the holding of money. The simplest rationale lies in the existence of some form of transaction costs in buying and selling assets other than money.[7] Putting money in the utility function will also generate portfolio diversification; this device is best thought of as being justified by the existence of transaction costs that are not explicitly included in the analysis, but rather implicitly treated as foregone utility. A third possible source of diversification is risk aversion, though here it is necessary to ensure that money is not a dominated asset.

Sidrauski (1967) has elucidated the very strict conditions under which the rate of inflation does not affect the level of output in a model with labor and capital as factors of production and money and capital as assets. Money is superneutral if the optimizing units in the economy are

sumption is designed to rule out, for the moment, real effects of anticipated inflation arising from the tax system.

7. At this stage the consumption loans model becomes more difficult to use, since it tends to emphasize the store of value function of money, while the transaction costs arguments rely on the medium of exchange function. See Bryant and Wallace 1978 for the attempted incorporation of money in a consumption loans model with other assets.

infinitely lived, if the quantity of real balances does not affect the economy's production possibilities, if labor is inelastically supplied, and if consumers have a constant discount factor for comparing utilities over time. The steady state capital stock is determined by the modified golden rule condition that the marginal product of capital be equal to the sum of the consumers' rate of time preference and the growth rate of population. Even this set of restrictions does not, strictly speaking, imply superneutrality, since economic agents are not indifferent to the rate of inflation.

Relaxation of the specified conditions will again produce nonneutralities of anticipated money. If labor supply is not exogenously fixed (Brock 1974), or if consumers do not effectively maximize over an infinite horizon (Drazen 1976), or if money enters the production function, money will not be superneutral. Nor does the superneutrality apply to the behavior of the economy before the steady state is reached (Fischer 1979a); more rapid rates of money growth tend to produce more rapid rates of accumulation of physical capital in the transition to the steady state.

Once there is a rationale for the holding of money, expansion of the menu of assets, held on grounds of risk aversion, introduces no fundamentally new issues. It is therefore useful to step back to examine the two basic mechanisms at work rather than continue to catalog possible nonneutralities. The first mechanism arises from the possibility that changes in the real return on holding money affect interest rates on other assets, thus portfolio composition, and possibly the rate of saving and labor supply. The second mechanism operates through the effect of an increase in the expected inflation rate on the level of real balances. Lower real balances may imply more transactions and less resources available for production; they may also produce wealth effects that will affect spending on goods and services and labor supply.

The empirical significance of these mechanisms is not known. But there is a priori reason to think the effects will be small. First, they do not all work in the same direction: the accumulation of physical assets induced by anticipated inflation tends to increase output, whereas the diversion of resources from the production of goods to the production of transactions tends to reduce final output. Second, the base on which the real balance effect works is small; the stock of non-interest-bearing money is less than M_1, since some implicit interest is paid on demand deposits.[8] Further, it is likely that explicit interest payments on demand deposits will soon become legal, leaving currency as the only non-interest-bearing nominal asset.

8. Startz (1978) estimates the implicit rate to be half the competitive rate.

Institutional Effects of Anticipated Inflation

Up to this point, we have confined the government to making lump sum transfer payments in determining the growth rate of money. We want now briefly to consider the real effects of anticipated inflation arising from the nature of the tax system and other government regulations.

There is first the inflation tax itself. Changes in the growth rate of money affect the real revenue the government obtains from the creation of high-powered money and make it possible to vary other taxes, given the level of government spending. Changes in the pattern of taxation will have real effects, though little more definite can be said without considering the details of the tax structure.

The primary nonneutralities of the tax system arise, however, from nonindexation of taxes. The major effects will arise from the payment of taxes on nominal, rather than real, interest (combined with differential rates of personal and corporate taxation), and from the use of historical cost as the basis for depreciation.[9] Each of these features of the tax system implies that increases in the anticipated rate of inflation would discourage capital accumulation. Similarly, despite changes in the method of financing housing investment in the last few years, anticipated inflation still has potentially large effects in reducing the volume of housing investment;[10] the effects may be attributed in part to the existence of government-imposed interest ceilings.

It is worth noting that the specified characteristics of the tax system and housing financing are part of the institutional setting of the economy that has not completely adapted to the existence of ongoing inflation. Their existence thus cannot be relied on as a permanent mechanism through which monetary policy will affect the economy. It is significant, however, that the institutional features remain at least partly in place after twelve or more years of continuing inflation. The costs of changing the institutions of an economy that are based on an implicit assumption of the stability of the value of money to those that are based on the recognition of ongoing inflation must be substantial.

The institutional nonneutralities discussed above tend to make increases in the anticipated rate of inflation reduce the rate of investment and subsequent output. The net effect of anticipated changes in money on output in the current and subsequent periods is thus difficult to predict a priori; it will also probably be a delicate matter empirically to isolate the magnitude of the mechanisms discussed in this section. One place to start is by examining the effects of anticipated changes in money on the real

9. These effects have been emphasized by Feldstein and others; see, for instance, Feldstein and Summers 1978.

10. Details are contained in Modigliani and Lessard 1975.

interest rate. In the next section we also discuss reduced form estimates of the effects of anticipated money on output.

But even if reliable estimates turned out to show that the nonneutralities of anticipated money are not trivial, it would still remain to make the theoretical case for the desirability of activist monetary policy. An initial reaction might be that the factors discussed in this section merely suggest that the growth rate of money should be set at that level which would produce the optimal quantity of money[11] and the economy otherwise left free of monetary interference. However, in a context in which there are other distorting taxes, the inflation tax should also in general be used to raise revenue. Nor, even ignoring the inflation tax, is the optimal quantity of money provided by keeping the growth rate of money constant if the marginal product of capital varies over time. The argument for an activist monetary policy would thus be derived from analysis of the optimal inflation tax: as government expenditure varies, and other disturbances impinge on the economy, the optimal use of the inflation tax would also change. The optimal growth rate of money would therefore change as the state of the economy changed.

There are three main conclusions from this section. First, there are sound theoretical reasons for thinking that anticipated money is not necessarily neutral. Second, we do not at present have empirical knowledge of the net direction and magnitude of the mechanisms underlying the neutralities. Third, there is no reason to think that an optimal monetary policy derived in a model in which nonneutralities are present, and in which revenue from the inflation tax accrues to the government, will be a constant growth rate rule. Put differently, considerations of the type discussed in this section do not attach any sanctity to the constant growth rate of money.

A fourth conclusion should also be drawn: While the nonneutralities of this section may eventually be important in designing a framework for monetary and fiscal policy, they are not of central importance to the debate over countercyclical monetary policy. We therefore turn to the nonneutralities of unanticipated money.

2   Nonneutralities of Unanticipated Money

Emphasis by Lucas (1973) and others on the importance of the unanticipated component of the change in the price level has led to empirical work, of which the best known is by Barro (1977a, 1978), which ap-

---

11. Friedman (1969) suggests that the optimum quantity of money obtains when the economy is satiated with real balances; this requires that money pay a real return equal to "the" real interest rate on other assets. The positive real return on money is achieved by producing deflation.

pears to show that only unanticipated changes in the money stock affect real output and that anticipated changes in money have no real effects. A finding that only unanticipated money affects the behavior of output would be significant for the conduct of monetary policy, though not decisive in establishing the desirability of a constant growth rate rule. The case for activist policy would then have to rest on the effects of the policy on the natural level of output and on its implications for price level behavior. The welfare case for a monetary policy that operates by surprise or deception appears to be a difficult one to make, so that the strong Barro position that only unanticipated money works would tend to support rules over discretion.

For the purposes of this paper, I want to show that Barro's results are not inconsistent with the view that systematic monetary policy can affect the behavior of output. I therefore do not have to enter into a detailed argument about the real meaning of Barro's results or even into the question of whether he has successfully measured expectations of the growth rate of money[12] though fundamental criticisms will doubtless center on this latter issue.

The key point in my argument is that anticipations of money growth for periods other than one year ahead (Barro uses annual data) are relevant to the determination of output. I believe that, to a useful first approximation, the long-run Phillips curve is vertical. That means that fully anticipated changes in the money stock would not affect unemployment significantly. But one can hardly imagine a change in the money stock that has always been anticipated: *every* change in the money stock must be unanticipated as of *some* earlier date. If the Fed can respond to disturbances occurring after decisions relevant to the determination of output are made, then it can systematically affect the behavior of output.[13]

The Barro Output Equation

I review Barro's procedure briefly in the text; more detail is provided in the appendix. Unemployment, or the deviation of output from trend, is explained in a regression using annual data with actual and unanticipated changes in the money stock as regressors. A single stable money supply rule was estimated and taken to have been used in forming expectations, based on information available one year ahead, of monetary

---

12. David Germany (1978) points out that the restrictions Barro needs to identify the coefficients on unanticipated money in his output equation are literally incredible: it is assumed that expectations are known (by the output regression runner) exactly.

13. This point is worked out in Fischer 1977a. That article implicitly accepted the view that systematic monetary policy would be used to "deceive" the private sector, rather than the view of the present paper that systematic policy can be used to produce desirable outcomes more cheaply than is possible with a passive policy.

growth over the period.[14] Barro finds that unanticipated increases in the growth rate of money significantly increase the level of output; the hypothesis that anticipated changes in money also affect the behavior of output is not accepted.

A relevant question about Barro's results from the viewpoint of activist policy concerns the time interval over which "unanticipated" is defined. In an earlier paper (1977) I argued that anticipations of the price level more than one period ahead might enter the output equation. Analogously, it is possible that expectations of the money supply formed two periods back, rather than one period back, could enter the output equation.

Using Barro's money supply equation, I have constructed two-period ahead forecast errors for the money stock and included them in the output equation. (Details are in the appendix.) As would be expected, the two-period forecast errors are collinear—though not perfectly so—with the separate one-period forecast errors over the same two years. The inclusion of a two-period ahead forecast error in the output equation reduces the standard error in that equation, but not significantly so. Replacing the first one-period ahead forecast errors with a two-period error reduces the standard error of estimate, though not significantly. I conclude that the data cannot tell us whether only one-year ahead or only two-year ahead errors in predicting money, or both, contribute to explaining the behavior of output—though if forced to choose, the data choose the two-period forecast error. My belief is that both types of forecast error are relevant; there is nothing in the Barro data to reject that view.

The reason the inclusion of the two-period ahead error matters is that it is very hard to argue that the Fed cannot use a monetary rule that reacts within a period of two years to new information. If the two-year expectation is somehow locked in (for example, in labor contracts), then the Fed has ample time to act to affect the behavior of output. That does not mean it *should* act, but rather that it can systematically affect output. Moving in the other direction, though, it is also difficult to believe that the Fed cannot within the period of a year systematically react to information that becomes available to it, after the one-year ahead expectations are locked in. That is, the length of the Barro period suggests that the Fed can systematically produce unanticipated money—by acting on information that becomes available within the year.[15]

14. In an earlier version of his 1977*a* paper, Barro showed that his results were not significantly affected if a money supply equation based only on data available up to the time an expectation was formed was used in generating the expected change in money.

15. It is, of course, true that whether or not the Fed can systematically produce unanticipated money depends on private sector contracting arrangements; I return to this point below.

This possibility raises the familiar mutual causation question, as a potential explanation for the apparent strength of the effects of unanticipated money. It is somewhat surprising that Barro finds a stable money supply process over a period during which the Fed moved from a policy of supporting interest rates to one in which it claims to pay attention to monetary targets; it is also surprising that there is no apparent role for interest rates in Barro's equation.[16] His results might reflect the effects on both money and output of movements of other variables that tend to increase output, with the Fed increasing money to smooth interest rates.[17]

The Lucas Supply Function

Given the uncertainties raised in the preceding paragraphs, it would be useful in judging the importance of Barro's results to know what mechanism might have produced them if they were true. The impact of an unanticipated increase in the growth rate of money by one percentage point produces an increase in output of over 1% in the current year, and nearly 1.2% in the following year. The Fed rolls high-powered dice.

There are two competing explanations for results of the type Barro has obtained. The first is the standard rational expectations supply hypothesis, which will be detailed below. The second is a Keynesian story, which attributes Barro's results to the stickiness of wages that are based on expected prices.[18] The first explanation tends to rule out a role for active policy, while the second does not. The Phillips curve is an implication of both stories and cannot be used to distinguish between them.[19]

In this section I discuss the Lucas supply hypothesis to see whether there is independent evidence suggesting that it underlies Barro's reduced form results. The Lucas supply function is:

$$(1) \qquad y_t = y_{nt} + b(P_t - {}_{t-1}P_t) + e_t,$$

where y is the level of output, y_n is the natural or full employment level of output, and P is the price level, each in logarithms; e is a disturbance term, and the notation ${}_{t-1}P_t$ denotes the expectation of P_t that is formed

16. See the comments on Barro's paper (chap. 2) in this volume by Robert Weintraub.

17. Preliminary evidence indicates that unanticipated increases in money (as measured by Barro) are positively correlated with unanticipated increases in short-term interest rates (the expected interest rate is calculated from the term structure), providing some support to the notion that increases in the demand for money partly produce unanticipated money.

18. Backward looking "catch-up" elements are also typically found empirically in the Phillips curve; Taylor 1979 has a model with overlapping labor contracts in which workers are concerned with relative wages, which is consistent with estimated Phillips curves.

19. I am grateful to Robert Hall for emphasizing this point.

on the basis of information available at time $(t - 1)$. The Lucas analysis is most accessibly developed in his 1973 article; the rationale for (1) builds on information confusions, which cause individuals to increase their supply of output when nominal prices increase, under the mistaken impression that the relative price of their output has risen.

The key element in the Lucas mechanism is the increase in the supply of output in response to a rise in the perceived relative price, a story that is most naturally told as the model of an individual supplier of labor services, for whom the price of output is the nominal wage. Lucas (1977) notes, however, a very similar mechanism would operate in the case of firms. The strength of the mechanism would be greatest in response to an increase in the perceived real wage that was thought to be temporary, for in that case workers would like to increase the amount they work in the current period (at a high wage) and substitute more leisure next period (when the wage is expected to be lower than its current level). An increase in the real wage that is expected to be permanent might not elicit any increase in output, since labor supply curves may even slope backward.

Doubts can be raised about the supply mechanism (1). First, as David Small (1977) has pointed out, the assumed reaction of workers to an increase in the current price level requires it to signal an increase (or at least not a large decrease) in the real interest rate; in a model in which monetary growth affects the real interest rate, monetary policy can negate the labor supply response to unanticipated inflation.[20] Second, the mechanism provides no real explanation of a relationship between unanticipated inflation and the unemployment rate—it appears that those who choose not to work when the perceived real wage falls would not be unemployed. Perhaps, however, the existence of unemployment insurance makes it profitable to appear to be unemployed even when workers desire to reduce the amount they work; in addition, movements in the participation rate, as in Sargent (1976a), might help explain movements in the unemployment rate. Third, if this mechanism were powerful, temporary income tax changes would be potent instruments for affecting the pattern of output over time—and there is little evidence of such potency. Fourth, given the crucial importance of the mechanism, the empirical support for it is small.[21]

Unanticipated Money and Sticky Prices

The evidence supporting the Lucas supply hypothesis is hardly strong enough to justify the view that it is the main mechanism underlying

20. Bulow and Polemarchakis (1978) have studied essentially this mechanism.
21. Lucas refers to his work with Rapping (1969), to work by Ghez and Becker (1975), and some more casual evidence. The Ghez and Becker evidence does not appear to bear strongly on cyclical labor supply substitution.

Barro's empirical results. Indeed, Barro's (1978) price equation reveals some stickiness of the aggregate price level, leading him to remark that the money-to-price link may be too weak to explain the estimated effects of unanticipated money on output.[22]

The stickiness of prices suggests that a Keynesian mechanism, in which changes in money affect aggregate demand, which affects employment, may be at work. The response of some prices, particularly wages, to changes in demand is sluggish relative to the period over which policy is formulated;[23] Sargent (1976a) finds that wage rates may be treated as exogenous in a quarterly macro model. The most plausible generalization of the Lucas supply function is probably this: the longer in advance a given type of change in the money supply has been expected, the greater the effect on prices relative to the effect on output, with the effects being proximately attributed to the stickiness of nominal prices fixed over different horizons.[24]

In the short run (maybe several years) in which prices are sticky, monetary policy can affect the behavior of output in the manner suggested by Keynesian disequilibrium analysis, in which quantities are not necessarily determined at the intersections of supply and demand curves. There is no presumption that any intervention can only worsen the situation in such circumstances.[25]

The conclusions from this section are that there is no strong evidence for the view that only unanticipated (with a one-year horizon) changes in the money stock affect output. The data are not strong enough to force acceptance of the view that it is one year ahead rather than longer or shorter forecast errors that are relevant to the behavior of output. Similarly, while there is some evidence supporting the Lucas supply mechanism, there is also evidence for price stickiness.

We are now free to discuss activist policy.

22. Since interest rates are held constant in Barro's price equation, a more complete analysis might reverse, or for that matter, strengthen, this conclusion.

23. Poole (1976) argues that there is some period short enough that the price adjustments assumed in the equilibrium supply framework do not operate.

24. This comment applies to the extent that money is neutral, price stickiness aside. In Fischer 1979b I show that when anticipated money affects output, prices may rise less the longer a given change in money has been expected—because the anticipated money then affects output more.

Taylor's 1979 model produces an adjustment pattern like that referred to in the text.

25. It can and has been objected to the view that short-run price stickiness implies that output is not optimally determined and can be predictably affected by monetary policy, that the private sector would not enter into arrangements that would "predictably" imply a deadweight loss (Barro, 1977b). By the same token, the private sector would presumably not enter into arrangements that leave it vulnerable to the effects of unanticipated money.

3   The Desirability in Principle of Activist Policy

The classical argument for government control of the money supply is that a fiat money system is unstable, tending to degenerate into a commodity money system. Historically, central banking developed in response to a slightly different instability: that of a financial system in which the quantity of claims on the existing stock of commodity money was larger than that stock. The Bank of England, for instance, was driven against its will to manage the London money markets by financial crises that threatened private sector financial institutions (Bagehot 1906, Sayers 1957). The private sector can manage financial panics,[26] but the nineteenth- and early twentieth-century record indicates that better management should not be difficult—though the Great Depression proves that worse management is also possible.[27]

At a general level, we can agree that if the government is to control the money supply, it should provide a stable monetary background against which the economy can proceed with its real business of producing and consuming goods. If there were no disturbances to money demand, arising from disturbances affecting the level of output or interest rates, or the random term in the demand function, a stable monetary background would be a stable (predictable) money supply. A constant growth rate rule would serve well.

But there are, of course, disturbances to money demand. In the long run these take the form of changes in the assets that constitute money. Historically, the process has been one of a broadening of the class of assets that serve as the medium of exchange. Price level behavior over the long term would become less and less predictable if monetary policy were devoted to control of the supply of an asset that constituted a decreasing proportion of the money supply. We therefore cannot expect that a constant growth rate rule, or for that matter any other rule, would remain inviolate over the long term; occasions would arise when it would be necessary to change the asset whose growth rate was being controlled.[28] Such changes hardly constitute activism, however.

The General Rationale for Countercyclical Monetary Policy

The important issues arise in the short run. Short-run disturbances to money demand arise both from goods market disturbances that affect the level of income and the interest rate and from random shifts in

26. Friedman and Schwartz (1963) suggest that the private sector would have handled what became the Great Depression better than the Fed had the latter not existed.

27. I assume that enough has been learned (and that institutions have changed), so that the Fed would not again act as it did in the early 1930s.

28. The 100% money plan would have difficulty in controlling the development of money substitutes.

money demand; the money demand function does not fit perfectly even for the sample period 1955–73. The evidence reviewed in section 2 suggests that by reacting to these disturbances, the Fed can affect the subsequent behavior of output, interest rates, and prices, even if the policy actions constitute a regular pattern of behavior and are in that sense anticipated.

I shall also argue that it is at least potentially desirable that the Fed seek to offset disturbances. The argument most usefully starts from the recognition that there would be no reason for disequilibria to emerge as a result of monetary disturbances in the absence of transactions and information costs. In the absence of such costs, the private sector would closely monitor the aggregate price level and aggregate money stock and make contracts contingent on them. Unanticipated money—or any other disturbance—would create disequilibrium, or an unsatisfactory state of affairs, for only as long as the arbitrarily short period over which prices and wages were fixed. There is, of course, noise in both price and money data, but some information is better than none.

It might be suggested that the private sector does not enter into complicated arrangements contingent on aggregate variables because aggregate fluctuations account for only a small part of the risk facing individual economic units. Such an argument is both correct and incomplete; it has to be combined with the obvious assumption that there are costs of acquiring and processing information, of writing detailed contingent contracts, and of reducing the length of contract periods, if it is to account for the nonexistence of the contracts that would render the private sector immune to aggregate disturbances.

The costs that prevent the private sector from insulating itself against aggregate disturbances lead also to temporarily sticky prices that produce the presumption that private sector output is not continuously optimal. Those costs are the underlying reason there is a potential role for activist monetary policy in attempting to offset aggregate disturbances.

If one takes the view that monetary management has the task of offsetting aggregate disturbances that the private sector has not made arrangements to deal with, the goals of policy are the standard ones of full employment (minimizing the deviations of the unemployment rate from the natural rate) and price stability.[29] Price stability is desirable in part for the reasons emphasized in the Lucas supply mechanism: it enables the price system to operate more efficiently.[30] But this cannot be

29. This sentence glides over some difficult issues, particularly in relation to price stability versus price predictability.

30. It has, of course, been recognized that a desire for price level stability would support an activist monetary policy even if anticipated money did not affect output (Sargent and Wallace 1975). But it is important to realize that price level *predictability*, as well as stability, can in principle be increased by the use of active feed-

the full explanation for the weight that inflation aversion has in public opinion polls.[31]

To say that monetary policy should have worthwhile goals is hardly a policy prescription. Detailed prescription cannot be expected from a paper that does not present an empirical model as a basis for prescription, though I do in the next two sections discuss general characteristics of desirable monetary policy. In principle, the optimal monetary policy to be used for stabilization can be studied using an appropriately specified macroeconometric model, which pays due attention to the effects of changes in policy regime on the structure of the model.[32] Such models are not inherently impossible to build.

4   Activist Policy in Practice

There is no inconsistency in accepting the general argument of section 3 for activist policy and in urging the immediate acceptance of a constant growth rate rule (CGRR). After all, we do not know the optimal activist policy. In this section I concentrate on a comparison among a number of monetary policies, leaving the rules versus discretion issue to section 5.

The first policy is the most difficult to describe: it is the current system, in which the Fed makes monetary policy as best it can, with input from business, academic, and other sources of pressure, and in ways that change over time. The second is the constant growth rate policy (CGRP) or a passive policy. Most studies of alternative monetary policies have compared these two, with history serving as the representation of Fed policy. Third I will consider a policy that is intermediate between the

---

back rules. The predictability at issue is that of prices in the more distant future. In a number of models, the one-period ahead variance of the price level is the same whatever the monetary rule that is being followed. But the uncertainty today about the level of prices in the distant future in general is greater if monetary policy does not respond to current disturbances than if it does attempt to stabilize prices. To the extent that price level predictability more than one period ahead is relevant to the allocation of resources, activist monetary policy might be desirable on those grounds alone.

31. Fischer and Modigliani (1979) list many of the real effects of inflation on the economy; these may in part account for popular attitudes to inflation, which are frequently ascribed to irrationality.

32. The warning in Lucas 1976 that the structure of econometric models will not remain invariant to policy changes applies also to the structure of contracts. The monetary policy of the last three decades has, by some accounts, been largely in error but the private sector has allowed itself to be left in the position where, by some estimates, a 1% unanticipated change in the money supply affects output by 1% within a year, and more the next year. If monetary policy were to improve, the private sector would make itself *more* vulnerable to the effects of unanticipated money, by adopting longer-term contracts and paying less attention to monetary variables.

first two—one in which policy is basically passive except in the face of major actual or anticipated disturbances.

The major arguments for CGRP as compared with actual policy are familiar from earlier discussions: they are that ignorance of the structure of the economy makes policy intervention destabilizing ("long and variable lags"); that most serious disturbances have been caused by inept policies; and that political pressures lead to monetary mismanagement. Underlying these arguments is an interpretation of the historical record that claims the Great Depression would have been more moderate had the Fed followed a CGRP (Friedman and Schwartz, 1963) and that macroeconomic behavior in a number of subsequent episodes would likewise have been better had the Fed been following such a policy (Friedman, 1960).[33]

At the theoretical level it is correct that increased uncertainty about the structure of the economy supports the use of more passive policies. Similarly, it is entirely possible for naive policies to be destabilizing. Whether ignorance and naiveté have in practice caused policy to be destabilizing and will do so in the future are difficult questions to answer. The historical record, to which we turn shortly, casts some light on these questions.

Before we examine the record, though, we have to ask whether the entire post-1913 history of the Fed, including the Great Depression, should be thrown into the scales, or whether it is reasonable to assume the Fed has learned something. As previously noted, I will proceed on the assumptions that the Fed can and has learned from history and that deposit insurance, memory, and the persuasive evidence of Friedman and Schwartz, will prevent a repetition of the behavior of the monetary authority during the early 1930s. Similarly, I believe that the Fed is now more aware of the potentially destabilizing influence of stabilizing nominal interest rates than it was in the sixties and that it pays more attention to the behavior of the monetary aggregates than it did.[34]

The Historical Record

The record of monetary policy up to 1960 was studied by Friedman (1960), who emphasized the debacle of the Great Depression and regarded post–World War II monetary policy as less obviously defective (p. 94).

The evaluation of monetary policy in the post–World War II period (or in any other period) presents substantial difficulties. The natural

33. Poole's contribution to this volume makes that claim for the 1971–75 period.
34. The need for this paragraph may not be obvious to all readers. However, some comments on the first draft of this paper persuaded me that the question of whether the monetary authority has learned anything is central to disagreements about CGRP.

way to proceed appears to be to use an econometric model to compare the historical performance of the economy with that which would have occurred under CGRP. Such experiments typically show actual monetary policy outperforming, or not being markedly worse than, a passive policy (for example, Modigliani 1977, Eckstein 1978[35]). Unfortunately these experiments are subject to the reservations emphasized by Lucas (1976) in his discussion of econometric policy evaluation.

The other method of evaluating policy is less formal. It is to select particular episodes for discussion, criticism, and comparison with the results of a passive policy. For instance, it is reasonably clear that the growth rate of money was too high in 1968 and early 1969 and that a policy that maintained the growth rate of money at, say, the average rate of the sixties would have been better.

Similarly, Poole provides an interesting evaluation of the 1971–75 period (see chap. 9). Poole argues convincingly that monetary policy was too expansionary in 1971–72, especially given the existence of wage and price controls. He also suggests that more expansionary monetary policy in the first half of 1974—as urged at the time by, for instance, Modigliani (1974)—would have produced substantially more inflation but little more output than actually occurred. He argues, interestingly, that the Fed could not really have followed a more expansionary policy in the first half of 1974 because such a policy would not have looked right at a time of high inflation and relatively low unemployment. He absolves the fall in monetary growth in the second half of 1974 from most of the blame for the recession. And he argues for a constant growth rate rule.

Although exercises of this type are subject to both the Lucas critique and selection bias, the argument is sufficiently interesting to be worth pursuing. The initial appearance is that Poole's analysis does not support the case for CGRP. The implication of Poole's argument is that monetary growth should have been reduced below the trend rate in 1971–72 to accompany wage and price controls, and it should have been increased above its trend level in the second half of 1974. (Poole seems to be agnostic about the first half of 1974.) If political forces indeed restrained monetary growth in the first half of 1974, then one of the major arguments for rules—that they remove the Fed from unfortunate political pressures—appears redundant.

However, there is more to be said in defense of CGRP. In the first place, although optimal policy in 1971–72 would not have been CGRP, the latter would have been better than actual policy. And second, it is

---

35. Eckstein's passive policy controls the growth rate of unborrowed reserves rather than M1. The growth rate of money under such a policy is not much more stable than the historical path.

open to proponents of CGRP to argue that there would have been no need for wage-price controls in 1971 if the rule had been in effect in the sixties.

Although Lucas's critique of econometric policy evaluation makes any statements about the historical record difficult to support strongly at this stage, the following remarks are in order. First, monetary policy in the post–World War II period has not on average been markedly worse than a constant growth rate rule, and has probably been somewhat better. Second, it is easy to find particular episodes for which one can confidently assert that actual policy was worse than a constant growth rate policy. Third, we can on general grounds be sure that a 4% growth rule would have produced a lower inflation rate between 1960 and the present than actually occurred. But without an econometric model, we do not know whether overall economic performance—including the behavior of the unemployment rate—would have been better under such a policy.

The historical record since World War II does not tell the unambiguous story that proponents of CGRP find in it, even though there are episodes in which CGRP would have been better than actual policy.

Modified Activist Policy

The arguments against activist policy outlined in this section, and the evolution of actual policy, point in the same direction—toward a policy that responds very little or not at all to minor actual and prospective disturbances, but with proportionately more vigor to actual and potential major disturbances. For want of a better term, I shall refer to this policy as modified activist policy, or MAP.

The arguments made by Friedman against activist policy are telling against fine tuning: given uncertainty about the structure of the economy, policy has to be cautious in reacting to information contained in minor disturbances, in part because data revisions are often large. However, there is no reason why policy should not react to major disturbances, actual or prospective, when it is clear that either expansionary or contractionary policy is required.[36] In saying this, I assume that major disturbances could occur even in the absence of government policy: the nineteenth- and early twentieth-century record suggests that possibility. If it should be the case that large disturbances have been the fault of the Fed, the absence or mildness of fine tuning would soon establish itself as a major success—unless political pressures make it impossible to run a cautious policy.

The discussion of the three policies of this section can conveniently be continued in the next section, under the heading of rules versus discre-

---

36. The monetary policy required in the case of a demand disturbance is usually clear, but the response to supply disturbances presents greater difficulties.

tion. In practice, a monetary rule would almost certainly be written as a constant growth rate rule, and discretion would mean continuance of the present evolving system of monetary control. In operation, a monetary rule would be much like MAP, for the rule would likely be adapted or changed in response to an anticipated or actual crisis.

5   Rules versus Discretion

The general issue of rules versus discretion in monetary policy amounts to the question of whether the Fed should be given a narrowly defined task by legislation specifying the behavior of variables fairly directly under its control (rules), or alternatively, should be left to decide the appropriate means of achieving ultimate targets of monetary policy (price stability, full employment, etc.) specified by legislation (discretion). As with most convenient distinctions, there is no hard and fast line: a rule that would leave the Fed with a minimum of discretion would prescribe the behavior of its own portfolio; the current situation in which various ultimate targets are mentioned in legislation, but the appropriate weights and the means of reaching those goals are not, gives the Fed a much larger measure of discretion. For convenience, we can draw the line between legislation that controls the behavior of a monetary aggregate (or several aggregates) as being a rule and legislation that prescribes the goals of stabilization policy without specifying the behavior of monetary aggregates as providing discretion.[37]

Any monetary rule would have to be amended as the financial system evolved, as we have already noted. Changes in the rule might also have to be made in the short run, if it proved defective in operation. Indeed, the proposal for a monetary rule is equivalent to the suggestion that monetary policy be subject to the same legislative process as tax changes unless it is seriously suggested that the rule be embodied in a constitutional amendment. The latter suggestion reflects excessive confidence (or hubris) in conclusions reached on the issues discussed in section 4.

Two complementary methods for changing the monetary rule suggest themselves. First, there could be hearings on the performance of the rule at fixed intervals: the Fed might be required to report regularly on the workings of monetary policy and make recommendations for changes. Second, changes could be proposed as the Congress or the Fed or any other agency saw the need.

37. On this definition, Henry Simons (1952) argued for discretion in the 1930s; his proposed monetary rule was that the Fed aim to achieve price stability. At the time he was concerned about the instability of the demand for money. He argued that an optimal system would have 100% money and a fixed amount of it, and he believed that such a system could eventually be set up.

The Case for Discretion

The benefit of discretion, or leaving monetary policy in the hands of the Fed, is flexibility. There are two aspects of flexibility. The first relates to the classic lender of last resort function of the central bank, in which flexibility enables the central bank to intervene in potential financial crises. Such intervention was useful in the Penn Central and Franklin National cases, even if the methods of intervention in the latter case were not optimal. In neither of these cases, though, did it seem that there was any threat of a run on high-powered money, and it may be that the advent of the FDIC has indeed removed the need for a lender of last resort. Further, a rule that fixes the growth rate of M1 would provide an element of built-in stabilization since increases in the demand for currency at the expense of demand deposits would be accommodated automatically. But the basic source of the instability that underlies a panic—the multiple expansion of credit—would not be removed by CGRR.

There is thus no certainty that panics would be avoided under CGRR and accordingly it is important that there be some agency in a position to deal with potential panics in the financial markets. The most natural agency for this purpose would be the Fed, which should have left open to it the possibility of discounting freely and/or conducting large-scale open market operations.

The second type of flexibility is that which permits the Fed to react to business cycle developments. The argument here would be that there might be business cycle developments to which the Fed should react and that the details are too subtle to spell out in legislation. If a rule were in operation, the Fed could ask the Congress for authorization to engage in extraordinary measures if the need were foreseen, but delays in the legislative process and uncertainty about its outcome might well exacerbate any underlying disturbance.

The loss of flexibility that a constant growth rate rule would imply for the Fed in dealing with run-of-the-mill small disturbances would probably not be any great loss; it would essentially be the end of fine tuning. But economic instability might be seriously worsened if the legislative process made it impossible for the Fed to react to a financial panic or to react in a situation, such as a deep recession, when action was clearly called for.

The Case for a Rule

The advantages of a rule are in large part the disadvantages of discretion. The alleged tendency of the Fed to undertake action that is too much and too late would be reduced by the introduction of CGRR, or any other rule, for the decision lag of discretionary policy would be avoided. Policies that reduce the money stock at a time when it should be increased—as during the Great Depression—would be avoided. The accountability of the Fed for its actions would be enhanced, since its task would be well defined. The record shows that CGRR would not have been much worse than actual monetary policy during the post–World War II period.

Another argument against discretion has recently been advanced by Kydland and Prescott (1977).[38] The Kydland and Prescott argument is essentially that the Fed always or usually has an incentive to change monetary policy (the argument is a general one that applies to any policy) once the private sector has committed itself to a set of plans based on given expectations of policy. For instance, to take a not irrelevant example, if the public has adjusted to a relatively low rate of inflation, it might be in the Fed's interest to accelerate the inflation rate, apparently improving the short-run situation.

If the Fed has discretionary power, it might sometimes face the incentive to exploit the short-run Phillips trade-off. By a similar token, it rarely seems a good time to reduce the inflation rate. But why should the Fed want to act in a way that invalidates the private sector's expectations. The typical argument is that the Fed reads the election returns and that it, discretely to be sure, does the bidding of the president. This argument implies the view, no longer novel, that political success can be bought by policy which is not in the public's real interest. (It also implies that the Fed can systematically affect output.) Although democracy is frequently invoked in the argument for rules, it is not clear what democracy requires in this case.

I believe there is in fact a conflict between the short- and long-run interests of the public in the political business cycle and that some weight should on that account be given to rules. But I would feel much easier about this argument for rules if I did not have the suspicion that it is a rationalization of the typical economist's belief (shared by the public) that inflation is a more serious problem than the revealed preference of the political process, or any serious economic analysis, suggests, and that inflation control has therefore to be imposed, if necessary by rule.

A Modified Constant Growth Rate Rule or MAP

Friedman (1960) made only modest claims for CGRR, namely, that it would prevent the Fed from making major mistakes. The serious draw-

---

38. A similar problem is examined in Calvo 1978. The remarkable feature of the Kydland-Prescott result is that it can apparently occur even if the policy authority is maximizing the expected utility of the representative individual, and if individual tastes are consistent through time.

back of a strict form of CGRR is the possibility that monetary policy will be immobilized precisely at a time when it is obviously useful.

The question that then arises is whether CGRR would not in practice be the best of all worlds, given the right of the Fed to ask for changes in the rule. There would then be CGRR in the ordinary course of events, and active monetary policy when circumstances warranted—which is precisely the modified activist policy described in section 4. However, given the delays of the legislative process, CGRR in practice could well be destabilizing,[39] particularly in the case of a financial panic.

A similar solution, which I favor, would leave the initiative for taking action with the Fed, but would maintain the presumption that in the ordinary course of events, monetary policy would be passive. Under such a solution, the Fed would be expected to maintain a constant growth rate rule and would be required to explain ex post (within some specified period) all deviations from the constant growth rate path to a congressional review panel.

This latter solution is very close to the current situation. It is beyond the scope of this paper, and my ability, to specify the legislative formula that would be required to make the Fed follow its targets more closely than it has since 1975. More Congressional supervision and more public explanation from the Fed of what it is doing are both to be welcomed in any event.

It is not clear to me whether the proposed policy is a rule or discretion. It is a rule in that it prescribes expected conduct for the monetary authority, but it leaves the Fed with sufficient discretion to take quick action if that is necessary.

6 Concluding Remarks

I will not repeat the summary of this paper, which is contained in the introduction. I want to make three final points. First, the purpose of the paper was to discuss the possibility of countercyclical, activist monetary policy in the light of developments in macroeconomics associated with rational expectations. Much of the paper was therefore devoted to the question of whether systematic monetary policy can have *any* real effects on output. Given the need to concentrate on that question, and the absence from the paper of a well-specified macro model, only the most general of policy prescriptions could be made.

Second, the reader will have been struck by the number of places in the paper at which it is asserted that there is no very strong evidence favoring one position over another. The only strong statement the evi-

39. Tax rates are not typically changed rapidly.

dence on adoption of a constant growth rate policy supports is that we do not know how such a policy would work. The conservative course is not to immobilize monetary policy when it might be useful in a recession or panic.

Third, the terms in which the argument is couched may seem unusual. But the general argument that is made for activist policy is not new. In Keynesian terms, the issue that is being discussed is whether "we should, in effect, have monetary management by the Trade Unions, aimed at full employment, instead of by the banking system" (Keynes 1936, p. 267). The answer given in this paper is that the central banking system rather than the private sector should provide monetary management.

Appendix: The Barro Output Equation

A typical Barro output equation, estimated from data in Barro (1978), over the sample period 1948–76 is:[40]

$$(1) \qquad \log y_t = \underset{(0.016)}{5.98} + \underset{(0.23)}{1.03 \, DMR_t} + \underset{(0.23)}{1.18 \, DMR_{t-1}}$$

$$+ \underset{(0.24)}{0.49 \, DMR_{t-2}} + \underset{(0.25)}{0.20 \, DMR_{t-3}}$$

$$+ \underset{(0.11)}{0.55 \, MIL_t} + \underset{(.0004)}{.035 \, t}$$

$$SER = 0.0168, SSR = .00622, DW = 1.81$$

In this equation, y is the level of real GNP, DMR is the unanticipated component of the growth in the money stock, MIL is a measure of the proportion of the prime age male labor force that has been drafted,[41] and t is time. If one adds the current and three lagged values of the actual growth rate of money to the regression (this is equivalent to including the anticipated component of the growth rate of money), the sum of squared residuals falls to .005872. An F-test indicates that the hypothesis that the anticipated component of money contributes to the explanation of the behavior of output, given the inclusion of the variables in (1), is not accepted.

Barro also estimates an equation in which the actual rather than unanticipated growth rates of money serve as regressors, and fails to accept the hypothesis that the coefficients on the anticipated and unanticipated growth rates are the same, for his sample period. I find that I do accept that hypothesis for the 1948–76 period, but the power of the test is very

---

40. This sample period was chosen because I later introduce a variable that was conveniently available only over these years.

41. Barro expresses some dissatisfaction over the inclusion of the MIL variable in the output equation.

weak. Further, there is really no good reason to have a null hypothesis that the coefficients on anticipated and unanticipated money are the same, since verticality of the long-run Phillips curve is inconsistent with that view.

As noted in the text, a more relevant question about Barro's results from the viewpoint of activist policy concerns the time interval over which "unanticipated" is defined. I have constructed a variable $2DMT$ that is the anticipation, based on information available at the end of period $(t - 2)$, of the growth rate of money in period t. The construction is straightforward insofar as the money rule depends on lagged growth rates of money. It also depends on the unemployment rate, for which I formed expectations using Barro's unemployment equation (1977a). Finally, the exogenous variables $FEDV$, MIL, and $MINW$[42] were assumed known with perfect foresight. As might be expected, the constructed variable is collinear with DMR (correlation coefficient of 0.65) and DMR lagged once (correlation coefficient of 0.82).[43] As might also be expected, the data are not able to tell us whether the two-period ahead unanticipated growth rate of money has significant independent effects on output. Adding the variable $(DM_t - 2DMT)$ to the Barro equation (1) reduces the sum of squared residuals from .00622 to .00547. If the current value of the DMR variable is then deleted from the regression, the sum of squared residuals rises only slightly, to .00553. Neither variable has a significant coefficient when both are included in the equation. We conclude that the data cannot tell us whether only one-year ahead or only two-year ahead errors in predicting money or both contribute to explaining the behavior of output.[44]

Comment   Robert E. Hall

It is noteworthy that Lucas and Fischer have no disagreement about the rationality of expectations, in spite of their very different views about the conduct of macroeconomic policy. The largest point of disagreement is the fixity of prices in the short run. Fischer believes prices to be sufficiently rigid over a span of, say, two years to provide a fulcrum for monetary policy to move real output. Lucas is skeptical both on the existence of such a fulcrum in all but the shortest runs and on the wisdom of encour-

42. For definitions see Barro 1977a, 1978.

43. The sample period 1948–76 was used because (DM-2DMT) was available only over that period.

44. F tests are inconclusive: given the inclusion of the two-year forecast error, the hypothesis that the DMR variable is irrelevant to the explanation of output is accepted, and vice versa.

aging the monetary authorities to make use of it. Neither is dogmatic on the point. Fischer recognizes the weakness of the evidence supporting the hypothesis that active monetary policy can smooth real output in a desirable way, while Lucas concedes the possibility of effective policies of this kind as a matter of theory.

Many speakers at this conference have emphasized the inadequacy of current knowledge on the key question of price rigidity. Though Lucas was a great pioneer in trying to make sense of the hypothesis within standard economic theory, he does not try to develop his views any further here. Fischer points out that many relevant transactions take place under contracts. It is costly to make these contracts contingent on aggregate economic variables apart from consumer prices. But this line of argument seems to start from a presumption that the natural noncontingent contract predetermines prices (or wages) and lets the buyer determine quantity later in response to further information. If such contracts are common, aggregate supply will be highly price-elastic, and a relatively Keynesian set of conclusions and prescriptions will follow. There is no good reason for this type of contract to be the starting point, though. As far as I can see, most contracts for goods have the simple form of predetermining both quantity and price. Nobody argues that this kind of contract yields Keynesian conclusions, and it certainly involves no expensive contingencies. In the labor market, contracts do seem to permit quantity variations during the contract, but they do not predetermine the wage. Rather, compensation varies with employment along a schedule established in the contract. At the theoretical level, this problem is studied in an important paper by Calvo and Phelps (1977) and in a subsequent paper of mine with David Lilien (1979). My own empirical work (1974) has shown the importance of variations in wage rates during the term of a union contract. Obviously, much more work needs to be done on this important question.

Fischer indicates the importance of the issue of the way that monetary policy affects real output with a lag. If the lag of two years arises because prices are sticky over a two-year period, then the scope for useful monetary policy is enlarged. If it arises because a monetary surprise brings about a predictable shift in the economy's equilibrium level of output, a very different and probably less activist prescription for monetary policy emerges. Without further assumptions, that data cannot distinguish these two hypotheses (Sargent 1976b). In the empirical work reported here, Fischer's implicit identifying assumptions relate to the irrelevance of fiscal and other variables in predicting fluctuations in real output. As he discovers, even these assumptions are inadequate to make the distinction. The problem can be put in the following ways: The two-year-ahead forecast error for money incorporates new information available this year and new information available next year. Essentially (but not exactly) the same information goes into the current one-year-ahead forecast error and into next year's one-year-ahead error. The result is severe multicollinearity among these three variables and the inability to distinguish the two hypotheses.

Fischer presents an admirably cautious discussion of the aggregate supply function that underlies Barro's evidence of monetary nonneutrality. As he points out, there are two leading explanations, one of Lucas's and a Keynesian alternative. I share some of Fischer's misgivings about the relevance of Lucas's model for, say, the American economy. I would add that Lucas's critical assumptions of the unavailability of information about the aggregate economy seem particularly inappropriate. But my own work (1979) has suggested that the necessary amount of intertemporal substitutability of labor supply may actually be present. I reach a mixed, but generally negative, verdict about the application of Lucas's model to the behavior of the U.S. economy, just as Fischer does. But Fischer does not apply the same level of criticism to the Keynesian hypothesis of wage-price stickiness. There is a slight suggestion in the paper that the Keynesian hypothesis must be right to the extent that Lucas is wrong. To my mind, we lack so far any presentation of Keynesian ideas on the same level of rigor and clarity as Lucas's work. The model implicit in most Keynesian work says that prices and wages are sticky *and* that labor demand, not labor supply, determines employment (this is certainly true for the basic IS-LM model). In the Keynesian story, the labor market operates off the labor supply function, for reasons which so far have not been successfully explained. It is not enough just to invoke the practical reality that wages and prices are sticky. We need to explain why demand wins and supply loses in the contest to determine employment in the face of stickiness. Obviously I agree with Fischer's basic theme that we are far from understanding the sources of monetary nonneutrality.

On the policy issues discussed by Lucas and Fischer, my own views are not especially strong and I do not have too much to say. I have learned that policymakers do not listen to unsolicited advice from economists. Economists are invited to advise in two very different circumstances. The Federal Reserve and the White House ask for recommendations about what to do in the next few months. Here the economist who replies that the wrong approach to policy formulation is being taken and that a simple fixed policy rule should be instituted in its place is never taken seriously and is never asked back. At those meetings, it seems to me, the best we can do is suggest that negative policy surprises not occur in recessions nor positive surprises in booms. I might even go a little further and recommend a positive surprise in a recession.

The second opportunity is congressional consideration of changes in the rule of policymaking. Congress has come close to imposing a fixed monetary growth rule in the past and it might again. Then I confess some ambivalence about the desirability of a fixed growth rule for monetary policy. On the one hand, I find Fischer's description of good discretionary policy very attractive. No rule can remotely approach the flexibility of an intelligent, well-trained, and well-intentioned human being. If I thought Stan Fischer were going to make monetary policy unilaterally, I would happily endorse his approach to the conduct of policy. On the other hand, it seems clear to me that we would have been much better off under a fixed growth rule than under the kind of discretionary policy we have had under the Federal Reserve system. By and large, money growth seems to have accelerated in booms and slowed in recessions, though the facts apparently admit several interpretations. Fischer's discussion seems excessively optimistic about our potential for reversing the dismal record of past discretionary policy.

Comment   Mark H. Willes

I suppose I have been asked to make some comments at this conference because, as a policymaker, I am a consumer of macroeconomic analysis. I cannot presume to discuss things at a sophisticated technical level. As a consumer, I feel the conference—specifically the two papers by Lucas and Fischer that I was asked to discuss—has provided several important contributions to the policy debate.

First, both of these papers highlight what seems to be a growing awareness that policymakers should not ask for policy solutions, because at the moment economists are not capable of providing them. It is true that Fischer says, and I think most of us would agree, that in principle there should be models available that can supply the policies we want. As he puts it, "In principle, the optimal monetary policy to be used for stabilization can be studied by using an appropriately specified macroeconometric model, which pays due attention to the effects of changes in policy regime on the structure of the model. Such models are not inherently impossible to build."

But his paper does not contain such a model, nor am I aware of any generally accepted model of that kind. In fact, the discussion of this conference points out to me, at least, the significant difficulties of both theory and estimation, which are yet to be overcome before such a policy model is in fact available. In the meantime, it seems to me that policymakers should not demand so much of policy advisors, and in return, policy advisors should not offer so much specific advice to policymakers. In this respect I find it encouraging that both Lucas and Fischer are properly humble and cautious in their policy prescriptions; Fischer, who comes out in favor of some "activist" policy, goes on to state that "fine tuning has to be cautious" and "fairly passive." Clearly, those are rather muted calls for action compared with some I have heard.

A second significant contribution to the policy debate, related to the first, that I see emerging from these two papers is a growing consensus that policymakers ought to be thinking not in terms of putting out fires but in terms of developing an acceptable and stable *process* or *rule* for setting monetary policy instruments.

Macroeconomists now seem to agree about what it would mean to have a *quantitative* solution to the problem of "making policy optimally," at least within the confines of a given institutional structure. First, it would be necessary to have in hand an econometric model (with actual numbers estimated for the parameters) that accurately describes how people would behave over an interesting range of alternative situations. Second, after the policymaker reveals his preference for alternative possible aggregate economic outcomes, determining policy becomes the (undoubtedly difficult) technical matter of deriving the "optimal control law" for the policy instruments that the authority controls. The control theory expert is clear in what he means by a "policy": it is a feedback rule or, in effect, an entire probability distribution for the government policy instrument, contingent on information that the authority will have in hand at the time that it must act. For a collection of mathematical equations to qualify as a model in the sense used above, it is necessary for it to describe peoples' economic behavior over the range of possible policies that the policymakers and their control theory experts want to consider.

Many of us in the late 1960s gave the impression that we possessed collections of equations (or soon would possess them) that qualified as models in this sense. Finding good methods for calculating the optimal feedback rules for those systems became an important topic.

As Fischer implies, however, it understates matters to say that the optimism of the late 1960s about the early successful completion of this research program has evaporated in recent years. Two related factors caused this. First, the best big models failed to predict important aspects of the 1970s, including unemployment-inflation interactions. Second, partly in response to the first event, the existing econometric systems could not be taken seriously as models of behavior that could be expected to hold up under a variety of hypothetical monetary and fiscal policies (feedback rules), as Lucas argued on theoretical grounds. As I understand it, Lucas's point was that for macroeconometric work it will just not do to formulate theories and econometric equations at a level that corresponds only to demand curves or supply curves. Formulating things at this level is too *shallow*, in the sense that economic theory predicts that peoples' dynamic demand curves and supply curves ought to change with a change in the nature of the environments that they face. But the changes in monetary and fiscal policy feedback rules necessarily occasion such changes in the environments that economic decision makers cope with. Therefore, their demand or supply curves, that is, their rules for setting decisions as functions of the things that they see, will change with a change in the policy rule.

One important negative implication of this argument of Lucas's is that big econometric systems in the style of the late 1960s cannot be regarded as *models* that will remain invariant under policy changes. This is because they consist only of collections of estimated demand curves and supply curves and nothing deeper. It follows that the systems of equations comprising most current econometric models are not suitable objects to hand over to a control theory expert for calculating the optimal rule. I find this argument of Lucas's compelling in its logic, even if it is disconcerting in implying that we are now much further from being able to promise a quantitative prescription for optimal monetary policy than we seemed to be ten or fifteen years ago.

An equally important positive element of Lucas's argument is his pointing the way to how macroeconometric work can be done in a manner designed to isolate those aspects of economic behavior that *will* remain invariant across different choices of policy rule. Put differently, the strategy must be to estimate objects that will enable us to predict how economic actors will change their dynamic demand curves and supply curves in response to changes in the random environments that they face. Ideally, this strategy involves rolling back what is estimated from the stage of demand and supply curves, to the stage of the parameters of the preference functions, production functions, and random elements that agents face. Then when agents are assumed to face new and different environments, predictions can be made about how their demand and supply curves will change. All of this is much easier said than done. Work along these lines is in its infancy and involves a number of difficult econometric and theoretical problems. Serious work along this line is being done at the Federal Reserve Bank of Minneapolis and elsewhere. But it is my understanding that we are a very long way from having a quantitative, empirically verified econometric model of the economy that meets the standards that have been delineated. Nevertheless, I have been encouraged by what I sense is a rather widely held view, at least by participants in this conference, of the need to build models in a different way from in the past and with emphasis on policy *rules*, rather than on ad hoc policy advice to meet short-run economic problems.

One final point flows from what I have said so far. Fischer seems to suggest that devotion to rational expectations implies that its adherents forswear the use of countercyclical stabilization policy. Coming from one of the hotbeds of rational expectations, may I say that such a conclusion is not required in principle. For example, as I understand it, Sargent and Wallace (1975) did not argue that *no* economic models could be imagined in which effective systematic countercyclical policy was feasible; rather, I understand the point of that paper to be that within the context of the simple model that they studied, it mattered a great deal for the choice of the policy rule whether expectations are assumed to be rational instead of being fixed in the face of alternative choices of rules. That main implication of their results would also characterize models modified to incorporate the various nonneutralities catalogued by Fischer. The potential existence of such nonneutralities has at least arguable implications for the present policy choice if one simultaneously admits that the currently available macroeconometric models cannot be used to analyze their quantitative importance. Even if one subscribes to some or all of the nonneutralities listed by Fischer, his declaration that "The rational expectations theory . . . has become and will remain the leading theory of expectations" in effect concedes that we are presently without a model for analyzing their quantitative dimensions and policy implications. Consequently, until such models are available, it would seem that the burden of proof might well rest on those who advocate activist policy intervention, rather than on those of us who argue for a rather steady policy course.

Comment   Peter Howitt

Although the conference revealed many important points of disagreement among the participants, I believe there are some important points of potential agreement that were not brought out in the discussion. The purpose of this note is to highlight some of these points.

The first point is that whatever course of action is pursued by the monetary authorities, it should be announced as clearly as possible and as soon as it is conceived. On the one hand, this point should certainly be acceptable to those who argue that announced monetary changes can have no real effects. According to this view the sooner and the more clearly are any given monetary changes announced the less potential harm they do. On the other hand the point should also be acceptable to those who believe that even announced monetary changes can have real effects. According to the most extreme version of this view, monetary actions will have the same real effects whether an-

---

EDITOR'S NOTE: This comment was submitted after the conference closed; it is included here because its contents are most closely related to the discussion of the Lucas and Fischer papers.

nounced or not, so that the policy of announcing any monetary changes, while it won't do any good, at least won't do harm either. The less extreme version, according to which expectations are formed rationally but money prices are constrained in the short run by the existence of long-term contracts, implies that this policy of announcing should improve economic welfare, because contracts signed after an announcement but before the corresponding policy change would otherwise have been inferred by agents can incorporate more accurate information as a result of the announcement, whereas other contracts will be unaffected.

Acceptance of this point of agreement implies acceptance of an even more important one—namely, that in response to any clearly recognized deflationary shock in aggregate demand the money supply should be increased above what it would otherwise have been. This may appear to be a contentious point that could be accepted only by an activist who denied the hypotheses of rational expectations and/or the Lucas aggregate supply function. But even to an advocate of these hypotheses the point is at worst innocuous. For according to his view, as long as the monetary change is announced, it can have no real effects; it does no good but it does no harm either. Indeed, if some weight is given to price stability as a goal, then even this extreme view implies that the policy, as long as it does not *over*react, will be positively beneficial.

This last point is even consistent with believing in rules rather than discretion, as long as the rule allows for feedback loops. It says that the rule ought to adapt to clearly identifiable deflationary disturbances.

There may be some doubt raised about whether or not such disturbances exist. I believe that this existence question is answered affirmatively by the single example of the events of late 1929 and early 1930. No one doubts that aggregate demand declined in this period in a way that could have been recognized in time to prevent the monetary collapse following October 1930, and not even Friedman and Schwartz argue that the decline was entirely attributable to monetary policy itself.

Some doubt may also be raised about how much of a reaction there should be. This depends upon one's estimate of the relevant parameters and the size of the shock. But the point is that in the face of such a deflationary shock it is hard to imagine how anyone's guess about the best monetary reaction could be other than positive. In any such situation there should be some positive reaction in the money supply that all among a finite number of economists agree is better than nothing.

Advocates of the rational expectations equilibrium approach may not appreciate being placed upon this common ground of agreement. But it seems to be implied by the logic of their argument. In my view this reflects a previously unseen aspect of the Sargent-Wallace proposition. The argument that systematic monetary policy is useless for affecting output also implies that it can do no harm to output. Thus while it warns of the potential limitations of activism, at the same time it strengthens the case for activism by showing how to avoid the potential dangers of which the rational expectations argument has warned, namely, by making sure that all monetary changes are announced.

General Discussion

In response to Hall's comment that in most labor contracts firms had to choose labor input at a wage that varies with the input level, Fischer said that the crucial issue was whether the overtime wage was based only on the amount of work, as he believed, or else changed depending also on the macroeconomic disturbance affecting the economy.

Lucas commented that there was confusion over what is required to make a case for activism. Such a case requires an argument to the effect that enough is known of the workings of the actual economy to permit successful activist policy, as opposed to purely hypothetical examples of economies in which activist policies might be successful.

Alan Blinder claimed that policy had not always been bad. Taxes were cut in 1964–65 and raised in 1968, as they should have been, though perhaps the tax increase had been delayed too long. Barro's reaction function, in which the Fed increased the growth rate of money when unemployment rose, showed that the Fed followed the tenets of good monetary policy as outlined in Robert Hall's remarks. Finally he noted that real output has been much more stable since World War II than it was before, and this was supposedly the period in which policymakers had followed Keynesian policies.

William Poole argued that there is an overwhelming case that a stable money growth policy would have been superior to the policies we have had. The one exception he saw to the optimality of stable money growth was that the central bank should intervene in liquidity and financial crises such as the Penn Central and Franklin National episodes. The overall goal of the central bank should be to avoid doing damage.

Herschel Grossman commented first on Fischer's paper. He presented two reasons why unanticipated money might affect output: (1) utilizing information is costly, in which case there is room for systematic monetary policy to have an effect, and (2) current information is noisy, in which case it does not follow that systematic monetary policy can have real effects.

Turning to Lucas's paper, Grossman remarked that while Lucas felt that we did not at present know enough to develop rules better than the Friedman rule, he himself doubted we would ever know enough to do so.

He was risk averse and was satisfied that the Friedman rule would at least prevent catastrophe. He did wonder whether there would be a transitional problem in moving to a constant growth rate policy.

Robert Gordon asked what basis Lucas had for the recommendation of balancing the budget on average, in contrast to Martin Bailey's conclusion that the optimal budget surplus could be positive or negative. He also commented that it would be useful to look at other countries, such as Germany, in studying labor contracts.

Robert Solow addressed himself to the political theory of fixed rules: Congress cannot legislate a permanent money rule because the next Congress may amend or repeal the legislation. It was only people present in the room who thought the money supply was (in a manner of speaking) the most important thing in the world and that it should be determined by fixed rules. If constitutional amendment were suggested to implement a money rule, we would be creating the precedent for constitutional rules for foreign policy, taxes, tariffs, and other matters that are at present adequately handled by legislation.

Solow added that modesty and caution in the making of policy did not necessarily imply sweeping changes such as a constant growth rate rule for money.

Karl Brunner said that the type of statement made by Solow should not be made without reading Buchanan and Tullock on the behavior of politicians and bureaucrats. He argued that it was perfectly legitimate to ask what the role of the government should be and what governmental actions should be constrained by constitutional rules.

Frank Morris said that the disarray of policymakers at present mirrored the disarray of economists; policy had currently to operate in a theory vacuum. He agreed with Hall that the rate of growth of money should be increased in recessions and decreased in booms. He thought that monetary policy rules make considerable sense in a stable environment, but not during an unstable period.

Phillip Cagan remarked that as a practical matter there was little difference between a nonactivist and mildly discretionary policy. To achieve a constant growth policy from where we were at present, he thought the best way was to slowly decelerate. Although this would result in a period of slack, when it came to be realized that policy had definitely changed, expectations would adjust and the economy would move more readily toward full employment with reduced inflation. He was not sure, however, that the initial period of slack would be politically acceptable.

Jerry Green discussed the nonexistence of full contingent contracts. He argued that if people are rational enough to form rational expectations, they should be able to write contingent contracts against major disturbances, but he doubted whether the welfare gains from these contracts could be sufficient to provide the incentive to write them.

References

Bagehot, W. 1906. *Lombard Street*. London: Kegan Paul.

Barro, R. J. 1976. "Rational Expectations and the Role of Monetary Policy." *Journal of Monetary Economics* 2:1–32.

———. 1977a. "Unanticipated Money Growth and Unemployment in the United States." *American Economic Review* 67:101–15.

———. 1977b. "Long Term Contracting, Sticky Prices, and Monetary Policy." *Journal of Monetary Economics* 3:305–16.

———. 1978. "Unanticipated Money, Output, and the Price Level in the United States." *Journal of Political Economy* 86:549–80.

Brock, W. A. 1974. "Money and Growth: The Case of Long-Run Perfect Foresight." *International Economic Review* 15:750–77.

Bryant, J., and Wallace, N. 1978. "Open Market Operations in a Model of Regulated, Insured Intermediaries." Research Department Staff Report no. 34. Minneapolis: Federal Reserve Bank of Minneapolis.

Bulow, J., and Polemarchakis, H. 1978. "Retroactive Money." Unpublished.

Calvo, G. 1978. "On the Time Consistency of Optimal Policy in a Monetary Economy." *Econometrica* 46:1411–28.

Calvo, G., and Phelps, E. S. 1977. "Appendix: Employment-Contingent Wage Contracts." In *Stabilization of the Domestic and International Economy*, edited by K. Brunner and A. H. Meltzer, pp. 160–68. Carnegie-Rochester Conference Series on Public Policy, vol. 5. New York: North-Holland.

Drazen, A. 1976. "Essays on the Theory of Inflation." Ph.D. diss., MIT.

Eckstein, O. 1978. *The Great Recession*. Amsterdam: North-Holland.

Feldstein, M., and Summers, L. 1978. "Inflation, Tax Rules, and the Long-Term Interest Rate." *Brookings Papers on Economic Activity* 1:61–99.

Fischer, S. 1977. "Long-Term Contracts, Rational Expectations, and the Optimal Money Supply Rule." *Journal of Political Economy* 85:191–205.

———. 1979a. "Capital Accumulation on the Transition Path in a Monetary Optimizing Model." *Econometrica*, forthcoming.

———. 1979b. "Anticipations and the Non-Neutrality of Money." *Journal of Political Economy* 87:225–52.

Fischer, S., and Modigliani, F. 1979. "Towards an Understanding of the Real Effects and Costs of Inflation." *Weltwirtschaftliches Archiv* 114:810–32.

Fisher, I. 1922. *The Purchasing Power of Money*. New York: Macmillan.

Friedman, M. 1960. *A Program for Monetary Stability*. New York: Fordham University Press.

————. 1969. "The Optimum Quantity of Money." In *The Optimum Quantity of Money*. Chicago: Aldine.

Friedman, M., and Schwartz, A. J. 1963. *A Monetary History of the United States, 1867–1960*. Princeton, N.J.: Princeton University Press.

Germany, J. D. 1978. "Can the Effects of Unanticipated Policy Be Estimated?" Unpublished.

Ghez, G., and Becker, G. 1975. *The Allocation of Time and Goods over the Life Cycle*. New York: Columbia University Press.

Hall, R. E. 1974. "The Process of Inflation in the Labor Market." *Brookings Papers on Economic Activity* 2:343–93.

————. 1979. "Labor Supply and Aggregate Fluctuations." Carnegie-Rochester Conference.

Hall, R. E., and Lilien, D. 1979. "Efficient Wage Bargains under Uncertain Supply and Demand." *American Economic Review*, forthcoming.

Keynes, J. M. 1936. *The General Theory of Employment, Interest and Money*. London: Macmillan.

Kydland, F. E., and Prescott, E. C. 1977. "Rules rather than Discretion: The Inconsistency of Optimal Plans." *Journal of Political Economy* 85:473–91.

Lucas, R. E., Jr. 1973. "Some International Evidence on Output-Inflation Tradeoffs." *American Economic Review* 63:326–34.

————. 1976. "Econometric Policy Evaluation: A Critique." In *The Phillips Curve and Labor Markets*, edited by K. Brunner and A. H. Meltzer, pp. 19–46. Carnegie-Rochester Conference Series no. 1. New York: North-Holland.

————. 1977. "Understanding Business Cycles. In *Stabilization of the Domestic and International Economy,* edited by K. Brunner and A. H. Meltzer, pp. 7–29. Carnegie-Rochester Conference Series on Public Policy, vol. 5. New York: North-Holland.

Lucas, R. E., Jr., and Rapping, L. A. 1969. "Real Wages, Employment and the Price Level." *Journal of Political Economy* 77:721–54.

Modigliani, F. 1974. "A Critique of Past and Prospective Monetary Policies." *American Economic Review* 64:544–57.

————. 1977. "The Monetarist Controversy, or Should We Forsake Stabilization Policies?" *American Economic Review* 67:1–19.

Modigliani, F., and Lessard, D., eds. 1975. *New Mortgage Designs for Stable Housing in an Inflationary Environment*. Boston: Federal Reserve Bank of Boston.

Phelps, E. S. 1970. "Money Wage Dynamics and Labor Market Equilibrium." In *Microeconomic Foundations of Employment and Inflation Theory*, edited by E. S. Phelps. New York: W. W. Norton.

————. 1973. "Inflation in the Theory of Public Finance." *Swedish Journal of Economics* 75:67–82.

Poole, W. 1976. "Rational Expectations in the Macro Model." *Brookings Papers on Economic Activity* 2:463–514.

Sargent, T. J. 1976*a*. "A Classical Macroeconomic Model for the United States." *Journal of Political Economy* 84:207–37.

————. 1976*b*. "The Observational Equivalence of Natural and Unnatural Rate Theories of Macroeconomics." *Journal of Political Economy* 8:631–40.

Sargent, T. J., and Wallace, N. 1975. " 'Rational' Expectations, the Optimal Monetary Instrument, and the Optimal Money Supply Rule." *Journal of Political Economy* 83:241–54.

Sayers, R. S. 1957. *Central Banking after Bagehot*. London: Oxford University Press.

Sidrauski, M. 1967. "Rational Choice and Patterns of Growth in a Monetary Economy." *American Economic Review Proceedings* 57:534–44.

Simons, H. C. 1952. "Rules versus Authorities in Monetary Policy." In *Readings in Monetary Theory*. London: George Allen & Unwin.

Small, D. N. 1978. "The Endogeneity of Rational Expectations and Labor Supply." Unpublished.

Startz, R. 1978. "Interest Bearing Demand Deposits." Ph.D. diss., MIT.

Taylor, J. B. 1979. "Aggregate Dynamics and Staggered Contracts." *Journal of Political Economy*, forthcoming.

8 What to Do (Macroeconomically) When OPEC Comes

Robert M. Solow

My assignment was to write a short paper stating the correct macroeconomic policy for 1974–75. This seems a straightforwardly simple task, so trivial, in fact, that one wonders why it has been assigned to two different people. Can it be that Poole and I will produce two mutually contradictory answers to so elementary a question?

In order to find out what should have been done in 1974–75, one needs only three bits of information. The first is a notion of what specifically happened in those years to make them worth thinking about. What (exogenous?) events made 1974–75 different from 1964–65, or from 1954–55? The second requirement is some sort of statement of goals. What objectives is macroeconomic policy supposed to achieve? Presumably, the correct policy is one that comes as close as possible to achieving them. The third and last requirement is a model of the economy. How will the economy respond to this policy or that policy or to no policy, under the circumstances that prevailed in 1974–75?

Once you know those three things, finding the correct macroeconomic policy is just a matter of arithmetic. That is why the task is so simple.

This being so, I shall stick pretty close to the issues of principle just listed, and I shall not try to specify the correct policy in numerical detail: the correct commercial paper rate, the correct full employment surplus, the correct excise on gasoline, and so forth. It would be silly to come all the way to New Hampshire to do arithmetic. The best thing to read on this subject is probably *Brookings Papers on Economic Activity*, number 1 (1975). It contains articles by Poole, Modigliani and Papademos, Okun, and Perry that do indeed consider alternative macroeconomic policies for 1974 in some detail. The same issue also contains an

EDITOR'S NOTE: The discussion for chaps. 8 and 9 appears in chap. 9.

excellent article by R. J. Gordon which does go after the issues of principle in the context of a two-commodity ("farm" and "nonfarm") model, and does it right. My analysis differs from his mainly in trying to place the problem in the framework of a completely aggregated macroeconomic model, just to see if it can be done that way. For general arguments, one can go back to Hicks (1965, chap. 7, and 1974, chaps. 1 and 3). For me and many others, a useful idea is the distinction made by Okun (1975, especially the clear analysis on pp. 376–78) between auction markets and customer markets, and their interplay. E. S. Phelps (1978) has analyzed the response-to-supply shock problem in a way which is more "neoclassical" than mine; his paper complements this one.

Initial Conditions

I turn first to the question, paraphrasing another famous query, what made that year different from other years? I propose to maintain the convenient fiction that 1973 was a year of macroeconomic equilibrium. It wasn't, as Poole points out clearly in his contribution to this book, but most of us have made worse assumptions from time to time. The unemployment rate was 4.9%; and since the benchmark unemployment rate used by the Council of Economic Advisors in calculating potential output for 1973 was 4.8%, the proportional gap between actual and potential GNP was estimated at less than half of 1%. Capacity utilization in manufacturing was fairly high, but generally not at bottleneck levels.

The fly in the ointment was that prices were rising. After two years in which the CPI rose at an annual rate of 3.4%, it jumped 8.8% in the four quarters of 1973. A lot of that reflected the rise in food prices; the nonfood commodities component of the CPI rose by only 5% in 1973, but even that was twice the 1972 rate. The food component of the CPI, which had risen 4.7% in 1972, went up 20.1% in the four quarters of 1973. Nevertheless, I will pretend that 1973 was an equilibrium year. My notion of macroeconomic equilibrium permits steady inflation, as will be seen. More to the point, I can conveniently merge the 1973 increase in the price of food with the other more or less exogenous forces that characterize 1974 and make it an interesting object of study.

To come to the point, the conventional wisdom about 1974 seems perfectly acceptable. The economy was hit by a number of shocks, each of which could be regarded as generating a one-time upward push on the domestic price level. The important shocks included the OPEC-enforced oil price increase, the lagged effects of the depreciation of the dollar in 1971 and 1973, the lapse of price and wage controls in 1974, and the worldwide boom in nonfuel mineral prices which began as the normal effect of an unusually synchronized increase in world demand on an industry with an inelastic short-run supply and turned into a speculative boom. To these four shocks we can add, as already mentioned, the sharp rise in agricultural prices beginning in 1973 and continuing into 1974, caused in part by crop shortages in the U.S. and in part by strong foreign demand, some of which resulted in turn from crop failures abroad.

It is an abuse of language to describe all of these as supply shocks. That is fair enough for the oil price increase, for the depreciation-induced rise in import prices, and for the crop shortage part of the food price increase. There were clearly demand-side elements in the cases of food and nonfuel raw materials. Even there, however, the supply shock characterization does only minor violence to the facts. Since the demand-side impulses originated outside of the U.S., it is not terribly misleading to classify the result as a rise in the world market supply price to U.S. consumers. It would certainly be a mistake to treat these sectoral impulses as if they were equivalent to bursts of generalized excess demand. Generally speaking, I will argue as if everything that happened was analogous to the oil price increase, so that the policy problem boils down to: What to do when OPEC comes? The real-life problem was more complex, of course, but the important issue of principle is the proper response to adverse supply shocks.

Here it seems worthwhile to anticipate the story a little. Suppose a monopolist is able to double the price of an important, almost universally used, input, and make it stick. If nothing else happens, or before anything else happens, the relative price of oil will have doubled, and the general price level will rise by a much smaller amount, depending on the weight of oil in the price index and on the particular sort of index being used. But of course other prices will change too. The rise in the price of oil will disarrange relative prices; somehow the prices of oil-intensive commodities will have to rise relative to those of other goods. There will then be further consequences through demand curves, longer-run reverberations, the whole panoply of general equilibrium effects. One can imagine all this working itself out without any further rise in the general price level, or even without any rise in the general price level at all. But one has to imagine it, because it is unlikely that any of us will live to see it actually happen that way.

If, instead, many nominal prices are inflexible downward, then the realignment of relative prices will be accompanied by a substantial rise in the general price level. This "inflation"—if that is the right word for it—will erode part of the original increase in the relative price of oil. Any sensible monopolist will respond by jacking up the nominal price of oil another notch and then the process may continue. What could have been a one-time rise in the relative price of oil can thus be converted into a fairly long process of continuing inflation. (I hope nobody rushes forward to tell me that the process can only happen if it is "validated" by the monetary authorities. *Das kennt jeder Esel*, as Brahms is supposed to have said to someone who made a similarly vapid remark after a concert.[1])

Here, for instance, is the course of the wholesale price index for fuels and related products and power divided by the all-commodity WPI:

Year	1970	1971	1972	1973	1974	1975	1976	1977
WPI	110.4	114.0	119.1	134.7	160.1	174.9	180.0	194.2
Fuels and related products	106.2	115.2	118.6	134.3	208.3	245.1	265.6	302.2
Fuels $\div$ WPI	96.2	101.1	99.6	99.6	130.1	140.1	145.1	155.6

Between 1973 and 1974, the nominal price of fuels rose by 55%. The relative price increased by only 30% because the whole WPI rose by some 20%. It took until 1977 for the relative price of fuels to achieve an increase of 55% over 1973, by which time the WPI was up almost 50% over 1973 and the nominal price of fuels was up by a factor of 2.25.

The point of this digression is to remind us all that the policy problem posed by an adverse supply shock is not to try to undo the real effects of the shock. There is no way that macroeconomic policy can replace lost wheat after a crop failure; if OPEC can raise the real price of oil and enforce the necessary restriction of output, then macroeconomic policy cannot make oil cheaper. The secondary effects on the price level and on aggregate output are the macroeconomist's real concern.

Goals

That brings us to the second element of a correct policy. What are the goals to be achieved or approached? Here a rough shorthand statement is probably almost as good as the optimal controlnik's objective function, and perhaps better.

I presume that a one-time increase in the price level is not a tragedy. You would hardly seek that outcome, but neither would you be prepared to sacrifice much real output to avoid or reverse it. Severe distributional effects could always be offset in other ways, if the political process were serious about equity. My impression is that it is not. Anyhow, I take it that a one-time rise in the price level can easily be tolerated.

Prolonged inflation, however, is painful. I persist in believing that the media and the political process grossly overstate the true social costs of 1970s-style inflation. Whatever esoteric things *we* have in mind when we speak of the real costs of inflation, the public has been allowed to think that a 6% rise in the CPI is a 6% reduction in real income, as if

1. Oder hat er eigentlich "Das weiss doch jeder Esel" gesagt, wie mein hochverehrter Kollege Professor Dr. Dornbusch glaubt?

we were buyers with fixed nominal incomes in a store whose prices have just been written up by six cents on every dollar. Nevertheless, any sensible policy calculation has to take into account the information about the public's sensitivities revealed by opinion polls. In various ways, inflation *is* painful, and the society is prepared to sacrifice real output to reduce it: not in unlimited amounts, but in perceptible amounts.

Output and employment are also valued, needless to say. Right now the pendulum seems to be swinging away from the standard objects of public expenditure toward private consumption and away from direct regulation of economic activity, but that is not likely to concern us in this context.

To sum up, the object of macroeconomic policy is to avoid prolonged inflation of the sort recently experienced, but without generating severe recession. I think 1974–75 qualifies as a severe recession for this purpose. So in fact we had the worst of both worlds.

A Macroeconomic Model: Output and Employment

The last required ingredient is a model of the economy. It would be easy to produce a model in which prices adjust almost instantaneously to shocks, markets clear essentially all the time, and the correct policy is to do nothing. The trouble with such a model is that it fails so transparently to reflect any actual economy. It therefore has to be supplemented by an elaborate pretense that what looks like involuntary unemployment is really voluntary, that what looks like idleness is really investment in human capital, that what looks like excess supply is really an optimal response to some epidemic misperception of the current state of affairs. I suppose it is a step forward to convert transparent failure into opaque failure. Nevertheless, I shall follow a different strategy and analyze the consequences of supply shocks in a model in which prices move only slowly in response to disequilibrium, so that markets do not necessarily clear in a time period long enough for macroeconomic policy to be effective.

The particular model I shall use is a slightly simplified and extended version of the one contained in Solow and Stiglitz (1968). It is simplified by the elimination of some unnecessary and distracting labor market dynamics, and it is extended by the insertion of something to play the role of the oil price. That 1968 model turns out to be almost identical in basic structure to the one analyzed by Malinvaud (1977). As already mentioned, a different but fundamentally consistent approach has been used by Gordon. With all this literature available, I shall be sketchy in outlining the model.

The representative firm produces a single domestic output (y) using inputs of labor (n) and energy (e), according to a well-behaved production function. The stock of capital goods is effectively constant in the short run and either user cost is zero or capital requirements are technologically fixed, so that capital can be ignored. The firm is a price-taker in all markets, and maximizes profit given the prices of output (p), labor (w) and energy (q). There arise routine demand functions for energy and labor, and a supply function for output, all functions of $v = w/p$ and $z = q/p$, the real wage and real price of energy. The supply of output is a decreasing function of v and z. It is plotted as a falling curve in the (v,y) plane for given z; a rise in z shifts the whole curve downward.

The demand for domestic output is a bit trickier, but I will skip all the details here. Assume that real aggregate demand depends on the real wage (positively, but perhaps weakly), the real price of oil (negatively, but perhaps weakly), real autonomous expenditure (a), and the real money supply ($m = M/p$). The rationale for these assumptions is, roughly speaking, that the propensity to spend wages exceeds the propensity to spend other incomes and that energy is "imported" from a sector that spends a large part of its proceeds elsewhere. Autonomous expenditure includes investment and the appropriate "weighted standardized budget surplus" to allow for the fiscal activities of the government. The real money supply enters for the usual reasons. For given z,a,m, the demand function slopes upward in the (v,y) plane, but the slope may be very flat if the various marginal propensities to spend are very similar. The curve shifts up with a rise in a or m, and probably down with a rise in z, at least in the short run, in which the elasticity of substitution between oil and other inputs is very small. (If the role of OPEC were being played by the domestic agricultural sector, one might want to vary these assumptions.)

I shall assume that the supply of labor is given and insensitive to the real wage in the short run; it will be obvious how to relax that assumption. Any reader of Barro and Grossman (1976) or Malinvaud (1977) will realize that one would have to doctor the aggregate demand function whenever there is unemployment. In general, output in the model economy cannot exceed full employment output, defined as the level of output producible with full employment of the labor force and with the level of energy imports that makes its marginal product equal to z, given full employment. With labor inelastically supplied, full employment output graphs as a horizontal line in the (v,y) plane and shifts down (slightly) for higher values of z. As this story makes plain, I am assuming that domestic firms can always satisfy their demand for energy at the going price.[2]

2. A complete anlysis of this two-factor model, with labor and "energy" treated symmetrically can be found in Robert E. Marks 1978. Marks does all the "Clowerization" of demand and supply functions that I treat cavalierly here.

As usual, whenever the market for output or labor does not clear, the actual volume of sales or employment is equal to the smaller of current supply and demand in that market. When there is excess supply of output, firms demand the cost-minimizing input bundle for producing the quantity of output demanded. When there is excess demand for labor, firms supply only what they can produce. The economy is thus always confined to the lower envelope of the three curves plotted in figures 8.1–8.3. The first diagram is drawn so that there is a unique point of full macroeconomic equilibrium (at E). For this to be so, fiscal and monetary policy, as measured by a and m, have to be just right. Starting from figure 8.1, an increase in m or a would shift the demand function up and lead to figure 8.2; a decrease would shift the demand function down and lead to figure 8.3.

For those who have read Malinvaud's book (1977) it may be useful to observe that, as one moves hypothetically from lower to higher real wages in figure 8.2, the economy moves from a state of Keynesian unemployment, to repressed inflation, to classical unemployment. In figure 8.3, the state of repressed inflation does not occur for the given a and m.

This model determines the state of the economy given the policy variables a and m, the real energy price z, and the real wage v (or, alternatively, given nominal autonomous spending $A = pa$, the nominal money supply M, and the absolute prices p, w, and q). It is fair enough to treat a (or A), M, and q as exogenous. As already suggested, I think the only defensible position is that p and w respond, at least a little, to the demand-supply balance in product and labor markets and to other forces as well; but their response is slow enough and weak enough so that neither market may clear for quite a long time. In terms of the model, the economy is always somewhere on the solid lower envelope curve in figures 8.1–8.3, but *where* on that curve it is to be found depends on the historically given w and p (and therefore v and z). More-

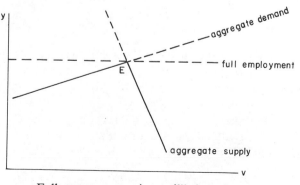

Fig. 8.1   Full macroeconomic equilibrium (at E)

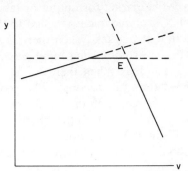

Fig. 8.2   An increase in real money supply or real autonomous expenditure causing an upward shift in the demand function

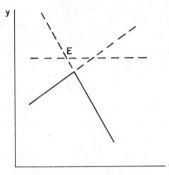

Fig. 8.3   A decrease in real money supply or real autonomous expenditure causing a downward shift in the demand function

over, the current state of the economy helps to drive w and p (and therefore v and z).

A Macroeconomic Model: Prices and Wages

I confess to a good deal of uncertainty about the correct way to model macroeconomically the determination of wages and prices. I have a lot of company. Anyone who professes certainty is pretty certainly wrong. In order to get on with it, I am going to make simple assumptions; I would be the first to admit that they could profitably be refined.

In particular, I shall adopt the formulation of Solow and Stiglitz (1968). The nominal wage is driven by a modified Phillips curve:

$$w'/w = h(n/n^s) + kp'/p,$$

where n^s is the (fixed) supply of labor, $h(.)$ is an increasing function that crosses zero somewhere, k is between zero and 1, and the prime denotes a time derivative. It is easy to think of plausible modifications of this equation and I could easily go along with most of them. There is debate about whether the price change term on the right reflects backward-looking catch-up effects or forward-looking expectations and about whether it should be represented in some more complex way. Some researchers prefer long lags (too long, in my opinion[3]) and some prefer rational expectations (too rational, in my opinion[4]). Within limits, one could allow for minor complications informally in using the model; but the simple formulation is easy to represent in a plane diagram. Even rational expectations would not make a drastic difference given wage and price stickiness.

For the price level,

$$p'/p = g(y^d/y^s) + iq'/q + jw'/w.$$

Here $g(.)$ is an increasing function, y^d and y^s represent aggregate demand and supply, and the two remaining terms allow for cost-side impulses. Presumably i is less than j, and j is between zero and 1. In any model in which markets do not always clear, a question arises about the proper definition of (unrealized) supply and demand and about the communication of excess supply/demand to the market. I think the broad issues to be discussed in this paper would come out the same no matter which reasonable position were taken on such matters.

I want to make one further drastic simplification. Each of the curves in figures 8.1–8.3 is parametrized by z, the real price of energy. If z were changing all the time, then all of those curves would be shifting all the time. To keep track of the model, one would need a third z-axis. To avoid that complication, I shall assume that the story begins with a one-

---

3. I have in mind the fact that the long lags often come from equations in which the dependent variable is a short-term interest rate. It is hard to believe that rates of inflation several years old contain information about the next quarter's rate of inflation (all that is relevant for a 90-day bill, say) not contained in more recent observations.

4. I regard rationality of expectations in the Lucas sense as an empirical hypothesis way over at one end of the range of possibilities. The other end of the range is occupied by simple rules of thumb. The a priori plausibility of rational expectations does not seem high; the empirical evidence in its favor that I have seen is very weak and very indirect, certainly no better than that for rules of thumb. Moreover, the hypothesis of rational expectations has not been able to account, so far as I know, for the wide dispersion of actually reported expectations at any instant of time, except by the undocumented assumption that information sets differ. But the differences in information would have to be incredibly large to account for the observed dispersion of expectations.

time jump in the nominal energy price q imposed by the external monopolist. There may be a corresponding jump in the domestic price level p, but it is incomplete, so that the net result is a jump in $z(= q/p)$. After that, I will take it that the monopolist is able to keep z constant, and does so. It is as if the original nominal increase had been calculated to be large enough so that, even after the initial jump in p, the real price of energy had settled right where the monopolist had wanted it in the first place. Earlier on, I pointed out that this was not the way things actually worked after 1973: the real price of oil kept rising for several years and became part of the stagflation problem of the 1970s. But it will be easier if we try to handle that sort of thing informally in discussing the model, rather than formally in the model itself.

With that simplification, the q'/q term disappears from the price equation, because it can be set equal to p'/p. The new coefficient j is really $j/(1 - i)$ and the new function g is really the old one multiplied by $1/(1 - i)$. I continue to assume that (the new) j is less than one.

Now the wage and price equations appear as two linear equations in w'/w and p'/p. They can be solved for w'/w and p'/p (provided $jk \neq 1$) and thus for $v'/v = w'/w - p'/p$. The determinants of v'/v are y^d/y^s and n/n^s (or perhaps better n^d/n^s if the labor constraint is actually binding so that $n^d > n = n^s$). These right-hand-side variables are themselves functions of v alone in this version of the model. So the end result is an equation of the form $v'/v = f(v)$, where f is a decreasing function. This gives the dynamics of the real wage. There is a critical real wage $\bar{v}$, the root of $f(\bar{v}) = 0$, which will be maintained if ever achieved. The key property of this stationary real wage is that pressures in the goods and labor markets are balanced; w and p may be inflating together or deflating together, but both at the same rate. If v is below $\bar{v}$, $f(v) > 0$ and v is increasing; if v is above $\bar{v}$, $f(v) < 0$ and v is decreasing.

The model is now essentially complete. The point (v,y) is always on the lower envelope curve of figures 8.1–8.3. At any such point we can calculate the direction and speed of change of v, and therefore the motion of the economy along the envelope curve: to the right if $v < \bar{v}$, to the left if $v > \bar{v}$. In the absence of shocks, eventually v tends to $\bar{v}$, and the economy to the corresponding state on the envelope.

In the parent paper of 1968, the model allowed for some very short-run inertia in employment and output, so that the current state need not always be exactly on the envelope. In that version of the model, the dynamics of the real wage can be described by an equation $v'/v = f(v,y)$, because v does not determine y instantaneously. The function $f(v,y)$ can be quite complicated in general, although it remains unambiguously a decreasing function of v. In Solow and Stiglitz (1968) it is argued that the locus $f(v,y) = 0$ is likely to be upward-sloping, with v increasing to the left of the curve and decreasing to its right. This more general version of the dynamics of v is represented in figures 8.4–8.6.[5]

Figure 8.4 reproduces figure 8.2, and superimposes four possible versions of the curve $f(v,y) = 0$. Any intersection like A,B,C, or D represents a stationary point for the real economy. Output, employment, and the real wage are constant. The nominal prices p,w, and q may be inflating or deflating, depending on the price and wage equations, but they are all inflating or deflating at the same proportional rate, so nothing real is happening. (Remember, since m and a are assumed to be constant in the background, this means that fiscal and monetary policy are passively accommodating the ongoing inflation or deflation.) A little further reflection shows that B,C, and D are stable points, while A is unstable. If we stick to configurations like B,C, and D then, after any shock the economy will gradually move toward such a (quasi) equilibrium.

A Stylized Story

Once upon a time, there was an economy in macroeconomic (quasi) equilibrium, at point E in figure 8.5. The market for goods and the market for labor both cleared. The real wage was constant, although the nominal wage and the price level may have been inflating (or even deflating) at the same proportional rate. If that were in fact so, then the central bank was keeping the real money supply constant and the fiscal authorities were keeping their net contribution to real demand (the real weighted standardized budget surplus) constant. And far across the sea, OPEC was maintaining the price of energy in fixed proportion to the price of domestic output. Time passed.

One fine day, OPEC announced a big increase in the price of energy. Always responsive to costs, the domestic price level jumped too, but not as much as the energy price, so there remained a very large rise in the real price of energy. What else is likely to happen?

1. The horizontal line (whose height measures net output at full employment) will drop because more gross output has to be paid to OPEC in exchange for energy and because the profit-maximizing input of energy falls. The size of the drop will probably be larger in the short run than in the long run as substitution effects strengthen with time.

2. The aggregate supply curve shifts down. With the stock of capital frozen in the short run, and labor and energy the only variable inputs, there is a rising marginal cost curve for domestic output. The supply

5. In simplifying the parent model for the purpose of this paper, I inadvertently overlooked the implied change from $f(v,y)$ to $f(v)$. Professor John B. Burbidge of McMaster University caught the slip and called it to my attention. I thank him for that and apologize to the reader. Luckily, the message of this paper is not affected at all. The reader can simply imagine the stationary-v locus to be vertical.

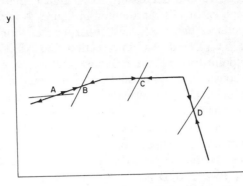

Fig. 8.4   Four possible versions of the curve $f(v,y) = 0$.

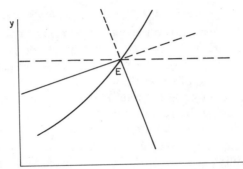

Fig. 8.5   An economy in macroeconomic (quasi) equilibrium, at
                    point E

curve in figure 8.5 may be regarded as showing, for given z and each v,
the output at which marginal cost equals price. The new higher value
of q implies higher marginal cost at each level of output. Since the initial
rise in p does not match the rise in q, marginal cost catches up with price
at a lower level of output for each value of the real wage. This could be
a very important element in the whole picture.

3. The aggregate demand curve will shift down if OPEC is not a big
buyer of domestic output. There is obviously a lot more to be said on
the demand side than this model is capable of saying, especially when
one takes account of effects through capital markets.

4. Unless fiscal and monetary policy accommodate the initial jump in
p, there is a further, and perhaps more important, force depressing the
aggregate demand curve. The real money supply will fall unless M jumps
along with p; and slow adaptation of nominal government spending, com-

bined with the normal progressivity of the tax system, will generate real fiscal drag.

5. If p jumps when q jumps, but w doesn't, or jumps even less than p, then v falls suddenly. The economy is displaced to the left along its (new) lower envelope curve. There is nothing in the model that requires the real wage to fall suddenly, but there is nothing against it either, and that seems to be what actually happened.

6. I am not happy with the part of the story that limits the initial response of the price level to a single jump that offsets part of the OPEC price increase, after which z remains constant and the price equation reverts to form. I have the feeling that there ought to be some residual cost push in there somewhere, but I do not see how to do it nicely without losing simplicity. Perhaps it is adequate to allow for a (temporary?) worsening of the price-Phillips curve by a NW shift of the stationary-v locus in figure 8.5. I am not too happy with this ad hoc device either, but it may be better than nothing. (Here is where Okun's model helps a lot.)

The net result of all this is figure 8.6. The old equilibrium point at E is drawn for reference. The new equilibrium is at G and, if nothing else happens, the economy will slide along the envelope curve toward G. I have drawn G on the falling part of the envelope to be compatible with the suggestion that the shift in the supply curve is the dominant geographic feature of the diagram. That could be a mistake if the contraction of the aggregate demand (described under 3 and 4 above) is strong enough.

Instead of a single initial point, I have drawn three possibilities, labelled F_1, F_2, and F_3. In the case of F_1, the initial reduction in v and

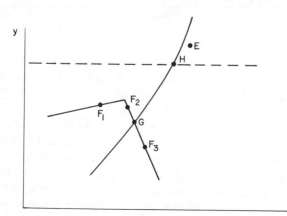

Fig. 8.6   The old equilibrium at point E, the new at point G, and a target equilibrium at point H

contraction of aggregate demand are enough to convert the supply shock into a state of Keynesian unemployment, with excess supply in both the goods market and the labor market. That seems a little unlikely in general, but perhaps the shocks of 1973–74 were extraordinary enough to have this effect. F_2 and F_3 are both, like G, situations of what Malinvaud (1977) calls classical unemployment: more goods could be sold at current prices, but price would exceed marginal cost at any higher output. In the case of F_2, even though there is excess supply of labor, the wage-Phillips curve generates enough wage increase and the excess demand for goods is slight enough that the real wage will rise and recoup some of its initial loss before stabilizing at G. In the case of F_3, there is enough excess demand for goods so that the price level will outstrip the nominal wage and the real wage will fall further toward G. Starting from F_2, output and employment fall along the supply curve as the real wage rises; starting from F_3, output and employment rise.

Evidently the model can generate a few different immediate outcomes, depending on quantitative details. But they have some important features in common. In the immediate aftermath of an adverse supply shock, output and employment are down, the real wage falls, and inflation accelerates. Only the last of these statements requires further comment. The initial cost-induced jump in the price level is certainly a contribution to faster inflation. At a point like F_2 or F_3 there is excess demand for goods (compared with balance at E) and that is a further contribution. At F_1, however, there is excess supply of goods, and always there is excess supply of labor. These work to reduce the rate of inflation. Finally, I have staged at least a temporary worsening of the short-run price equation, represented in figure 8.6 by the fact that the stationary-v locus passes to the left of E. It would take a very steep wage-Phillips curve to overturn the presumption that inflation accelerates initially.

Policy

At last I come to the question; but by now the answers are obvious.

I take it that the aim of macroeconomic policy is to steer the economy to a point like H in figure 8.6. The level of income at E is no longer attainable. In accepting H as a reasonable target, I am taking it for granted that nothing can be done about the location of the stationary-v curve, or about wage and price behavior in general. It is possible, of course, that when the extra cost-push effects of the energy price rise have worn off, the curve will drift back to its old position through E and the eventual target equilibrium will be a bit to the right of H. But anything that could have been done by way of policy to modify wage and price behavior post-OPEC could have been done pre-OPEC. This is a separate matter. I do not discuss the possibility of settling for some lower point on the stationary-v curve with a smaller rate of inflation because I want to avoid the tiresome argument about the existence or nonexistence of a long-run trade-off, or about the length of time before the trade-off evaporates.

I have already argued that it would be a mistake to try to reverse the initial one-shot increase in the domestic price level stemming from the representative firm's attempt to evade the cost increase imposed by OPEC. It is not so damaging as to justify the loss of real income that would be necessary to roll it back from the demand side. Indeed, if the initial point were like F_1, there would be a presumption in favor of accommodative fiscal and monetary policy to cancel the secondary reduction of aggregate demand caused by the fiscal drag and the reduction of the real money supply induced by the immediate price increase. (Between the end of 1973 and the end of 1975, real M2 fell by 3 or 4 percent; if potential output rose by a routine 6 or 7 percent during those two years, then the equivalent reduction of the real money supply was more like 10%. It is equally commonplace that progression in tax rates added some unintended fiscal drag.) If the initial point were like F_2 or F_3, then immediate replacement of lost aggregate demand would add little or nothing to output, but would, by adding to excess demand for goods, worsen inflation. Eventually, however, on the way to equilibrium at H, most of the dissipated aggregate demand would need to be replaced via expansionary fiscal and monetary policy: most, but not all, because the target is H, not E.

I am inclined to believe that there was a large component of Keynesian unemployment in 1974, so that expansionary fiscal and monetary policy would have been effective in raising output and employment at least temporarily. If that were all, however, the economy could only have inflated its way toward G.

If the economy is to be steered toward equilibrium at H, then somehow both the aggregate demand and aggregate supply curves have to be made to pass through H. It should come as no surprise that the correct adaptation to an adverse supply shock requires a component of supply management. The obvious tools would have been reductions in payroll taxes and in excise taxes. In the absence of any broad-based federal excise tax, the natural recourse would have been to federally financed reductions in state and local excises. I presume that a negative federal excise tax is too unorthodox to live. (If OPEC and the other disturbances catalogued earlier are the wave of the future, then there may be some case for the creation of a broad-based federal indirect tax, just so that it can be used routinely as an instrument of stabilization policy.) Of course, such policy moves have demand effects too, and these would have to be reckoned into the overall calculation and supplemented or offset depending on the rest of the fiscal-monetary package.

Aggregate supply-oriented policies have the additional advantage of shifting the balance in the goods market so that even if output is temporarily demand-limited, there might be some reduction of inflationary pressure.

In the event, of course, we got mindless demand contraction, as if the inflation of 1974 were a reflection of excess demand, followed by only slightly less mindless demand expansion, with results that are obvious to everyone. Well, almost everyone.

Comment   Neil Wallace

Several times in the course of this conference, it has been noted that the conference is less about rational expectations than it is about the macroeconomic implications of non-price-rationing—so-called sticky prices, or, as I would prefer to put it, queue or first-come, first-served rationing. Yet, the discussion has not gone much beyond that remark.

I prefer to speak of there being queues rather than sticky prices because sticky prices have various implications, not all of which still need explaining. Thus, sticky prices give rise to the Phillips curve. This correlation contradicts the pre-signal-extraction full employment models, according to which any change in aggregate demand is felt entirely in prices and not at all in real output. But business cycle correlations are explained by models built along the lines of Lucas (1972). It is sticky prices which result in queues or first-come first-serve allocations that we have not explained. And queues are what many of us mean by involuntary unemployment.

I will comment in a general way about the modeling of queues. This is relevant for Solow's paper, because he would, I think, defend the macroeconomic model he uses on the grounds that it or something like it—say, some version of the model described by Malinvaud (1977)—adequately accounts for non-price-rationing or queues.

The general problem posed by a phenomenon like queues can be put as follows. The only economic model that we know a fair amount about is the Arrow-Debreu general competitive equilibrium model. But many important phenomena are not accounted for by that model. Examples are queues, money, and limited liability. I want to approach the discussion of how to model queues by considering ways of modifying the Arrow-Debreu model.

In modern expositions of the Arrow-Debreu model, we distinguish between the *physical environment* of the model and the *competitive scheme*. The physical environment consists of the technology, the total resources, and the preferences of the agents. A specification of the physical environment implies a set of feasible allocations and the subset of those that are Pareto optimal. The competitive scheme consists of a description of who owns what, of price-taking behavior, and of market clearing. When competitive equilibrium exists, the theorems of welfare economics connect up the allocations implied by the competitive scheme with the set of Pareto optimal allocations implied by the physical environment.

The competitive scheme can be criticized for not being an explicit noncooperative game. Put differently, it can be criticized for requiring the services of an outside agent, the Walrasian auctioneer. But recent work shows that there are explicit noncooperative games whose equilibrium allocations approach those of the competitive scheme as the number of agents approaches infinity (see, for example, Townsend 1978). This justifies studying the sort of model Solow uses by posing the question: Does it depart from the physical environment of Arrow-Debreu, from the kinds of noncooperative games implicit in Arrow-Debreu, or from both? Admittedly, to ask this question is, in effect, to require that outcomes implied by models which are described as being disequilibrium models should nonetheless be equilibria for *some* game in *some* physical environment. But without such a requirement for what constitutes a model, one cannot argue that the structure of the model is invariant in the face of alternative policies and one cannot appraise alternative policies in terms of the Pareto criterion.

Solow's model and ones like it have the following structures: starting with arbitrary prices, one assumes that agents optimally choose quantities taking those prices as given and, perhaps, taking into account that they may be rationed. The resulting quantities imply excess demands, which, in turn, imply new prices via assumed price adjustment rules. Since the physical environment of such models is not described as being different from that of the Arrow-Debreu model, the claim must be that there is some game whose equilibrium in the physical environment of Arrow-Debreu yields the above structure and, in particular, the price adjustment rules and the rationing schemes.

While we cannot rule out the possibility that the sort of model Solow describes is the equilibrium for some game, there are reasons for doubt. Although many different games can be formulated for a given physical environment, there have to be some standards for what constitutes an equilibrium concept for a game. Any equilibrium concept would seem to involve optimization on the part of agents and some notion of consistency between the environment agents think they are in and the environment implied by the outcome of the game. (By the way, to impose rational expectations is to impose some degree of such consistency, but it would be a great mistake to think that one achieves overall consistency by taking some so-called macroeconomic model and altering it along the lines of Sargent and Wallace 1975.) Thus, if there are price setters, it has to be shown that the environment is such that the price adjustment rules in Solow's model are optimal courses of action for them. But as Gordon and Hynes (1970) argued, that seems doubtful. In any case, the efficient way to proceed is to start with the description of the game and to see what it implies.

More fundamentally, though, there is reason to believe that phenomena like queues will not be adequately modeled without departing from the physical environment of Arrow-Debreu. Everyone concedes the need for models that assign a smaller allocative role to markets than does Arrow-Debreu. Such models would, in a sense, explain which markets exist and which do not and would likely assign some allocative role to devices like queues. It seems obvious that such models will have to depart from the costless multilateral communication implicit in Arrow-Debreu. When one examines how much information is costlessly exchanged in the explicit noncooperative games whose outcomes mimic those of the competitive scheme, one begins to appreciate how much costless communication is implicit in Arrow-Debreu (again, see, for example, Townsend 1978).

While analogies are dangerous and this one particularly so since Solow is from MIT, it is as if Arrow-Debreu is economics without friction in the same sense as there is physics without friction. And as there are many physical phenomena unexplainable in terms of physics without friction, so there are many social phenomena unexplainable in terms of economics without friction. While not much is implied by saying that the modeling of queues calls for an economics with friction, the notion that we must depart from the physical environment of Arrow-Debreu in order to model queues does suggest that we not make policy recommendations based on a vision of what is feasible and optimal in the Arrow-Debreu environment. A model with friction will not imply the same set of feasible allocations as a model that is in all other respects similar but has no friction.

What seems to divide those at this conference are our guesses about the macroeconomic implications of models that will successfully confront phenomena like queues. Some of us believe such models will have macroeconomic implications much like those of Solow's model. Others believe such models will have macroeconomic implications much like those of Lucas (1972). Since I belong to the latter group, let me say why.

So far I have discussed the modeling of queues per se. In an important sense, though, it is not queues per se that constitute the problem for macroeconomics. Rather, it is the way the lengths of queues vary over time and in a way related to aggregative variables like the price level and the government deficit. A model of queues per se need not be able to address this cyclical variability. But a combination of the elements that give rise to queues per se and the informational constraint elements in Lucas (1972) will, I think, explain cyclical variation in the lengths of queues. My guess that the macroeconomic implications of models of queues will be much like those of Lucas (1972) is based on my belief that the informational constraint ideas in Lucas will be fruitful in explaining the cyclical variability of queue lengths.

In general, I would have liked to see much more of this conference devoted to discussions of why we differ so much in our guesses about the macroeconomic implications of models of queues. We seem, instead, to have spent quite a bit of time both in the papers and in the discussion simply announcing our guesses.

References

Barro, R. J., and Grossman, H. 1976. *Money, Employment, and Inflation.* Cambridge: Cambridge University Press.

Gordon, D. F., and Hynes, A. 1970. "On the Theory of Price Dynamics." In *Microeconomic Foundations of Employment and Inflation Theory,* edited by E. S. Phelps, pp. 369–93. New York: W. W. Norton.

Hicks, J. R. 1965. *Capital and Growth.* London: Oxford University press.

———. 1974. *The Crisis in Keynesian Economics.* Oxford: Basil Blackwell.

Lucas, R. E., Jr. 1972. "Expectations and the Neutrality of Money." *Journal of Economic Theory* 4:103–24.

Malinvaud, E. 1977. *The Theory of Unemployment Reconsidered.* New York: Wiley.

Marks, R. E. 1978. "Non-renewable Resources and Disequilibrium Macroeconomics." Ph.D. thesis, Stanford University.

Okun, A. M. 1975. "Inflation: Its Mechanics and Welfare Costs." *Brookings Papers on Economic Activity* 2:351–90.

Phelps, E. S. 1978. "Commodity Supply Shock and Full Employment Monetary Policy." *Journal of Money, Credit, and Banking* 10:206–21.

Sargent, T. J., and Wallace, N. 1975. " 'Rational' Expectations, the Optimal Monetary Instrument, and the Optimal Money Supply Rule." *Journal of Political Economy* 83:241–54.

Solow, R. M., and Stiglitz, J. E. 1968. "Employment, Output, and Wages in the Short Run." *Quarterly Journal of Economics* 82:537–60.

Townsend, R. M. 1978. "Equilibrium with Endogenous Marketeers." Carnegie-Mellon University Working Paper.

9 Macroeconomic Policy, 1971–75: An Appraisal

William Poole

I was invited to examine the macroeconomic policy of 1973–75, but limiting the analysis to those years runs the risk that the major lessons of this period will be lost. Since the events of 1973–75 cannot be understood without reference to the highly expansionary policies of 1972 and the disruptive impact of the wage-price controls introduced in August 1971, I have taken the liberty of redefining my topic.

The controversy over policy in this period centers on monetary policy in 1974. In the first major section of the paper I sketch the policy activists' position on this controversy—the position that the oil price shock should have been accommodated by extra monetary expansion. The next section of the paper contains three subsections in which I provide my thoughts on the monetary, fiscal, and price control policies of the 1971–75 period. The final section contains some general observations on the lessons of the period.

The Activists' View of 1973–75

Since this paper might have carried the title, "The Case against the Case against Macro Policy in 1973–75," I might as well begin my discussion by outlining what I understand to be the typical activist position on macroeconomic policy for 1973–75. Hoping to use a reasonably neutral and descriptive term, I have called this position "activist" rather than "conventional" or "Keynesian," but a case might be made for these other terms.

This paper was half completed when I read the paper by Robert Lucas prepared for this conference. The Lucas paper has certainly helped me to clarify my thinking about the lessons to be learned from the 1971–75 experience.

In any event, the dispute centers on policy, and especially monetary policy, in the first half of 1974. The activists' view is that policy was far too tight at that time. Using the most recently revised quarterly average data, M1 and M2 growth rates from 1973:IV to 1974:II were 5.9% and 8.5%, respectively.[1] The monthly average federal funds rate was pushed from 8.97% in February 1974 to 12.92% in July 1974. While the change in the federal funds rate was large, and the July 1974 peak was historically high, the M1 and M2 growth rates in the first half of 1974 were not low by long-term historical norms and were essentially unchanged from their respective growth rates over the preceding year.

The argument that money growth in early 1974 reflected a very tight monetary policy depends on the observation that growth in real balances was abnormally low. With the GNP deflator rising at a 9.5% rate from 1973:IV to 1974:II real M1 growth was −3.6% and real M2 growth was −1%. The policy significance of this observation, however, depends on the assertion that the inflation of the period was largely exogenously determined by supply shocks; the rising price of oil was not offset by declines in other prices because in the short run many prices are downwardly rigid. If this view is accepted, then it appears to follow without further argument that nominal money growth was too low in early 1974. The Federal Reserve, on this argument, should have adjusted upward the rate of growth of nominal money balances to maintain at least some growth in real balances.

While I do not accept the view that the price level can be taken as exogenous for policy purposes and will discuss the issue below, at this point it is worth noting that the logic of the activist position requires indictment of monetary policy in 1972. At the same time price controls were exogenously forcing down the rate of inflation, nominal money growth was accelerating. From 1971:IV to 1972:IV, M1 and M2 grew at 8% and 10.6% rates, respectively, while the GNP deflator grew at a 4.1% rate. The economy expanded excessively rapidly, and in early 1973 the unemployment rate dropped below 5%. The 1972 controls price shock should have been accommodated by lower money growth.

While most activists do condemn 1972 monetary policy, as I understand their position the magnitudes involved require that the greater criticism be applied to policy in 1974. In 1973 unemployment was only slightly less than the natural rate and so excess demand is capable of explaining only a small part of the 1973–74 acceleration of inflation— perhaps only half of one percentage point. Since controls are estimated to have reduced the price level to a point about 2% below what it other-

---

1. These growth rates, along with all other growth rates reported below, are continuously compounded annual rates of growth.

wise would have been at the end of 1972,[2] the breakdown of controls per se could account for at most a 4 percentage point acceleration in the inflation rate in 1973—two percentage points of return to the underlying inflation rate of about 6% plus 2 percentage points catch-up. In addition, some extra inflation may have resulted from controls mismanagement. The off-again, on-again phases and freezes of 1973 generated some production inefficiencies and some anticipatory price increases.

In sketching the activists' position I hope I have not set up a straw man; I certainly have not intended to do so. This position does not require that the inflation rate be completely insensitive to business conditions. Indeed, most of those adhering to the activists' position believe in a Phillips curve, although one that is fairly flat in the short run. The key feature of this view is not that unemployment is irrelevant to inflation but that in 1973 and the first half of 1974 unemployment was so close to the natural rate that the acceleration of inflation must be attributed primarily to exogenous food, fuel, and controls mismanagement supply shocks.

Destabilization Policy 1971–75

An important lesson from 1973–75, I believe, is that destabilizing policies really are destabilizing. This lesson cannot be understood by concentrating on the period 1973–75 alone; the events of 1971–72 must be examined at the same time. Monetary policy, fiscal policy, wage-price control policies, and normal business cycle dynamics interacted with each other in a highly destabilizing manner. The supply shocks were of some importance but mostly because of the controls. The nature of these policies and their interactions will now be sketched.

Monetary Policy. Over the period 1971–75 the money stock followed a classic destabilizing pattern. To avoid getting bogged down in numbers I will concentrate on M2, but the timing of accelerations and decelerations of M1 was broadly similar.

After growing at a trend rate slightly below 9% in 1970–71, M2 growth accelerated to a rate of 10.6% between 1971:IV and 1972:IV. This acceleration may be regarded as highly expansionary for three interrelated reasons. First, continuation of the 9% rate of M2 growth would have been consistent with a cyclical recovery. The rate of inflation was gradually creeping down before controls were imposed and would have continued to do so had controls not been imposed. With the inflation rate creeping down, a 9% rate of M2 growth already reflected a monetary policy consistent with rapid expansion in real output.

Second, wage-price controls did, I believe, suppress inflation for a time. For a given rate of nominal money growth, the suppression of inflation generated larger real money growth and, therefore, tended to stimulate real output growth. And third, nominal M2 growth did not remain at 9% but accelerated to 10.6%. With the GNP deflator rising at a 4.1% rate between 1971:IV and 1972:IV, real M2 balances grew at a 6.5% rate over this period.

The acceleration of money growth in 1972 was clearly a mistake—as I believe most policy analysts will agree. But it should be understood that this mistake was partly caused by the introduction of wage-price controls in 1971. The Federal Reserve was under considerable political pressure not to "scuttle prosperity" through tight money, especially after price control policies were introduced to solve the inflation problem. In addition, as I have argued elsewhere,[3] the Federal Reserve was concerned that holding money growth down would require interest rate increases that would undermine political support for "tough" wage and price standards.

Following its 1972 acceleration, M2 growth returned to a rate only slightly below its 1970–71 rate—8.5% from 1972:IV to 1974:II. This lower rate collided unavoidably with the price and output effects of the 1972 acceleration. Real balances in early 1973 were above those desired in equilibrium. An attempt to maintain the higher real balances through higher growth in nominal balances would have led to an even greater acceleration in inflation.

This view, of course, is disputed by those who argue that the evidence from Phillips curve studies indicates that unemployment was not low enough to cause a substantial acceleration in inflation. But it is impossible for the usual Phillips curve approach to deal adequately with changing inflation expectations. Surely, if ever there was a time when a substantial outward shift in the Phillips curve occurred because of rising expectations of inflation, then that time would be 1973. The transition from Phase II to Phase III was widely interpreted as a relaxation of controls, and controls were in any event breaking down in many areas because of growing shortages of goods.

While very little is known at the empirical level about the dynamics of adjustment, I believe that some degree of overadjustment in the price level is quite likely. As inflation in 1973 worked down the level of real balances, inflation also served to reduce the desired level of real balances by raising the cost of holding money. Given the path of nominal money

3. William Poole, "Burnsian Monetary Policy: Eight Years of Progress?" *Journal of Finance* 34 (May 1979):473–84.

balances, inflation was partly self-generating for a time. But the process, while oscillatory, was not unstable; eventually the price level increased to the point where excess real balances were eliminated.

As real balances were further reduced by inflation in 1974, aggregate demand weakened. This process was then aggravated by the unambiguous monetary policy mistake of permitting a sharp decleration in money growth in the second half of 1974. Between 1974:II and 1975:I, M2 growth averaged 6.2% annual rate. Without this deceleration the recession would not have been quite as bad as it was, but it seems unlikely that the recession profile would have been much different if 8.5% M2 growth had been maintained.

Fiscal Policy. Fiscal policy from 1971 through 1974 was destabilizing although, in my opinion, of much less quantitative importance than monetary policy. As estimated by the Federal Reserve Bank of Saint Louis, the high employment budget deficit was $7.8 billion in 1971. During the boom year of 1972 the high employment deficit was $15.5 billion. As the rate of growth of real output fell in 1973 and became negative in 1974, the high employment budget deficit fell to $4.6 billion in 1973 and in 1974 turned into a surplus of $1.1 billion. Fiscal policy provided no stimulus during the contraction phase of the business cycle, although it did turn expansionary at about the time of the recession trough in 1975.

Many observers have noted that the major explanation for the contractionary course of fiscal policy in 1973–74 is the high elasticity of federal revenues with respect to nominal income. Inflation-generated increases in nominal income yielded continuing growth in real tax revenues at rates above the growth in real GNP.

Although fiscal policy was operating as an automatic destabilizer in 1973–74, it would in principle have been possible for discretionary policy changes to offset the automatic destabilizers. But in the inflationary environment of 1973–74, tax cuts seemed out of the question politically. This observation makes clear the importance of designing a fiscal policy structure with desirable operating properties—a structure involving automatic stabilizers. The key fiscal policy lesson from this experience is the importance of indexing the tax system.

Wage-Price Controls. The macroeconomic effects of wage-price controls are, I believe, generally underestimated. There are certainly many stories about inefficiencies caused by the last set of controls—new apartments sitting idle for many months because of controls-induced shortages of plumbing fixtures, and so forth. It is, I suspect, no accident that productivity growth was subnormal, even adjusted for normal cyclical patterns, in 1973–75.[4]

4. See George L. Perry, "Potential Output and Productivity," in Arthur M. Okun and George L. Perry, eds., *Brookings Papers on Economic Activity* 1977, 1:11–47, especially 34–38.

Analysis of controls is of great importance in assessing the argument for monetary accommodation of the "oil shock." It is crystal clear that price controls and quantity allocations magnified the problems caused by the OPEC price increases and the oil embargo. Few will forget the disruptions caused by the unavailability of gasoline in the winter of 1973/74, but a few numbers will serve to indicate the magnitude of the regulatory disaster.

First, when the embargo began in October 1973, the U.S. petroleum industry had already been disrupted by controls and spot shortages of petroleum products had appeared. Total inventories of crude oil and petroleum products had declined by 3% in the 12 months ending 5 October, 1973. The embargo ended in mid-March 1974, but, because of the regulatory fiasco, inventories had been accumulated rather than run down during the embargo. At the end of March 1974 total inventories were 6% above their levels a year earlier; gasoline inventories were about 7% higher while distillate fuel oil inventories were almost 20% higher. While price indexes for petroleum products in this period were probably lower than they otherwise would have been by virtue of the oil price controls, the disruption of the production process must surely have raised the prices of other goods. Without price controls the erosion of real balances in the first half of 1974 might have been smaller.[5]

The disruption argument is reinforced by the fact that industrial production reached a peak in November 1973 and then declined substantially in each of the next three months. This output decline cannot possibly be attributed to a decline in real money balances; if the numerator of real balances had declined rather than the denominator increasing, no one would have predicted that industrial production would start falling with a one-month lag.

Without relaxation of controls monetary accommodation of the oil price shock would have been less successful than the activists' position might suggest, even accepting the assumptions of that position. During the embargo larger aggregate demand would have increased the size of the petroleum products shortage and, presumably, the shortages of goods whose production is heavily dependent on petroleum products. Thus, more of any nominal aggregate demand stimulus would have been dissipated in price increases than relationships estimated in noncontrol environments might predict.

After the embargo, assuming continuation of price controls on domestic crude and petroleum products, stimulus to aggregate demand through extra monetary expansion would also have been dissipated in

5. The inventory figures in this paragraph are from Richard B. Mancke, *Squeaking By: U.S. Energy Policy Since the Embargo* (New York: Columbia University Press, 1976), table 2.1, p. 24.

price increases to an unusual extent. With the price of domestic crude controlled but the prices of labor and other inputs to crude oil production not controlled, and with a growing gap between the controlled price of "old" oil and the expected future price of oil, demand stimulus would have tended to reduce domestic crude production further. To the extent that aggregate output rose the extra petroleum demand would have been satisfied by extra imports. These two extra sources of demand for petroleum imports would have made the foreign exchange value of the dollar depreciate more rapidly and would, therefore, have quickly increased the prices of many tradable goods.

The 1973–74 experience shows that price controls can leave an industry highly vulnerable to disturbances. While this point may be disputed by price control advocates who insist that the problem was not with controls per se but with their administration, I believe that administration of controls by a competent independent agency would have caused basically the same problem. The 1960s guideposts were justified in part by the argument that they would help to prevent "premature inflation"—price increases that occurred before capacity production was attained. The U.S. oil embargo experience provides a clear example of the benefits of firms maintaining some margin of excess capacity, excess capacity that could not exist with controls under the premature inflation doctrine.

Whatever the merits of my analysis of the probable performance of an independent controls agency, experience with price controls in oil and many other industries demonstrates that controls cannot be kept out of the political process and that the political process does not produce even remotely sensible controls decisions. Controls are futile and disruptive, period. And they spill over to affect traditional stabilization policies as my earlier comments on Federal Reserve efforts to limit interest rate increases in 1972 pointed out.

Some General Comments on 1971–75

I have insisted on discussing the period 1971–75 rather than just 1973–75 because the problems of the later years cannot be understood without reference to the earlier years. The entire period is especially interesting because it shows how policy was constrained in 1973–75 by policies followed in 1971–72 and earlier and by market expectations concerning future policies.

The 1973–74 experience with fiscal policy is helpful in explaining a poorly understood point about monetary policy. Although monetary policy is supposed to be flexible, it is in fact subject to the same types of political constraints as fiscal policy. For a clear example of these constraints, consider the allegation made by some that Federal Reserve policy in 1972 was politically motivated to help the reelection of Richard Nixon. In the absence of "smoking gun" evidence such a charge can be neither proved nor disproved and so is not a good subject for scholarly inquiry. What can be investigated, though, is the impact of such charges on monetary policy. My distinct impression from following monetary policy over a period of years is that Federal Reserve officials do feel constrained to follow policies that "look right" to the public and the Congress. With respect to stabilization policy, the Fed probably does have more room to maneuver than Congress has, but the difference should not be exaggerated.

By concentrating on the analysis of discretionary policy, economists have neglected study of the actual operating properties of monetary and fiscal policies determined importantly by feedback from the political process and from the reactions of those dealing in speculative markets. The recent concentration of some economists who used to be called "fiscalists" on discretionary monetary policy reflects, I suspect, a feeling that in the United States discretionary fiscal policy is a lost cause politically. Thus, there is no point in criticizing fiscal policy for failing to offset the oil price shock. But recognition of the impossibility of well-timed discretionary fiscal policy, instead of generating renewed interest in fiscal policy by formula flexibility, has led fiscalists to turn their interest to discretionary monetary policy without recognizing that the same issues arise in both policy areas.

Fiscal policy can be used, and has been used, to pump up expenditures and cut taxes in an election year, but those playing the game had better play with a certain amount of discretion. Somewhat higher political standards are demanded of U.S. monetary policymakers, as the controversy over 1972 policy makes clear. My guess is that at many points in time monetary policymakers have freedom roughly comparable to that of election-year fiscal policymakers.

The activists who advocated 12%–15% money growth in the first half of 1974 are in the same political boat as those who advocate special tax rebates. No matter how sound the analysis, tax rebates payable on the Monday before the first Tuesday in November of an even-numbered year just do not look right, and neither does a special, one-time dose of extra money growth when the inflation rate has hit double-digits and the unemployment rate is about 5%. A substantial increase in money growth in early 1974 could have generated political charges that the Fed was trying to prop up a weakened Republican party before the fall elections; it could also have triggered sharp declines in the stock, bond, and foreign exchange markets as investors increasingly feared a further acceleration of inflation. Such events would have forced the Federal Reserve to follow more stringent policies.

Experience with wage-price controls contains the same lesson. To the economist, nothing is more natural than to raise price ceilings whenever shortages develop, provided, of course, that the control agency has investigated the shortages and determined that they are not "artificial" or "contrived." But politically there is no question that the most difficult time to raise price ceilings is when there *are* shortages.

In a democratic society the behavior of all public officials is severely constrained by some combination of explicit legislation and implicit norms. Even policymakers with apparently unlimited discretion on paper are substantially constrained. The key feature of the implicit norms relevant to discretionary policymaking is that the norms, like explicit legislation, are determined in advance of the events to which they apply precisely so that the policymaker will not be able to pursue personal objectives inconsistent with his public responsibilities.

Advocates of discretionary policy have concentrated their analysis on uncovering the economic structure and on diagnosing disturbances so that the optimal policy response can be calculated period by period. Although this analysis has suffered from the failure of the models employed to handle rational expectations issues, model builders are acutely aware of the need to improve their models and are constantly trying to do so. But advocates of discretionary policy seem almost oblivious to the need to think about the analytical implications of being forced by the political process to follow policy rules that sharply limit discretion. A simple example is that most advocates of price controls would probably abandon the policy altogether if told that no price ceiling could be adjusted by more than 6% per year.

Although I do not have great confidence in my positive political analysis because my "knowledge" consists of nothing more than undocumented impressions, I think I know something about the norms applying to particular policies. In the policy area I know best—monetary policy—I am convinced that a lack of public appreciation for the lags in monetary effects and excessive attention to interest rates generates a monetary policy that is naturally procyclical. Political norms do not by any means rule out policy responses to special events. In the monetary policy area there is a well-established class of special events known as "financial panics" under which central banks not only can act but are expected to act. The Federal Reserve's response to the Penn Central failure in 1970 was certainly consistent with this implicit rule. A similar analysis applies to Federal Reserve support of the Franklin National Bank in 1974, although here the Fed had to be concerned about the charge that it was bailing out the bank's owners and management at the public expense. The public correctly perceives that some public officials are scoundrels; until oil shocks and similar events are placed in a broad class of events subject to norms defining the appropriate policy response, policymakers will not be able to respond to such disturbances to the full extent indicated by "all available information."

I suspect that a strong and politically astute Federal Reserve chairman could break the procyclical pattern of general monetary policy, but I have more confidence that a well-designed legislated policy rule could provide a permanent improvement than that we will be fortunate enough to have an endless string of highly competent Federal Reserve chairmen. Given the vehemence with which so many activists complained about monetary policy in 1974, I am surprised that so few of them share this view.

The research agenda implied by this discussion has two major items. At the level of economic analysis per se there is need for examination of alternative policy rules. This item does not, or need not, reflect ideological commitment to rules and ideological opposition to discretion but rather the empirical proposition, which is subject to investigation, that discretionary policy in the United States has been subject to political processes that produce a suboptimal policy response pattern.

The second item on the research agenda is an improved understanding of the nature of the policy response patterns generated by the political process. Positive analysis of the political process is of interest for its own sake but is also important for the economist as a policy adviser. One of the arguments against legislated policy rules has always been that it takes discretion to enact legislation, and discretion can repeal legislation. The argument is correct, but incomplete. Legislation does make a difference; laws are not typically ignored or abandoned on short notice. Indeed, this point is recognized by rules opponents who argue that legislated rules will lock us into harmful and outmoded policies. The economist as policy adviser needs to know something about the political process so that he can propose rules that are consistent with it.

If asked to speculate on the nature of the optimal monetary policy rule I would first emphasize that it is a mistake to approach the problem as one of designing a rule expected to be optimal for all time. The operation of any rule is bound to generate evidence pointing toward modification of the rule. In addition, since public attitudes change through education and experience, a desirable rule that is not politically feasible now may become so later. The policy problem is not that of devising an optimal policy rule but rather that of devising an improved rule that can evolve over time as evidence accumulates and public perceptions change.

The events of 1971–75 strengthen the case for adopting a steady growth monetary rule. Given the lack of public understanding of the lags in the effects of monetary policy changes, a reactive rule designed with lags in mind seems unlikely to survive politically. While a steady growth policy may not survive politically either, it at least has a better chance than a reactive rule that almost certainly will at times appear perverse to the layman. In addition, a reactive rule is clearly subject to opportunistic tampering since the evidence on the length of the lags in policy effects is not strong enough—probably because the lag process is not at all stable —clearly to justify one particular reactive rule over another.

The political question in the design of policy rules is one of feasibility in the fundamental rather than the partisan sense. Successful policy advisers have always operated with an intuitive feel for political processes, but surely the methods of social science can add much to our understanding. Multiple regressions and explicit policy rules will never replace the policy adviser who has brilliant political intuition but they will make it possible to pass along a certain amount of knowledge from one generation to the next.

Comment   James L. Pierce

Poole's paper provides a thoughtful appraisal of macroeconomic policies over the years 1971–75. Poole had been asked to analyze the policy implications of OPEC but concluded, quite correctly I believe, that the macroeconomic effects of OPEC cannot be understood adequately without appraising the initial conditions for the macroeconomy prior to the formation of the oil cartel. These initial conditions can be appreciated only after examining the macroeconomic policies of earlier years, which can hardly be viewed as exerting a stabilizing influence on the economy. The imposition of price controls in 1971 and the highly expansionary monetary and fiscal policies that followed produced economic distortions and inflationary pressures that, in turn, led to the subsequent relaxation of price controls and rising inflation. The economy possessed an unusually bad set of initial conditions upon which were superimposed the quadrupling of oil prices in 1973. The surge of inflation that followed produced highly restrictive monetary and fiscal policies. The economy responded to the shocks—both external and self-inflicted—by producing the worst collapse of real output since the 1930s. Poole concludes that matters had gotten out of hand and that political considerations helped to turn policy restrictive in 1974. He argues that a more steady monetary policy during the entire 1971–75 period would have been beneficial for the economy.

In reaching his conclusions, Poole revives the old question of rules versus authority in the execution of monetary policy. He concludes that rules seem preferable to the kinds of macroeconomic policies that have actually evolved. In the current context, the issues can be developed by asking the question: Are there shocks, such as the one created by OPEC, for which it is appropriate and desirable for policy to react? Solow answers yes, the government should have moved to offset the aggregate demand effects of OPEC. For him an activist policy is desirable. Poole is a little less clear on the answer to the question but points out that previous policy errors seriously affected the conditions in the economy upon which were superimposed the actions of OPEC. Poole seems to be arguing that policymakers cannot be trusted to pursue activist policies. Political and other factors can prevent the appropriate activist policies from being pursued.

The argument for rules to constrain the execution of monetary policy has been made forcefully and repeatedly by Milton Friedman. A description of the kinds of rules that might be applied are summarized in the paper by Lucas. There are two elements in the argument for rules. First, policymakers often cannot be trusted to do the right thing because of political and other noneconomic factors. Second, there is such ignorance of the true structure of the economy that activist policy strategies produce economic consequences that are inferior to the consequences of pursuing a simple rule. There is ample evidence to support the first argument. The second argument is more difficult to analyze, but it can be shown for certain models with stochastic structures, under certain conditions, pursuit of a rule can produce "optimal" policy. These results, however, hold for well-behaved stochastic disturbances and have nothing to say about the kind of shock produced by OPEC. There was no way to anticipate that shock, but once it occurred there was ample evidence that it produced a disturbance to aggregate demand that could have been offset to a degree by more expansionary policy. This is Solow's point. To be sure, ignorance of the exact effects of expansionary policy would limit the extent of the policy move, as would the political problems discussed by Poole. But despite these limitations, pursuit of a policy rule in the face of OPEC-type shocks represents a very restrictive policy.

It appears that the economy would have been better off if the Fed had moved to offset part of the decline in aggregate demand that resulted from the increase in the price of oil.[6] In my opinion it would have been desirable and politically feasible for the Fed to have pursued such a policy *if* it had announced what it was doing. In particular, it would have to explain that it was not "accommodating" the inflation but rather acting to cushion the economy from the collapse in aggregate demand that occurred in 1974.

A particularly unfortunate consequence of the monetary policy of 1973–74 was that it was extremely difficult for private agents in the

6. For a discussion of the kinds of policy responses that might have been appropriate see Pierce and Enzler, "The Effects of External Inflationary Shocks," *Brookings Papers on Economic Activity* 1974, 1.

economy to figure out what the monetary policy strategy was. It seems fair to say that these agents were surprised both by OPEC and by the monetary policy that followed it. Previous experience strongly suggested that monetary policy would have been accommodative in the sense that the Fed would have limited the increases in the interest rates that accompanied the surge of inflation and scramble for credit. Agents were surprised and often chagrined to learn that the Fed had changed the rules of the game. Short-term interest rates were allowed to rise at unprecedented speed. As a result, many agents got caught with the need to roll over short-term liabilities at rapidly rising cost while seeing the yields on their longer-term investments not rise in commensurate fashion. Turmoil resulted, and at times it became extremely difficult for many firms to roll over their liabilities. The uncertainties and confusion about monetary policy interacted with the uncertainty and confusion stemming from OPEC, price decontrol, and all of the other factors that were hitting the economy. During the episode, the policymakers, both fiscal and monetary, were either silent about their intentions or were issuing the kind of optimistic claptrap that one has come to expect from Washington. Thus, the statements from policymakers coupled with actual policy actions heightened uncertainty.

During the period from late 1973 through late 1974, monetary policy was for the first time on an M1 target. That is to say, the Fed was actually trying to achieve an M1 growth of 6% or less as opposed to just making public utterances about money targets. This shift in policy strategy was unprecedented and produced many surprises in financial markets. Solow's analysis and the results from many other plausible models imply that a fixed target for money is inappropriate when external supply shocks occur. It is interesting that it was in response to such a shock that the Fed decided to pursue an M1 strategy. Perhaps this shift makes Friedman's point: central bankers are not to be trusted. A smoother policy as suggested by a rule would be preferable in many cases to the kinds of policy we can apparently expect.

But literal application of a policy rule through law or constitutional amendment is likely asking society to perform a lobotomy on itself because the patient will feel happier that way. Such radical procedures do not seem justified. It does seem justified to push for more orderly and predictable policies but to expect policy to cushion the effects of external shocks. I believe that disclosure of policy strategies and intentions is the best way to accomplish these ends.

It was disappointing that neither Poole nor Solow really addressed the basic issue raised by the proponents of rational expectations. Private agents do attempt to interpret current policy and they attempt to anticipate future policy. A more stable policy is a more predictable policy and agents can accommodate their actions to it. Even if policy were always "wrong" in a predictable way, perhaps agents could counteract at least some of its effects. But unfortunately policy is often unpredictable. A mildly "activist" policy would be unpredictable to the extent that shocks to which it responds are unpredictable. But if agents could have a reasonable expectation that policy would at least move in the right direction following discrete and unusual events such as OPEC, the economy would almost certainly be better off than by slavishly following a fixed rule.

General Discussion

Benjamin Friedman said he would try to connect his discussion of the Solow and Poole papers with the earlier discussion of the Lucas and Fischer papers, during which it seemed generally agreed that monetary policy in 1974–75 was poor. The growth rates of money (M1) on an annual basis (annual average M1, year over year) were 6.7% in 1971, 7.1% in 1972, 7.5% in 1973, 5.5% in 1974, 4.4% in 1975.

He suggested four possible reasons for arguing that policy in 1974–75 was poor:

1. The growth rate of M1 was not moved to 4% quickly enough.
2. The growth rate of M1 was moved to 4% too quickly.
3. Because oil prices had risen substantially, it was a bad time to go to a 4% money growth.
4. Policy erred by thinking in terms of a 4% rule at all.

Despite the agreement that policy was poor, Friedman sensed strong disagreement about why; indeed, some people who criticized policy seemed reluctant to say why. Friedman himself preferred the fourth answer: he thought policy in the first half of 1974 had been in error in allowing interest rates to rise so high. He dissented from the view that either policymakers or economists were more aware now of the need for caution and prudence than they had been in the 1960s. William McChesney Martin was hardly incautious. What has changed is the base against which caution is judged: it used to be interest rate movements and it is now money growth. He thought a more prudent approach would recognize that both money growth and interest rates conveyed information to policymakers.

Robert Hall noted that calculations made by him and Knut Mork, as well as work by Eckstein, suggested that OPEC was responsible for only a part of the fall in real GNP in 1974 and 1975. For that reason he thought that a small increase in unanticipated money would have accommodated the OPEC shock. Hall noted that there had in addition been a dramatic unexplained drop in productivity in 1974–75. A third reason frequently given for the recession, the drop in inventory investment, was not well understood but could not be regarded as exogenous.

Robert Gordon said that of the 12% price rise in 1974, 6% could be attributed to inherited expectations and excess demand, 1% to food, 2% to energy, and 3% to the end of controls. He felt that Solow had missed a key issue by not considering the sensitivity of the real wage to aggregate demand. The United Kingdom, Italy, Canada, and Sweden had all pursued policies of accommodation in 1974 and 1975, real wages had not fallen at the time, and more severe recessions followed later. Switzerland and West Germany had elected to take their medicine early.

Alan Blinder thought that 3.4% would be a better estimate of the effect of energy price increases on the overall CPI. He added that close to 100% of the acceleration of nonfood and nonenergy inflation from February to October of 1974 was a result of the lifting of controls. He agreed with Poole that controls were a bad idea and that economists should say so. But he disagreed with Poole's view that economists should worry about political constraints on policy: economists should advocate what they believe to be optimal policies.

Phillip Cagan agreed that the direct effects of energy and oil price increases had been small but said that pursuing those increases through stages of processing would account for ⅜ of the price rise. He added that the difficulty of measuring the size of the shock made it difficult to know how much accommodation should have been provided.

Robert Weintraub also felt that the effects of the oil price increase were larger than Hall and others suggested. As a crude approximation, the increase in the price of imported oil multiplied by the share of such oil in GNP would account for a 4.4% price rise. On the timing of policy, he felt that monetary policy had been particularly poor in late 1974, when fiscal policy was also contractionary. Finally, he remarked that changes in monetary policy did not require constitutional change: the Fed could operate by following legislative rules, or rules of its own choosing.

Frank Morris said it was not true that the Fed had started following a monetary growth rule in late 1974. They had started in 1972 but had mistakenly thought the natural rate of unemployment was between 4.5% and 5% rather than 5.5%. By 1973 they were aware they had made a mistake. He thought monetary policy in 1973 had been reasonable, although the food price rise was a surprise. Monetary policy in the first half of 1974 had been satisfactory but other conditions, especially inventory overaccumulation, made the recession inevitable. Monetary policy had erred in the second half of 1974: the size of the recession had been underestimated and monetary policy turned around too late.

Robert Solow said that zero accommodation was not necessarily a good approximation to the best policy merely because actual policy had not been particularly successful. He also remarked that policymakers pretend to be constrained to get themselves off the hook when policy is criticized.

William Poole responded that he still did not believe it useful to recommend policy without regard for public attitudes.

List of Participants

Professor Costas Azariadis
Department of Economics
University of Pennsylvania
Philadelphia, PA 19174

Professor Robert Barro
Department of Economics
University of Rochester
Rochester, NY 14627

Professor Olivier Blanchard
Department of Economics
Harvard University
Cambridge, MA 02138

Professor Alan Blinder
Department of Economics
Princeton University
Princeton, NJ 08540

Professor Karl Brunner
Graduate School of Management
University of Rochester
Rochester, NY 14627

Professor Phillip Cagan
Department of Economics
Columbia University
New York, NY 10027

Professor Rudiger Dornbusch
Department of Economics
Massachusetts Institute of Technology
Cambridge, MA 02139

285

Professor Martin Feldstein
Department of Economics
Harvard University
Cambridge, MA 02138

Professor Stanley Fischer
Department of Economics
Massachusetts Institute of Technology
Cambridge, MA 02139

Professor Jacob Frenkel
Department of Economics
University of Chicago
Chicago, IL 60637

Professor Benjamin Friedman
Department of Economics
Harvard University
Cambridge, MA 02138

Professor Robert Gordon
Department of Economics
Northwestern University
Evanston, IL 60201

Professor Jerry Green
Department of Economics
Harvard University
Cambridge, MA 02138

Professor Herschel Grossman
Department of Economics
Brown University
Providence, RI 02912

Professor Robert Hall
Department of Economics
Stanford University
Stanford, CA 94305

Professor Peter Howitt
Department of Economics
University of Western Ontario
London, Ontario
Canada

Dr. John Kraft
National Science Foundation
Washington, DC 20550

Dr. David Lindsey
Board of Governors of the Federal Reserve System
Washington, DC 20551

Professor Robert Lucas
Department of Economics
University of Chicago
Chicago, IL 60637

Professor Bennett McCallum
Department of Economics
University of Virginia
Charlottesville, VA 22901

Dr. Charles McLure
National Bureau of Economic Research
Cambridge, MA 02139

Dr. Frank Morris
President, Federal Reserve Bank of Boston
Boston, MA 02106

Professor Charles Nelson
Department of Economics
University of Washington
Seattle, WA 98195

Dr. Dan Newlon
National Science Foundation
Washington, DC 20550

Professor Michael Parkin
Department of Economics
University of Western Ontario
London, Ontario
Canada

Professor Edmund Phelps
Department of Economics
New York University
New York, NY 10003

Professor James Pierce
Department of Economics
University of California, Berkeley
Berkeley, CA 94720

Professor William Poole
Department of Economics
Brown University
Providence, RI 02912

Professor Edward Prescott
Graduate School of Industrial Administration
Carnegie-Mellon University
Pittsburgh, PA 15213

Professor Michael Rothschild
Department of Economics
University of Wisconsin
Madison, WI 53706

Mr. Mark Rush
Department of Economics
University of Rochester
Rochester, NY 14627

Professor Robert Russell
Council on Wage and Price Stability
Washington, DC

Professor Paul Samuelson
Department of Economics
Massachusetts Institute of Technology
Cambridge, MA 02139

Dr. Frank Schiff
Committee for Economic Development
Washington, DC 20006

Professor Robert Shiller
Department of Economics
University of Pennsylvania
Philadelphia, PA 19174

Professor Robert Solow
Department of Economics
Massachusetts Institute of Technology
Cambridge, MA 02139

Professor John Taylor
Department of Economics
Columbia University
New York, NY 10027

Professor Neil Wallace
Department of Economics
University of Minnesota
Minneapolis, MN 55455

Dr. Robert Weintraub
House Banking Committee
Washington, DC 20515

Dr. Mark Willes
President, Federal Reserve Bank of Minneapolis
Minneapolis, MN 55480

Index